All at once the dinks in front of us open up with small arms fire. We drop to the ground and return fire. If that isn't enough, we're getting shot at from our rear! And to make matters worse, the damn dinks are also shooting B-40 rockets at us. One of the rockets hits right behind P. R. and me, knocking us to the ground. But, somehow, we get away without a scratch.

I start to get up, when I hear a bullet whiz by my ear. I turn and see the new sergeant, with his M-16 pointed at me. My heart almost stops. He is on his knees, and his eyes have a wild look. I yell at him to shoot toward the front. I just know he's going to shoot me. But he turns away and starts shooting in the right direction.

TIME HEALS
NO WOUNDS

Jack Leninger

IVY BOOKS • NEW YORK

This book is dedicated to the fighting echelon, the small percentage of Vietnam veterans who know what it was like to be in actual combat; to those who walked the thin line between life and death, kill or be killed; to those of us who knew the importance of being in the right place at the right time, split seconds, faith, luck, and the other ingredients of survival.

To those who served in the "Forgotten Division" (4th Infantry Division), which operated in the largest AO (area of operations) in Vietnam, eight thousand square miles.

To those who served in the 1/12th Infantry Battalion, the "Red Warriors," who for two decades have been warriors without a war.

But, most important, this book is dedicated to those I knew and served with in B Company, 1/12th Infantry from September 1968 through August 1969.

Ivy Books
Published by Ballantine Books
Copyright © 1993 by Jack Leninger

All rights reserved under International and Pan-American Copyright Conventions. Published in the United States of America by Ballantine Books, a division of Random House, Inc., New York, and simultaneously in Canada by Random House of Canada Limited, Toronto.

Library of Congress Catalog Card Number: 93-90208

ISBN 0-8041-0916-8

Manufactured in the United States of America

First Edition: August 1993

IN REMEMBRANCE

Dean H. Johnson	KIA	March 8, 1969
Raymond Bethea	KIA	March 9, 1969
Clarence Burleson	KIA	March 9, 1969
Jerry MacDonald	KIA	March 9, 1969
Edward Millison	KIA	March 9, 1969
Clarence Nofford	KIA	March 9, 1969
Robert Pretto	KIA	March 9, 1969
Thomas Turner	KIA	March 9, 1969
Raymond P. Johnson	KIA	April 1969
Lawrence Budzinski	KIA	April 24, 1969
Randall Ruggs	KIA	April 24, 1969
William Stout	KIA	April 28, 1969
Michael Heath	KIA	May 31, 1969
Patrick Hagerty	KIA	May 31, 1969
Prentiss Harris	KIA	May 31, 1969
James Leonard	KIA	May 31, 1969
Kenneth Scurr	KIA	May 31, 1969
William Sewell	KIA	May 31, 1969
Stephen Turzilli	KIA	May 31, 1969
Philip Weir	KIA	May 31, 1969
Garry Barbee	KIA	Aug 2, 1969
*Byron Calkins	KIA	May 31, 1969

And to any of the fifty-four WIAs who may have died of their wounds. Once they left on the medevac chopper, we never heard anything about them, and we never knew if they made it home all right. To those who made it, please get in touch!
*attached (HHQ)

"68–69"
VIETNAM
THE WAR THAT I SEE

Ants and leeches,
C-ration peaches
Shovels and picks,
mosquitos and ticks
Twisted limbs, dead trees,
colored and fluorescent leaves
Orange fires burning,
compasses keep turning
Young men wearing old faces,
broken boot laces
Helicopters and planes,
no buses, no trains
Packages and letter mail,
bending and winding trails
The ground is my bed,
humans lie dead
Sometimes crying, sometimes laughing, always swearing,
people back home caring?
Living on top of bunker-covered hills,
white and orange malaria pills
Hunger and thirst,
it's my life I care about first
Choking dust and caked-on mud,
feet filled with whitish crud
Days without washing,
blue line crossings
SPs and fours and fives,
this is how we really survive
Hot humid days, cold wet nights,
illumination flares cast eerie light
Helmets and backpacks,
ammo-filled racks
Bunkers built with sandbags and logs,
jungle sometimes thick as dense fog
Rolling green hills, on top of lush green valleys,

cities with corrupt back alleys
Torn and filthy OD green shirts,
four young men sent out on SRPs
Climbing, stumbling, and falling,
"Incoming" someone calling
Frightened and scared,
but always prepared
Sunset brings a constant fear,
St. Jude protect us for one year
Convoys through battered towns,
pictures of buddies wearing frowns
Kids yelling "Chop Chop,"
rice is the only crop
Blood and sweat,
its patrols I regret
Rifles spitting lead,
someplace someone lies dead
The glowing redness of burning logs at night,
the distant sounds of a firefight.

> JACK LENINGER
> B Company, 1st of the 12th Infantry,
> 4th Infantry Division
> Written November 1968 through January 1969
> (Kontum Province, Vietnam)

CONTENTS

ACKNOWLEDGMENTS

Many people, in many different ways, helped me to write this book.

Some provided vital information. Others gave encouragement. Without their support, I never would have been able to finish what I started seven years ago. I am deeply indebted to my wife Joyce for her love and understanding through this ordeal. My utmost thanks to my best friend Bob Armstrong and his wife Sue. A special thanks to Henry Mayer, Assistant Chief, Military Field Branch, Military Archives Division, National Archives, and Michael Miller, Archivist. A special thanks to: W. A. Anderson (Chief, Access and Release Branch), Steve Eldridge, and Miriam Friend (Acting Chief, Research), all from the Department of the Army, Office of the Assistant Chief of Staff; to Janice McKenny, Historical Services; Richard Christian, U.S. Army and JSESG; Del Malkie, Director Public Affairs Defense Mapping Agency; Carolyn Graham and Peggy Cox, Military Operations Branch, National Personnel Records Center. I also want to thank those who provided eyewitness accounts: Bill Butler, Ed Medors, and Roger Ranker of the 1st Platoon; Robert Noel of the 3d Platoon; Phil Patrick, our company commander. Also, those who provided information and facts when memory eluded me: Larry Bond, Ken Comeaux, Joe Fegan, Ray Frederick, Lloyd Pelky, Luke Whitaker, Jack Regan, Wayne Kahre, Bud Kutchman, and Jack Shoppe. Also, a thanks to Ed Pozdoll, Mike Janeczko, Bill Russell, and Kevin "Bronx" O'Brian for their contributions. And last, but not least, a thanks to Mike Ranger, who told me to keep to the story.

PREFACE

This is a story of the sixties, a decade that has never really ended, a period of time that changed millions of people's lives forever, physically and psychologically.

I was born January 21, 1948, and was inducted into the army April 10, 1968. In 1948, the U.S. Supreme Court abolished religion in the public schoolroom, the United States formally recognized the new republic of Israel, Columbia Records introduced the 33⅓ RPM long-playing record, and the *Chicago Tribune* prematurely elected Thomas Dewey to the presidency. The fifties brought the Korean War, rock 'n' roll became the new jive, and grease became a way of life.

Then came the sixties, a time I find hard to leave. The sixties saw the assassinations of John F. Kennedy, Martin Luther King, Jr., and Bobby Kennedy. The sixties also brought riots, demonstrations, the generation gap, a man walking on the moon, the dynasty of the Packers, the Miracle Mets, the Beatles, Rascals, Cream, Smokey, the Temps, and the Four Tops. But to me the single, most important event of the sixties is my year in Vietnam, 1968–1969.

Jack Leninger

AUTHOR'S NOTE

This is the story of what happened to me in Vietnam. This book also contains a few eyewitness reports from my friends, which have not been altered in any way. I spent seven years recreating and researching this book, which is now a part of history. By using operational reports, morning reports, daily journals, newspaper articles, maps, and my memory, I was able to travel back through time to retrace that year I spent in hell. At times, I put the manuscript down for days because the truth of what went on was too painful. The events and characters are all real.

Other books have been written about Vietnam; some believable, others not. I wanted to write something unique, by showing what was going on in the whole division, what was going on in my battalion and in my company, so the reader can understand the whole picture. What you hold in your hand is a historical autobiography of me and a hundred thousand grunts just like me. I hope it may help others to realize what we endured and to understand us.

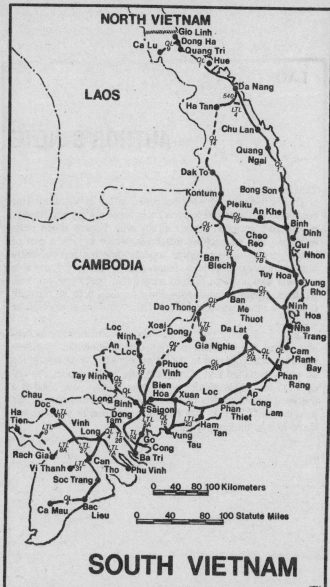

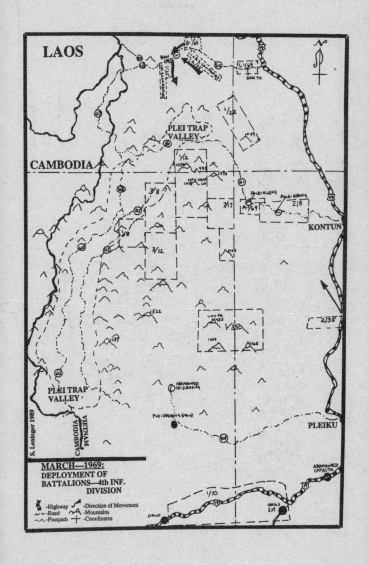

MARCH—1969:
DEPLOYMENT OF
BATTALIONS—4th INF.
DIVISION

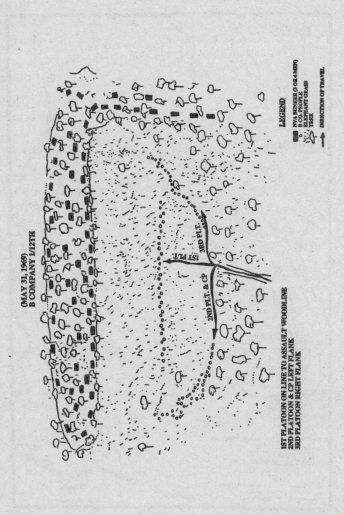

(MAY 31, 1969)
B COMPANY 1/12TH

3RD PLT.

1ST PLT.

2ND PLT. & CP

LEGEND

NVA BUNKER (3 OR 4 MEN)
B CO. PEOPLE
ELEPHANT GRASS
TREE
DIRECTION OF TRAVEL

1ST PLATOON ON LINE TO ASSAULT WOODLINE
2ND PLATOON & CP LEFT FLANK
3RD PLATOON RIGHT FLANK

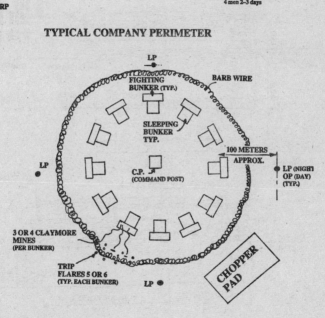

SRP
(Short Range Patrol)
2000–2000 Meters
3 or 4 sent out
different directions
4 men 2–3 days

● SRP

TYPICAL COMPANY PERIMETER

LP

BARB WIRE

FIGHTING
BUNKER (TYP.)

SLEEPING
BUNKER
TYP.

100 METERS
APPROX.

C.P.
(COMMAND POST)

LP

● LP (NIGHT)
OP (DAY)
(TYP.)

3 OR 4 CLAYMORE
MINES
(PER BUNKER)

TRIP
FLARES 5 OR 6
(TYP. EACH BUNKER)

LP ●

CHOPPER
PAD

● SRP

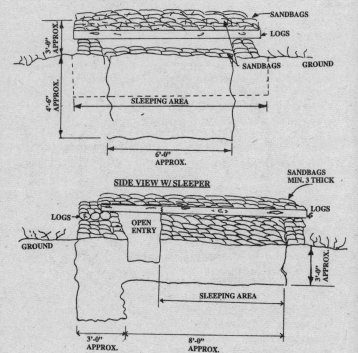

**TYPICAL FIGHTING BUNKER
(FRONT VIEW)**

SANDBAGS

LOGS

3'-0"
APPROX.

SANDBAGS

GROUND

4'-6"
APPROX.

SLEEPING AREA

6'-0"
APPROX.

SIDE VIEW W/ SLEEPER

SANDBAGS
MIN. 3 THICK

LOGS

LOGS

OPEN
ENTRY

GROUND

3'-0"
APPROX.

SLEEPING AREA

3'-0"
APPROX.

8'-0"
APPROX.

Chapter I

INDUCTION

On January 30, 1968, the "National Liberation Front" (NLF) and North Vietnam launched the Tet Offensive against all major cities in South Vietnam, including an attack on the U.S. embassy in Saigon. While U.S. troops drove them out, and General Westmoreland called it a "go-for-broke effort" that failed, among most politicians and the public, the Tet Offensive shattered any belief in an approaching U.S. military victory in Vietnam. But I showed no fear in going into the army; I felt it was my duty. And I'm sure that thousands of guys who went had visions of becoming an Audie Murphy.

April 10 of that year had not been just another sunny day, for me—it was the day that my parents and girlfriend drove me to the VFW Hall on Des Plaines Avenue near Madison Street, Forest Park, Illinois. Right around the corner was Draft Board 107, where I had to be at 9:00 A.M. The VFW served a free breakfast for those who were inducted in the area. There were about sixty of us; a few I knew from my high school, Proviso East. The area that Board 107 focused on included Forest Park, Oak Park, Maywood, Melrose Park, Broadview, and North Riverside. The good-byes were said to my family and friends. My mother and my girlfriend were crying, and I kissed and hugged them both, telling them not to worry, that I would write and call when I got situated.

The bus started down Madison Street, and fifteen minutes later, we hit the border of Chicago. We gazed at the charred buildings that had been burned during the riots when Martin Luther King, Jr. was assassinated six days prior. It's hard to describe the way I felt. I was excited, unsure of the future, proud that I was going, dumbfounded for not knowing why I was going, intrigued with the thought of being a hero if I went to Vietnam.

We reached the induction center, filed off the bus, and started induction—filling out forms most of the day. One clear folder with some forms in it also had a blue card that said USMC. Only a few of us got them, and I didn't want to go into the Marines, so when the sergeant walked out of the room, I said, "Does anybody want to go into the Marines?" One guy said "Yeah," so I passed him the card.

We left the induction center late in the afternoon and traveled by bus to O'Hare Airport. I was fine until we reached the plane. I was nervous because it was my first flight. The takeoff was fine, and I remember looking out the window at the flickering lights below. Then I remembered that we still had to land, so I prayed for a safe landing with no rain. I had white knuckles and locked knees, and I had to go so bad that I thought I'd wet my pants. I stayed glued to my seat until we landed, which we did safely. Where we landed, I didn't care. We were somewhere in Louisiana.

We boarded another bus that took us to the Fort Polk Induction Center. The warm wind blowing through the pine trees made an eerie, howling sound, like the soundtrack for a horror movie. About midnight, we were finally assigned to a barracks, and I had no trouble falling asleep.

The next few days were spent at the Reception Center, where our heads were shaved and we were issued fatigues, boots, etc. For the first few days in the army, not only do you look like an idiot, but you act the way you look. I was saluting corporals, sergeants—anything. "Dick-head" seemed to be the army term for new recruits.

We spent about ten days at the Reception Center; every day the same: getting shots, and taking tests for placing us in a Military Occupation Specialty (MOS).

We had three straight days of written tests, and on the third day, when we were really sick of them, the army slipped in one that seemed ridiculous. It had questions like (1) If you were walking down the street with your mother and somebody walked up and hit her, what would you do? As I remember them, the answers went something like: (a) I would beat the hell out of the guy; (b) I would do nothing; (c) I would turn and run the other way. Any normal guy would answer (a), of course. There were about twenty questions, each like the first. Obviously the army wanted to know if its young soldiers

would retaliate under certain circumstances. If we were infantry material. I guess I scored well, as any other normal guy.
Little did I know at the time that this test probably determined
my MOS after basic training.

At Fort Polk, we all pulled KP (kitchen police)—nobody
could get out of it. In our spare time, what little we had, a few
of us played basketball for two dollars a game. I was the only
white guy playing. I had played with Brothers at Proviso East,
and I could play hoop, usually scoring on anybody. My defense sucked, but I wasn't afraid to crash the boards or to
drive. I earned respect one game by hitting six shots in a row
from the corner, and Cherry, the guy covering me, was from
Detroit. He said, "Motherfucker, you won't get any more." I
didn't, but I already had six baskets, and we won. Cherry and
I became good friends after that.

We finally were assigned to our basic training companies
about April 20. I was assigned to Company C, 3d Battalion,
1st Basic Training Brigade. The guys I was assigned with were
all from the Chicago and Detroit areas, and most were all right
guys. I basically hung around with two guys named Joe from
Melrose Park and a couple of others, one a brother from
Maywood.

To me, basic training was a joke. The army did get us into
shape and taught us discipline, but a lot of the training was stupid, just petty harassment, push-ups, and having to answer
"Yes, Drill Sergeant" or "No, Drill Sergeant." No matter what
you did, you were the grass and the drill sergeant was the lawn
mower. *One* button unbuttoned, a shirttail out, boots not laced
correctly, pants not bloused—they caught everything. And they
accomplished what they set out to do—filled us out and got us
pissed off.

Most of basic was physical, doing PT (physical training)—
low crawl; run, dodge, and jump; mile run; the bars; sit-ups;
push-ups. All PT exercises were graded at the end of basic
training. Forced-marching, double-time to the rifle range. Waking up at 4:30 in the morning and running two miles before
breakfast. After breakfast, we did two hours of calisthenics,
and we learned very quickly not to chow down too much or
else we threw up during calisthenics.

At first I hated what GIs have always called "shit on a shin-
gle" (creamed "chipped beef"), but after a while, I got used to
it. The only thing I never learned to like was liver and onions,
which the cooks sometimes tried to pass off as hamburger. Of

course, we could tell it by the smell before we even walked up the mess hall stairs.

After two weeks or so, we started to march and to double-time to the rifle range—about five miles each way—with M-14 rifles. About midway through basic, we qualified with the M-14. The target distances varied from 50 meters to 350 meters. We had about seven seconds to find the target and shoot. I hit fifty-seven targets out of a possible eighty-four, which was good enough to qualify me for sharpshooter. Sixty would have made me an expert. Big deal, it meant I could buy a sharpshooter pin at the PX and wear it with the National Defense Service ribbon on my dress greens or khakis.

A few days later we went to "quick kill," where we learned to shoot by reflex at targets that popped up in the dark. One day we went to throw hand grenades, and I almost ended my army career early. I held the grenade, pulled the pin, and let the handle go—while still holding the grenade. You know, like John Wayne. Well the DI almost croaked. He screamed, "Throw it!" When I did, it exploded in midair. Then the DI kicked me right in the behind while screaming, "Don't ever do that again or you're going to kill yourself and somebody else, you stupid dick-head!"

The next day we practiced getting gassed. We were standing in line waiting to go into the shed when one of my friends said, "Let's sneak out of line, run into the woods, and circle around to the back and pretend we went through." I agreed to chance it, and we snuck out and circled around to where everybody was coughing and choking. We joined in the coughing and gagging, and we never got caught.

I wrote my parents and my girlfriend about once a week, keeping them informed about the training routine and what was happening with me and my buddies. We were confined to our barracks until about the fifth week of training when we got a pass for the weekend. A few friends and I headed for Lake Charles. Forget Leesville, the nearest town to Fort Polk. "Diseaseville" was loaded with bars and whorehouses. A few of us wanted to get as far away from the base as possible because we thought our chances to meet women would be better. The trip to Lake Charles took an hour by bus, and once there, we went to a lounge for a few drinks and to find some women.

During basic, I usually didn't think too much about my girlfriend—or any other girls—probably because I was just too busy. But when "The Tighten Up" by Archie Bell and the

Drells came on the speakers, I asked a girl to dance. We moved around the floor for a couple of songs, and I soon found out her name was Mary. She said that she was a model in Houston. But she lived in Lake Charles. I met her family when she invited me to dinner. But she was a typical southern belle, looking to get married; I wasn't. I saw Mary every weekend for three weeks and we got close, but not close enough.

The next couple of weeks, we were winding down basic training, getting closer to graduation and finding out what was in store for us.

During the night infiltration course, we had to crawl under wire while the instructors shot tracers about fifteen feet overhead. It looked a lot closer than that as we low-crawled past sandbagged holes where explosives were detonated. The point of it all was to get us used to live fire, but at the time I thought it was pretty stupid, like the skimpy training in hand-to-hand combat, and bayonet training. For training with pugil sticks, they paired up guys, gave each of them a wooden staff with padding on the ends, and football helmets with face guards. It was supposed to train us like using bayonets, with thrusting and blocking, etc., but it always ended up in a wild, swinging melée as we tried to knock our opponent's head off. Once I got hit so hard that my helmet turned completely around. Everybody else was laughing, but I didn't think it was very funny. I was dazed and confused.

We went on bivouac once, eight of us to a tent. We were issued blanks for our M-14's, but we did little more than sit around and talk. Even though we were told not to bring one, I had taken along a flashlight.

That night in the woods, I turned it on to check our tent and found that we were practically surrounded by scorpions. I almost died. So did everyone else. So much for getting any sleep. There was no way we were going to lie down.

While we were in the bush, June 5, Senator Robert Kennedy was assassinated in Los Angeles; he had just won the California primary.

At about 10:00 P.M., a few of the drill sergeants came around and fired M-14s. They were supposed to be the enemy, but they weren't very effective. So we laughed and fired back. We stayed awake all night, telling jokes, bullshitting, sweating, and checking the ground every so often for scorpions. I couldn't wait until June 14 when we were to graduate basic and, hopefully, go on to better things.

Our orders came down the week of graduation, and I found out that I was staying right there in North Fort Polk (Tigerland) for training in MOS 11B10—"eleven bush" or "eleven Bravo"—infantry. I was to report the following Monday, so I got no home leave. Eight more weeks would pass before I was able to go home. My chances of going to Nam had jumped to about 90 percent, but of 250 of us who went through basic together, only 18 were going to North Fort. That's about thirteen percent, so I was separated from most of the guys I was close to. Friday, June 14, 1968, we graduated basic, looking good in our khakis with light blue scarves and blue fourragere. Marching by units past the reviewing stand did send chills up my spine. We were young and proud. My girlfriend came down to visit, and I asked her to marry me. She accepted and called my mom right away to tell her. I knew then it would never happen.

After she left, I took the bus from South Fort to North Fort, which took all of ten minutes. We were put into groups. Carrying our duffel bags over one shoulder, we marched in formation down the road and under a wooden arch about fifteen feet high that straddled the road. On it was painted TIGERLAND with different infantry division insignia. I was assigned to Company B 3d Bn. 3E, AIT [Advanced Individual Training] Bde.

The sergeant yelled out, *"I want you troops to growl* every time you pass under this structure. Let me hear you!" We looked at each other, then we let out a feeble growl. He said, "I can't hear you." We growled louder. Some guys snickered, and I asked the guy next to me, "What the hell is going on?" He answered "Grrrrr," and we laughed. I guess it was supposed to mean we were mean as tigers, but I wasn't convinced. Basic had only whipped us into shape, which was step number one. It wasn't serious enough yet. I was only twenty years old, about average for those who served in Vietnam, and at that age, it was hard to get serious about anything. We weren't men yet, we were green, olive drab. Most of us didn't even know why we had been drafted, but we felt that accepting "the call" was our duty. Most of us had been brought up during and after World War II when patriotism was at the max. I didn't even know about the Korean War until I was in high school. Our history textbooks hardly mentioned it, although 54,246 Americans were KIAs and 103,000 WIAs.

AIT (Advanced Individual Training) wasn't too different from basic, although there was less physical conditioning and more training with weapons. In AIT we trained with the M-16, which felt like a plastic toy, compared to the M-14. But about then, my attitude changed somewhat; I had more confidence in myself because I'd gotten through basic without any help from anybody—that was something to build on. Still, I failed to realize that after eight more weeks I'd most likely be going to Vietnam. I still felt that the training was all a game.

The barracks were old in North Fort. Guys had trained for World War II and Korea in them, and they hadn't been remodeled. I wondered how many others had gone through them and off to war. We still had to pull fire watch the way we had in basic training. One night, my sleep was shattered by someone yelling. When I woke up, guys were running around with brooms, swinging madly at bats. I sat in my bunk and laughed. A few of the guys were really scared of the little monsters; I guess they'd seen too many Dracula movies.

The next few weeks, we spent a lot of time marching to the rifle ranges to handle different weapons. A few of them, we fired only once. We each fired one M-79 (40mm grenade launcher) round at an old APC (armored personnel carrier). We fired about ten rounds each on the .50-caliber machine gun. We learned about the M-19 LAW (light antitank weapon) but never fired it. Instead, a sergeant gave us a demonstration and fired it at the same APC. The beginning of July we fired the M-16 for qualification. I hit thirty-eight targets—good for Marksman. The following week came the M-60, on which I fired 138—good for Sharpshooter. The M-60 was the most fun.

When they gave us a weekend pass, I went to Lake Charles with a big buddy of mine. At about six foot three and 240 pounds, his nickname was obvious—"The Bear." But he could really dance. And he could shoot pool as well as I could, so we took a few guys for some dough. He was usually a gentle giant, but he *could* be as mean as a bear. He treated me like his little brother, always looking out for me. He called me his "little buddy."

About this time, I stopped seeing Mary. I called my girlfriend, who spent every Saturday with my mom. I had started to get cold feet about marriage. If I was headed to Vietnam, it would be hard enough for me—why should I put her through it? Besides, I didn't want to be attached to just one girl

now in case something happened. And I didn't want to put
pressure on either one of us. If she really loved me, she could
wait until I came back—a year wasn't too long.

We spent about another week with the bayonet, the drill sergeant yelling over a loudspeaker, "What's the spirit of the bayonet?" We would answer, "To kill." He'd ask again, "To
what?" We'd answer "To kill." The sergeants would also try to
light a fire under us by talking about "Jody," the guy who
takes your girlfriend away back home. Even when we were
marching, we would sing "Ain't no use in going home, Jody's
got your girl and gone . . ."

The last couple of weeks, we trained on map reading, first
aid, and survival. For the survival course, we were taken out
into the woods by truck and dropped off. Bleachers had been
set up for us to sit on while we were lectured all day about survival in the wilderness, eating roots, bark, bugs, whatever.
How to find the north star and read moss growing on a tree.
The climax of the lecture at the end of the day was the sergeant's ripping a live chicken's head off with his bare hands;
the blood just spurting all over him. A few guys in the stands
got sick, but I thought his act was funny. Even with its head
gone, the chicken kept flopping away, kicking its feet.

We knew something was up when the trucks didn't come
back for us. Then we were told that we had to walk back to
the trucks through the woods while trying to avoid getting captured by armed soldiers who were hidden throughout the area.
The army called it "escape and evasion."

It was dusk by the time we started off in small groups. I was
with the Bear and about five others. I picked up a stick the size
of a baseball bat, just in case. Just before dark, we reached a
road; it looked perfect for an ambush. Across the road on the
other side were small bushes and trees. Two guys went across
to check it out. They signaled for us to come across, but halfway across, the trees erupted with small-arms fire. It scared everybody, and we took off in different directions. I ran about
twenty yards down the road and into the woods—right into
one of the sergeants holding an M-16. He said, "You're captured, son."

"Come on take me, motherfucker," I said. "I'll knock your
head off." I held up the stick to take a swing at him.

"But you're captured," he said.

I said, "Yeah, you're right," and took off running.

I ran for about five minutes, and then I realized I was alone, and it was dark. I rested behind a tree and listened; the only thing I heard was my heart pounding. Then I started to walk, trying not to make any noise and stopping every few steps to listen. I heard nothing. Every so often, I would run a short distance to keep warm. I went on that way until, at almost 9:30 P.M., I reached a clearing. Through the trees I saw a light about two hundred yards away. I ran across the clearing to a bush but stopped when something ran out the other side, startling me. I ran again toward the light and found it was on a blacktop road. About a mile away, I saw some taillights. I followed the road until I could make out that the taillights were on troop transports! I had made it. I was so happy when I got closer and saw some of the guys standing around. One of them said, "Hey, Little Buddy." It was the Bear.

I walked up and asked where he'd been. He replied, "Beats me; when that shit happened, I just took off; the others got caught."

The truck was only half full. When we reached the barracks, we saw the others who were captured; they were full of mud. I found out that the ones who had been captured had to lay in mud with their hands and legs tied up. Others had to kneel on bricks. In the shower, we all exchanged stories, then as soon as I hit my bunk, I crashed out till morning.

The last week of AIT, I received my orders for Vietnam. I was glad because I had wanted to go there from the beginning. Saying good-bye to the Bear was hard. He was going to Europe, and I never saw him again. On home leave, I tried to tell my girlfriend that we had to wait for marriage; that was not easy. She told me she wouldn't wait. I told her fine, and that was that. At the airport, leaving my mom was hard because she was crying. I promised her I'd be back and told her I loved her. I shook hands with Dad and my brother, turned, and walked down the ramp to the plane, destination Fort Lewis, Washington.

Chapter II

ARRIVAL

I left for Vietnam on September 10, 1968, from Fort Lewis, Washington, with new fatigues and boots. I remember seeing Mt. McKinley, beautiful and ominous, covered with snow, as we passed by it, wondering about the future. In a little while, we would be on the other side of the world, fighting an unknown enemy in an unknown land.

Sixteen hours later, we landed in Tokyo to refuel, so I bought a postcard to send to my parents. I told them not to worry, that I would write when I got settled in Vietnam. I was really intrigued by Japan, what little I saw of it from the airport. We stayed about an hour and a half in the airport and then boarded the plane for another three- or four-hour flight. Next stop, Vietnam.

They switched stewardesses in Tokyo, and we had Japanese girls, who were beautiful.

It never really dawned on me until that flight from Tokyo to Vietnam that we were a planeload of about 280 GIs, mostly nineteen- and twenty-year-olds, being thrust into a war. We knew nothing about the country we were headed to: the people, the culture, or the language. How were we going to communicate with them? From what I had learned in training, the enemy wore black pajamas, was ill equipped, and fought mostly at night. I was sure that we were better trained, that we were superior in every aspect. I also worried about what to do if they started shooting at us when we landed? What do we do? We have no weapons. Since nobody had told us anything about what would happen where we landed, what else was I supposed to think?

My thoughts vanished when we were told to fasten our seat belts. I was glued to the window. My hands turned clammy, and my heart pounded against my chest. The plane started to descend at Cam Ranh Bay, and I couldn't believe my eyes at what I saw—it was huge, located on the coast of the South China Sea where the blue waters gently rolled up to white sandy beaches, which stretched inland a few miles, surrounded by dark green mountains. As we approached the runway, I could see people on the beach and in the ocean, swimming. I thought, what kind of war is this? This place was beautiful.

The plane landed, and I got up out of my seat. My legs felt like rubber as I shuffled down the aisle to the doorway. My feet hadn't even touched the first step down the ramp when I was hit by a gust of hot air, like someone's opening the door of a pizza oven. The air had a stench somewhere between bad body odor and burning shit. It was so humid that I was sweating by the time I reached the bottom step, where we filed onto buses. They had screens over all the windows and looked like prison buses.

As we boarded the bus, I asked the driver, "Why the screens? The army afraid we're going to run away?"

"It's so nobody throws a grenade into the bus," he answered.

The bus took us across the airstrip and down a road past a few Vietnamese women in black pajamas and coolie hats. I knew the old women couldn't be the enemy, but I hated them because they were part of the reason we were in Vietnam. We were taken to a reception center that had a group of wooden barracks with bunkers next to it.

We filed off the bus and into one of the buildings to change our U.S. dollars to MPCs (military payment certificates). Funny money we called it. Before we cashed in our money, we had to sign a statement that we had no U.S. currency in our possession. If you did and got caught, it would be an instant court-martial, and you'd spend some time in LBJ (Long Binh Jail). Of course, when you got out of jail, you still had to spend a year in country. I had a twenty- and a ten-dollar bill hidden between the pictures in my wallet as emergency money. I left it in there and changed about eighty dollars into MPC. They never checked my wallet, so I slid.

After changing our money, we were taken to a barracks and told it would be a few days before we would be assigned to our units. Well, that meant one thing in the army for sure—details! They weren't going to let us just sit around. One guy asked a sergeant about our getting issued rifles; that's when we were told we'd get them at our units. There we were in the middle of a war zone, without rifles. I guess if something happened, we could have hit the enemy with our duffel bags. We didn't think we were safe, but the army did, seeing that we were in such a huge camp. But we didn't know for sure. Shit, I was scared.

As I walked around the steaming reception area, I saw there were a few hundred new guys just waiting, most staying out of the sun. But I thought that if I stayed in the barracks, I'd get nabbed for some detail. Sure enough, as I was walking to a snack shack for a Coke, a sergeant nabbed me and about ten others. He lined us up, and I got on the right end. When he said, "Left face!" I was at the end of the column, out of sight. The sergeant went to the front and yelled, "Forward march," and the file took about four steps forward. But I took four back, about-faced, and ran to get my Coke.

That night I couldn't sleep; I lay in my bunk, thinking about what the future was going to bring. I wanted to get out of Cam Ranh Bay. The heat lingered inside the barracks, and I could hear the sounds of distant guns.

The next day dawned without a cloud in the sky, and after chow, I went back to my bunk and lay down. I dozed off. I was awakened by, "On your feet, soldier." I looked up to see some asshole sarge. It figured, he got three of us. He marched us to the shit house, and then said, "One of you go get the gas over there," and pointed to a jeep. I went for the gas while the others went to get the shit out of the shit house. The looks on their faces showed their disgust as they carried that half fifty-five-gallon drum full of shit. I poured the gas on the shit, then threw in the match. As the smoke rose, my eyes shifted from the black billows into the dark blue morning sky, to the dark mountains in the distance where the war was, the war that I would see soon. I prayed that God would watch over me and St. Jude protect me.

The next day I received orders: 4th Infantry Division, Pleiku, Camp Enari. I didn't know where Pleiku was, so I asked the guy next to me, and he said, "I think it's in the Central Highlands."

I asked, "Where is that?"

"Central, man."

I got it: center of the war.

They drove us to the airstrip where a four-engine turboprop, green-and-brown camouflaged C-130 was sitting. In a C-130 you can sit along the wall or on nylon-strap seats running down the middle. I sat along the wall of the plane, which could carry about forty or so troops. When we took off, the plane made so much noise I thought it was going to fall apart. Then, when we got airborne, so much vapor was coming out of the lines that ran along the fuselage that it scared me. I thought we had sprung a leak somewhere, for sure. There were no windows to see through, only a few small portholes, so I just stared at the interior of the plane. Compared to the jet we had flown over on, the C-130 was pretty crude. But we landed safely at Pleiku.

We were trucked from the air force base through Pleiku. Looking out the back of the deuce-and-a-half, I saw a city with open trenches that ran along the road where people relieved themselves in public. Run-down shacks were store fronts; hundreds of bicycles, motorcycles, and three-wheeled vehicles poured choking smoke into the air; crowds of people were all over. People wearing black pajamas with coolie hats, and kids who looked like they spent all day rolling around in the dirt. Most of the people were barefoot.

The truck snaked through Pleiku, then went west on a two-lane blacktop road. With lush green valleys and rolling green hills, the countryside was picturesque. After about twenty minutes, we hit Camp Enari, a huge base a few miles in diameter that was surrounded by rows of barbed-wire barricades. The perimeter also included lookout towers that had heavily sandbagged bunkers. The towers had machine guns. At one end of the perimeter was a tank battalion, and there was also an airstrip. I was told that fifty-five-gallon "foo gas" cans were buried right below the surface as antipersonnel weapons. And there also were hundreds of trip flares. Each bunker along the perimeter had about eight claymore mines in front of it.

We went through the gate and down the road, passing wooden barracks. Each battalion had its own section. We passed by the PX, the EM club, and a swimming pool—a swimming pool! We ended up at the 4th Division Reception Center, where we were assigned to a temporary barracks, and I finally had a chance to shower. We ended up staying in the reception center for three days because of a monsoon rain—a three-day downpour—and I got nabbed once for KP. Everything turned to mud, and the trenches around Camp Enari turned into rampaging rivers. One day we were watching the rain fall when a three-quarter-ton truck trying to cross a bridge got washed away in an instant. The driver and passenger disappeared in the churning water. It was over in seconds.

After three days, I received orders to report to Headquarters Company, 1st Battalion of the 12th Infantry.

The 1/12th was about six blocks from the Reception Center, and a deuce-and-a-half took a few of us there. After we signed in with the company clerk, we stored our duffel bags and were issued rucksacks, M-16, ammo, canteens, ponchos, poncho liners, helmets, and some C rations. At formation the next day, we were told to get our equipment, as we would be going out to the field to our companies. It was finally happening, and I was glad; I was anxious to get away from all the rear-echelon bullshit.

At the airstrip we boarded a Chinook ("Shithook") helicopter, a large troop-transport helicopter with two rotors. The Shithook was a loud bastard, and it vibrated like hell. We landed about forty-five minutes later at the Ban Me Thuot area of the Darlac Plateau, which was south of Pleiku about eighty miles, about twenty-five miles from the Cambodian border. We crouched against the powerful prop wash of the Chinook, holding our helmets, trying to protect the back of our necks from flying debris that felt like it was being shot from BB guns, and trying not to breathe so we wouldn't get the shit in our noses and throats. (The 4th Infantry Division area of operations in II Corps extended from Dak To in the north to Duc Lap, about twenty miles southwest of Ban Me Thuot [called "Bang My Twat" by GIs] in the south, all areas approximately west of Highway 14, except that around Pleiku it took in Mang Yang Pass and valleys to the south, between Pleiku and An Khe.)

AVDDH-CC-XH
SUBJECT: Operational Report of the 4th Infantry Division
           for Period Ending 31 October 1968, RCS
           CSFOR-65 (R1) Aug 1, 1968 thru Oct 31,
           1968

2. (C) Intelligence.
   a. General: At the beginning of the reporting period, the major enemy threat had shifted to DARLAC as a result of the 1st NVA Division having withdrawn from KONTUM Province in June and moved into DARLAC Province in July with the mission of taking BAN ME THUOT. By the middle of August, the enemy was conducting his final recon-

naissance of the city, with the 66th Regt north of the city, the 320th Regt to the west, and the 95C Regt to the south. With the arrival of the 4th Division units in the BAN ME THUOT area, however, the enemy was forced to switch his objective, and he redeployed the 320th and 95C Regts to DUC LAP. After unsuccessfully attempting to overrun DUC LAP sub-sector Headquarters and SF Camp, the enemy withdrew into Base Area 740.

In the Tri-border area, the 101D Regiment in late August made an abortive ground attack on DAK SEANG SF [Special Forces] Camp and a number of attacks by fire on DAK SEANG and FSB's [fire support bases] in the area.

In early August the 24th Regt relocated from north of KONTUM City to the vicinity of the PLEIKU-KONTUM Province boundary, east of Hwy 14N. They attempted three ambushes in late August. ARVN Elements inflicted heavy losses on the 24th Regt in August and September engagements east of Highway 14N between PLEIKU and KONTUM Cities.

The 18B and 95th Regts, which moved to Base Area (DUC Co) 701 West of DUC CO from the coast in July, did not return to the coast in September as anticipated, indicating that they may be assigned to the Highlands for a long offensive.

(1) KONTUM: In marked contrast to past patterns of enemy operations in the Highlands, KONTUM Province witnessed only limited enemy activity after early August, and at the end of the reporting period was opposed by the smallest number of NVA forces since prior to the Battle for DAK TO during November 1967.

Activity during the month of August was centered in the DAK SEANG area. After a feint at friendly firebases in the BEN HET area on the night of 14 Aug by means of heavy weapons attacks by the 40th NVA Arty [artillery] Regt, the 101D NVA Regt launched a savage attack on the DAK SEANG Special Forces Camp on 18 Aug. A sweep of the area following the abortive assault netted 39 enemy bodies and 12 prisoners. This attack signaled the initiation of the Third General Offensive in KONTUM Province. The 1st

Bde CP [command post] received a rocket attack on 22 Aug, and KONTUM City was hit by rockets and mortars on 23 Aug. It is significant that the attacks by fire were not followed by major ground contact as was the case during the TET and Second General Offensives. This would indicate that the VC and NVA forces simply were not strong enough to carry out full-scale coordinated attacks as they had previously. The attacks by fire continued on a daily basis in the DAK SEANG area during the remainder of August, but dissipated to sniping in the DAK TO area and mining activity and sporadic harassing attacks in the KONTUM City area.

(2) PLEIKU: In early August, the 24th NVA Regt moved from KONTUM Province and positioned itself along the PLEIKU-KONTUM boundary near Highway 14N. They were identified in a contact on 16 August when a two-company size ambush on Highway 14N resulted in 41 NVA killed. Documents captured in a sweep of the area identified the K-5 Bn, 24th Regt. Another two-company size ambush on 23 Aug, and subsequent platoon to company size contacts with CSF [camp strike forces], and ARVN units, produced PWs who identified all three Bns of the 24th Regt. The mission of the 24th Regt at that time was the interdiction of Highway 14N.

A newly formed Local Force Bn, designated the X-45, was identified by documents on 19 Aug. The X-45 Bn is located north of EDAP ENANG, between Highways 19W and 509, and has the mission of attacking the EDAP ENANG and THANH GLAO Resettlement Villages, as well as harassment of Highway 19W. Another Local Force Bn, the H-15, was identified for the first time since TET.

Enemy local force, sapper and artillery units harassed allied installations in the PLEIKU City area in late August. On 23 August, elements of the 31st Bn, 40th Arty Regt launched a total of 45 rounds of 122mm rocket fire from the west and north in conjunction with squad to platoon size sapper attacks against installations in the PLEIKU City area. On 12 Sep, Camp ENARI received approximately 25 rounds of 122mm rocket fire, all of which landed outside of the perimeter.

The infiltration and resupply route across southern PLEIKU Province remained active. Intermittent contacts have been made with transportation units providing supplies to the 95B Regt.

The 95B NVA Regt continued to operate on the eastern boundary of PLEIKU Province. The 5th Bn, 95B Regt continued its mission of harassment of vehicular traffic along Highway 19E. However, there was very little enemy activity along the highway, and recent indications are that the 95B Regt has moved east into BINH DINH Province and may in the future assume another mission.

In July, the 95th and 18B Regts moved from their areas of operation in PHU YEN and KHANH HOA Province into Base Area 701 in CAMBODIA. They remained in that location until approximately 1 Sep when the 95th Regt moved south to join the forces threatening DUC LAP.

(3) DARLAC: An increase of contact with small enemy forces and a large number of agent reports during the first part of July provided the first indications that a buildup of enemy forces was taking place in DARLAC Province. On 21 July 68 a rallier who returned to TRANG PHUC SF Camp revealed that the 1st NVA Div was preparing for operations in DARLAC Province. He also said the 66th Regt was moving one day behind the Division's HQs. In the latter part of July, captured documents and an increased number of contacts with infiltrating forces confirmed the presence of the 1st NVA Div and support elements in DARLAC. By the end of July the NVA forces were in position for the planned attack on BAN ME THUOT, the 95C Regt was located on the high ground approximately 15 Kms south of BAN ME THUOT, and the 320th Regt was located on the DARLAC/CAMBODIA border west of BAN ME THUOT.

On 9 August a PW [prisoner of war] was captured west of BAN ME THUOT by A/2-35 Inf. He revealed that BAN ME THUOT would be attacked in the latter part of August from three sides by three regiments and local force battalions. He had been with a 200 man reconnaissance force that had reconnoitered BAN ME THUOT on all sides for the impending attack. He identified the 66th Regt, 320th Regt, and

E-2 Regt (AKA 95C) as the major units to take part in the attack on BAN ME THUOT.

During the first part of August a decrease in enemy activity was noted throughout DARLAC Province. There were indications that preparations were being completed for the attack on BAN ME THUOT. After repeated light contacts with enemy reconnaissance elements north, south and west of the city in mid-August, however, reconnaissance and sensors revealed a shift of major enemy elements toward DUC LAP.

A large scale ground attack was launched against DUC LAP SF Camp and DUC LAP Sub Sector on 23 August. The initial battle lasted until 26 August when the attacking forces withdrew to CAMBODIA to regroup. The 320th Regt and 95C Regt were identified as the attacking units by documents and PW's. PW's captured in the contact revealed that the 1st NVA Div was preparing for the attack on BAN ME THUOT when US and ARVN forces discovered their position. The objective was immediately changed to DUC LAP. The 66th Regt was left in the BAN ME THUOT area to maintain pressure there.

A PW who was captured by 2-35 Inf on 21 Sep in the DUC LAP area revealed that the 95th Regt of the 5th NVA Div had moved to the DUC LAP area to participate in the attacks there. Also, the 66th Regt moved from its location in Base Area 238, north of BAN ME THUOT, to the DUC LAP area.

The 4th Inf. Division was involved in "Operation Binh Tay-MacArthur." The mission was to conduct reconnaissance and surveillance of the Cambodian border and destroy NVA/VC units within the assigned area of operations, block enemy infiltration routes from Cambodia/Laos across the central highlands to protect coastal provinces where most of the population was. Conduct spoiling attacks and ambushes. Destroy enemy base areas and supply installations, detect and eliminate Viet Cong infrastructure (which was collecting taxes in some places 3 to 4 times what the GVN was collecting, providing food for their increasing numbers of VC and NVA regulars infiltrating about 10,000 to 20,000 per month into the south and creating "liberation fronts" aimed at all classes of the society: doctors, teachers, students, farmers, etc., the "liberation front" controlled about 60% of the population of 15 million.) To clear, secure and assist in developing the tactical area of responsibility. To support Vietnam's EDAP ENANG resettlement program. Be prepared to deploy forces for reinforcement of Camp Strike Forces, Regional and Popular Forces, critical signal sites and sector sub-sector headquarters within II Corps and provide a battalion size reserve to I Field Force. The 1st Brgde was in Northern Kontum Province, the 3rd Brgde was split between Kontum Province and Western Pleiku Province. And our 2nd Brgde which was Task Force Bright (consisting of 1/12, 1/22, 2/25, 4/503 ARVN (infantry) battalions AC07-17CAV, DCO 1/10CAV, C-4-42 ARTY, B/2-9 ARTY, D/3-319 ARVN ARTY, C/1-92 ARTY) in Darlac Province.

From Ban Me Thuot, five of us were going to B Company, so we boarded a Huey helicopter that took us to where B Company was located. I thought I was going to have heart failure on that Huey. There were no doors and we sat with our legs dangling in midair while two door gunners, one on each side, scanned the jungle over the barrels of their M-60s. In the middle of the helicopter there were C rations and water bladders for B Company. The copter was so loud, we had to shout to each other. And the vibration through our rear ends made us feel like we were moving closer to the edge. Throughout the flight, I had a death grip on the C ration crates piled in the center of the chopper. I wondered if anybody ever fell out?

Eventually the helicopter banked to the left and started to descend. As we came in, I saw a round clearing cut into the jungle, with sandbagged bunkers and purple smoke rising from a landing pad. Guys were sitting on bunkers, others milling around without shirts, looking up at the chopper. The chopper landed, we got off, and it took off, kicking up a cloud of dust and stinging dirt. Everyone around the pad was looking at us like we were freaks. I felt really out of place. My hands and armpits were sweating like mad. One sergeant told the guy who brought in the chopper to take us FNGs up to the captain's hootch. As we were walking to the middle of the position, I asked the guy taking us there, "What is an FNG?"

In a slow Louisiana drawl, he said, "Fuckin' new guys."

We reached the center of the perimeter where the captain was. There were about ten people, a few were lieutenants and

E-6s, sitting underneath a couple of poncho liners. The captain said, "Welcome to B Company, glad to have you aboard, I'm Captain Burton." He pointed at me. "You go to 1st Platoon." The others were told to go to the 2d and 3d Platoons.

The staff sergeant (E6) of 1st Platoon came up to me and introduced himself, but I forgot his name right away. He told me I'd be in 3d Squad, and to go down to the bunker line and find the 3d Squad's leader, an E-5 named Dean Johnson. I trudged off to the bunker line to where he told me. When I got there, four guys were sitting around cooking C rations.

I went over to the E-5 and said, "Dean? The platoon sergeant said I should report to you."

"Take your pack off and sit down, relax." he said.

"I heard that right," I said. I sat down.

Dean (D.J.) introduced me to the three men sitting there, Happy Jack, Little George, and Bill. He said the others were on patrol and I would meet them in a few days. We started talking. Dean was from Maine, George Thompson was from Detroit, Jack Regan was from Malden, Massachusetts and Bill Warner was from Connecticut. As we talked about our home towns, the tension that was in me went away, and I started to relax. After ten minutes, I could tell these guys were all right.

After a while I said, "Hey, Little George!" He was black, about five feet six and 110 pounds, with a smile that went from ear to ear.

"What you want?" he replied.

"R-E-S-P-E-C-T." We laughed and I asked, "Little George, how's this company?"

"This company is cool, a lot of good guys here. There's a couple assholes, but the majority are okay."

"How's our battalion, the 1st of the 12th?"

"Well, we are supposed to have our shit together, in fact we are supposed to be one of the best units in the 4th Division, and our company is supposed to be the best out of the 1st of the 12th, so take it from there."

That made me feel good.

After a while, Dean came over and plopped down. He told me I would pull bunker guard that night with Bill and that we would alternate watches during the night. He'd be with Little George. He continued. "You'll be doing this a few days, and then when our patrol comes in, you'll have to pull LP [listening post] because it's our squad's turn."

I thought I was lucky because my squad leader was laying

everything on the table. I could tell he was intelligent and that he didn't want to rush me into anything. He also emphasized that he wasn't sending me on patrol because he wanted me to get used to the surroundings first. "A patrol," he explained, "is four guys sent out about three thousand meters. They stay out two nights, about forty-eight hours, and they carry a radio." He added that the company had just started pulling SRPs (short-range patrols) a few weeks earlier. He said that the patrol acted as an early warning. If something was headed toward the company, the patrol would be able to sound a warning. The SRPs were also used to observe enemy movement. He ended by saying, "Don't worry, we call our squad the lucky 1/3 elephant [instead of element]—1st Platoon, 3d Squad—13! That's lucky!"

That night, while I pulled bunker guard with Bill for two hours, we talked about where we were from, our families, girlfriends, music, what groups we liked, sports, etc., anything that would make the two hours go by quicker. I also spent a lot of time staring at the millions of stars in the sky—I'd never seen so many stars in my life.

During our watch, Bill told me about Dean.

"Dean has got his shit together; he's probably the best sergeant in this company. You," he said, "you're lucky to get in this squad. The guys you came in with aren't as fortunate as you."

Talking with Bill was just what I needed. I was confident, I was proud, anxious to prove myself, to earn the respect of the other guys. The following day, we sat around, filled sandbags, and just talked. It was over one hundred degrees, no wind, just hot, burning sun. In one day, I learned a lot about the guys. About two in the afternoon, I was sitting with Little George, and I started to sing, "I Wish It Would Rain," the Temptations' hit.

"How you know that?" he said.

I said, "I'm a blue-eyed brother, and I got so much soul, I can't even control."

He busted out laughing, saying, "You're okay, man, you're okay. You got a good voice, man. We'll get together with some brothers and do some jammin'!"

That night, I pulled bunker guard with Little George and learned a lot about him, his family, girlfriends. Every so often, we'd look through the Starlight Scope out at the perimeter wire to see if anything was happening, but nothing was.

The following day, the other guys from our squad came in, and I met Jerry Sehman, Ray Bethea ("Ray B."), Ken Thomas, and Jim Leonard, who was from the second squad. I also met guys in our platoon's machine-gun squad, who were in the bunker next to ours. They were Luke Whitaker, Wayne Kahre, Flynn, and Steve Turzilli, and a few others. While we filled sandbags and laid some barbed wire to fortify our position, we sweated our asses off in the heat. After the third day, we were running low on water. We were told more was coming, but it never arrived, and we all ran out of water that day. That night Dean told me I'd be pulling LP (listening post) with Ray B. A listening post was two men hidden outside the perimeter with a radio. If it heard someone headed toward the perimeter, the LP warned the company. Dean showed me how to operate the radio; he told me the CP (command post RTOs) would ask us for sitreps (situation reports, that is, what was going on). He also explained that the LPs were called Tiger 2, 3, 4, etc.

"They'll call you about every twenty minutes and say, 'Tiger 2, or 3, or 4, this is Tiger 1. Sitrep.' You squeeze the handset twice to answer that you're okay and that the situation is normal. If you hear anything suspicious, call Tiger 1 immediately and tell them who you are and what you hear. They will instruct you. Got it?"

"Should we shoot?" I said.

"No, you'll give away your position. Throw a grenade."

Ray B. and I picked up the radio and headed out of the perimeter through the wire, zigzagged our way by the trip flares and claymore mines into the jungle about thirty meters, and set up. Ray was a real smart-ass black militant who put out bad vibes to everyone. We sat there, not talking. He told me he would take first watch; I didn't want to argue, so I let him have it. I wasn't sleepy, so I pulled watch with him for the first two hours. I was a little scared as this was my first time out of the perimeter, but I wasn't scared about gooks sneaking up; I was worried about snakes, scorpions, spiders, or whatever else the jungle had in it.

About an hour into my watch, I started getting tired, and it was very hard to stay awake. The jungle sounds of crickets and other critters, almost lulls you to sleep, like the sounds of waves rolling lazily onto a beach. It was so dark, I couldn't see a thing except the glowing of my watch. I pulled my watch without any mishap, giving the sitreps on the radio by squeezing the handset talk-button twice. Ray had last watch, from four to six, but I woke up a few times. When I whispered, "Ray, you awake?" I got no answer. He was sleeping! I had to shake him to get him up. I was so thirsty I couldn't even spit. I chewed gum, but even that didn't help much. Daybreak came; we packed up and moved back into the perimeter after it was totally light out so nobody would think we were gooks and blow us away.

At our bunker, everyone was awake and stirring around, breaking off small chunks of C-4 (plastic explosive) to use as fuel for cooking C rations.

When I asked about water, D.J. said, "Who knows? They were supposed to have been here yesterday." Then he said, "If they're not here today, we have no choice but to drink that." He pointed to a puddle of water next to the bunker that was a milky white from shaving cream and who knows what else.

Bugs were floating on top, and it looked disgusting.

That day, because we had no water, we took it easy and tried to stay out of the sun. We did not move around too much. Of course, no water came, so we had to take our water from the puddle. D.J. had us put small gray halazone pills in it to kill whatever was in the water. I put four tablets into the canteen, shook it up, and presto chango; it tasted like liquid shit, but it was wet. We finally got water the next day. For the next few days, during the day we filled sandbags and laid barbed wire. Little George introduced me to more of the guys from the 3d Platoon.

One night, Little George told me a few guys were going to get together and jam (sing), so we went over by the 3d Platoon area. It was 6:00 P.M., and there were about ten of us, Harris, Claiborne, Little Joe, Griff, Billy Sewell, and a few others. For most of the songs we sang, I took the lead. All of the others sang the "shuwaps" or "*do do wa*'s." We had a hell of a time singing, laughing, joking, and goofing off. We sang "My Girl" (Temps). "Oh Baby Baby", "Going to a Go-Go" (Smokey), "What's Your Name?" (Don and Juan), "Wish It Would Rain" (Temps), "Hold on I'm Coming" (Sam and Dave), "This Old Heart of Mine" (Four Tops), "Blue Moon", "So In Love." Any songs that we didn't know all the words, we threw words in. We sounded good.

Before I knew it, it was 8:00 P.M.; we'd been singing for two hours, but it seemed like only ten minutes. Unfortunately we had to break off and go back to our bunkers for bunker guard. The next day a few white guys ignored me when I said hello, and I got stares all day long. So I asked Little George what was going on?

"I guess they don't like you hanging around us brothers," he said.

"Fuck 'em," I said. In high school, I fought blacks, whites, dagos, hillbillies, drunks, dopers, etc. There were assholes no matter what their color or ethnic group. I took people for what they were, not what color or nationality they were.

That day, I made my first mistake in Nam. With my shirt off most of the day, my shoulders and back got burned, and blisters formed on my shoulders. The 1st Platoon's medic gave me some salve and a couple of aspirins. He told me that I'd screwed up and there wasn't anything he could do. I'd just have to smile through it. That night I couldn't sleep; I had chills, hot flashes, and the sweats. I still had to pull bunker guard. Morning came, and we were sitting around cooking C rations when Dean came down from the CP and said, "We're moving out in half an hour so pack up."

"Oh, shit, I have to put on a pack?" I said.

He shrugged and said, "What can I tell you?"

I had nobody to blame but myself for getting sunburned. I put salve on my shoulders and got my shit together. When I asked Dean how far we were going, all he could say was, "All day and all tomorrow." We were headed for Duc Lap (southwest of Ban Me Thuot), two klicks east of the Cambodian border.

(4th Infantry Division Operational Reports Lessons Learned Period Ending Oct 31, 1968)

DARLAC PROVINCE

(1) The 95th Regt moved to the DUC LAP area in September, but was contacted only sporadically.

September and October saw a general withdrawal and re-alignment of B-3 Front forces. The 101D Regt vacated the Tri-border area and moved south, probably to Base Area 701. The 24th Regt moved out of country and probably returned to its normal resupply area in Base Area 609. The 66th Regt moved from north of BAN ME THUOT to the area north of DUC LAP.

KONTUM PROVINCE

For the first three weeks of September, friendly installations in the DAK SEANG area continued to experience almost daily attacks by fire, light contacts, and probes. In late September, however, enemy activity rapidly decreased, and Red Haze, APD sensings, and visual reconnaissance detected the withdrawal of the 101D Regt from the DAK SEANG area into LAOS. Activity generally increased south of DAK TO as a result of NVA efforts to reuse the old PLEI TRAP Road, specifically its northern and eastern extensions. The KONTUM City area remained relatively active during September. Two rocket attacks, numerous light harassing attacks, and several attacks by fire on friendly locations north of the city were received.

PLEIKU PROVINCE

Contacts continued throughout September. On 22 Sept a HOI CHAHN [defector] from the K-5 Bn, 24th Regt stated that 390 men from the K-4 Bn and 150 men from the K-5 Bn were killed by recent airstrikes. He also stated that the K-6 Bn was operating west of Highway 14N, north of PLEI MRONG. This was confirmed by contacts with US and CSF units north of PLEI MRONG in late September and early Oct. It now appears that the 24th Regt has withdrawn into CAMBODIA for resupply purposes.

All I could do was wrap a towel underneath the straps of my rucksack to soften the load on my shoulders. We tore apart our bunker, saddled up, and started to hump out in single file. In the first forty minutes, I tripped and fell three times. The total weight of my pack, which held two two-quart water bladders, three one-quart canteens, and three days of C rations, my personal stuff, writing paper, etc., poncho, poncho liner, one claymore mine, three trip flares, one hand-held flare, twenty empty sandbags, four bandoliers of ammo (twenty-eight magazines with eighteen cartridges in each), was about seventy pounds. I also had a pistol belt with two ammo pouches containing six M-16 magazines with two grenades on each. Each squad carried a pick, shovel, two axes, and three machetes.

My shoulders were burning from the blisters broken by my pack. The pain felt like thousands of needles being stuck into my shoulders and back. It hurt so bad, I thought I was going to pass out. I forced myself to push on; hell, I couldn't fall out;

I would lose face with the other guys. My fatigues were soaked with sweat; my arms and hands had small cuts all over from the jungle vegetation, which seemed to reach out and rip my skin open for violating its turf.

Vines with small three-prong claws, razor-sharp leaves, small thorns on stalks of other vegetation. It was very easy to trip with all of that stuff growing. The bush was so thick, sometimes, that the pointmen, instead of hacking madly at foliage, would just take a few steps back and hurl their bodies into the vegetation to knock it down. Travel was slow, and the line of men acted like an accordion: sometimes we were a couple of feet apart, and then, all of a sudden, we would be stretched out ten or twenty meters, and we would have to hurry to close the gap.

We humped all morning. We broke once, around noon, for some quick chow. I sat down, exhausted; my shoulders and back hurt like hell. The blisters were raw, and I asked Bill Warner to put more salve on my shoulders. My legs were tightening up. I hurt all over, and the air was like a steam bath.

After about forty minutes, it was saddle-up time again. I felt like screaming, and the pack felt like it had doubled in weight. I had thought after basic and AIT that I was in pretty good shape. Bullshit. I was not prepared for humping the bush. The first time was the hardest because you didn't know what to expect. We humped the rest of the day until about an hour before dark when we set up a makeshift perimeter and had some C rations. We didn't dig in because there wasn't enough daylight. We still had to pull watch, which was harder than hell after pushing our bodies to their limit for about eleven hours. We'd humped two or three klicks (two or three thousand meters), which didn't seem far unless you took the terrain into account. My back and shoulders were so sore, I had to sleep on my side. Sleep, at least, was no problem. I drifted off, thinking about what I had endured. I felt proud of myself for holding up under the most painful conditions I had ever experienced. I'll never get sunburned again, I promised myself. Night zoomed by after my watch, and before I knew it, nighttime shadows disappeared. It was dawn, the last day of September.

After eating a light breakfast, we saddled up and moved out. We humped all morning until we reached a blacktop road, which turned out to be Highway 14, a couple of miles southwest from Duc Lap. Cautiously, we moved across the road. We saw a few peasants walking, some riding bicycles, just going about their daily chores. The company set up about fifty meters from the road. We dropped our packs; the company put out a few LPs (listening posts), and we cleared away the jungle for our perimeter, cut fields of fire, dug bunkers, and cut trees.

Our squad was split into threes. Three of us cleared vegetation, three went to cut trees, three started to dig. Using a machete with Ray and Bill, I had to clear vegetation. I enjoyed it. We also set six or seven trip flares and four claymore mines out away from our unfinished bunker. That night was the first time I heard heavy artillery fire since I'd arrived in B Company—artillery barrages and occasional rifle fire a few miles away, toward Duc Lap. A few moments later, I saw Spooky for the first time (Spooky was an AC-47, a two-engine, World-War II vintage, propellor-driven cargo aircraft, converted to carry three miniguns and searchlights). When Spooky was growling, all you heard was a *brrrrr*, and it looked like the sky was spitting red. Every fifth round from the miniguns was a tracer.

The next couple of days were spent carving our niche into the jungle, building bunkers, connecting the bunkers with a trench, and clearing more of the jungle away from the perimeter to provide better fields of fire. Two more guys joined our company that first week in October. They were Greg Gates (Double G) and Eddie Medors from London, Ohio, which brought our squad, the 1/3 element, to eleven. The days were hot, about one hundred degrees, with high humidity. Drinking water always went quickly.

One day I was sitting on our bunker, filling sandbags with Double G, when I heard what I thought was a helicopter coming in. "Here comes a chopper."

"You better duck," Greg said.

I said, "What for?"

"Duck!" he said.

I did, and looked up because the noise was getting louder, *wap, wap, wap*—it was a bug about the size of a plum with what looked like two sets of wings. Greg and I were awed as it flew by.

"What the hell was that?" I said.

Greg shrugged, then Dean, who was sitting on the ground, said, "That, my friends, was a helicopter bug."

I looked at Greg and said, "Makes sense," and we both laughed.

That was the beginning of bizarre encounters with creatures

that lived in the jungles of Nam. About dusk, we were all sitting around the bunker bullshitting. We heard from the jungle, "Re-up, re-up, fuck you, fuck you," and we all starting laughing.

"That's the re-up lizard and the fuck-you bird, listen," D.J. said.

It happened again, "Re-up, re-up," "Fuck you, fuck you." I couldn't believe it, but it happened. Weird, I thought, but par for the course; if any army recruiter ever asked me to re-up, I would certainly tell him, "Fuck you," for sure.

The following day was hot as usual, but the weather changed for the first time in about three weeks. My fatigues looked like I'd just crawled out of a gutter on West Madison street, and I'm sure I smelled like it, too. But so did everyone else; we hadn't washed for three weeks.

It was right after we had lunch that someone yelled, "Here it comes." I looked up and saw rain in the distance coming towards us. A few guys stripped down, bare ass to the wind, holding a bar of soap, looking toward the rain approaching from the north.

Bill stripped down so fast you'd have thought his clothes were on fire. I followed and stood on top of the bunker clutching a bar of Ivory soap. The rains came quickly and hard. At first the rain was cold, but it felt great. "Lather up, but *quick*," Bill yelled over to me.

I thought I did, but as soon as I got lathered up, my hair full of soap, the rain just stopped. Bill was laughing his ass off. There I stood, naked, soaped up to the max. The sun came out and almost immediately caked the soap. All I could say was, "What the hell?" as I looked anxiously to the north. About ten minutes later, the rains came again, and this time, I quickly washed off.

That night it rained all night, turning our perimeter into a sea of mud and water. It rained a steady downpour for the next three days, and the weather got cold, or seemed cold, probably because we were soaked for three days. The fighting trenches became rivers, and our bunker had water in it up to our knees; our air mattresses became life rafts. On bunker guard, we wrapped up in ponchos and poncho liners and sat looking out into the dreary blackness, every so often hearing rats as big as cats rattling cans in the garbage sump.

Mostly, we thought about home, waiting anxiously for the weather to break so the army could fly in mail—mail was almost as important to us as food and water. It was our only link to the World. I hadn't any contact with my parents, brother, friends, or girlfriends since I'd mailed postcards from Tokyo and a short letter I'd sent them from Camp Enari to give them my address. I was only in country about a month, and already I was lonely, depressed, cold, hungry, and scared. Nothing dangerous had even happened yet, but I knew it was just a matter of time.

Chapter III

THE SRP

After four days, the rain let up enough to allow us to send out a few SRPs (short-range patrols). Each platoon sent out two SRPs, so everyone would alternate going out. Dean came over to me and said, "Saddle up. You're going on SRP, not with me, but with Jim Leonard, Doug Gilbert, and Ken Comeaux. I have to take out another patrol, but don't worry, Jim is one of the best in the platoon."

Well, I knew it would come sooner or later. I just wished it could be a little later.

When the squad leaders were called up to the CP to get briefed, I packed my gear and walked over to the second squad's bunker to wait until Jim came down from the CP.

He looked at me and said, "You got pace count."

"What's that?" I said.

"You keep track of how many steps we take from the perimeter," he answered.

"No sweat."

Then he added, "You bring up the rear and make sure no one comes up behind us." He put on his pack and said, "Okay, let's hit it."

Ken Comeaux was point, Doug Gilbert carried the radio in front of me, and Jim Leonard was second in line. We started out down a path that zigzagged through the barbed wire and trip flares, then out past some guys chopping down trees.

"Take care," someone said, as we passed, about one hundred meters from the perimeter. Then we were swallowed up by dense jungle. We stopped, and Jim whispered to me, "Keep count." I nodded my head okay and looked at my watch. It was about 8:30 A.M.

Ken was walking point and hacking wildly at the undergrowth blocking our way in every direction. Moving through a thick jungle was slow and tedious. We were tripping and falling, swearing under our breath, getting cut on the hands and arms by all the vines, thorns, and razor-sharp leaves. We tried to hold to a straight azimuth by the compass that Jim would whip out every fifteen minutes or so. About every half hour, he unfolded the map and figured out where we were.

The maps that we used weren't very accurate because they had been made from the air. We continued, stopping every so often to check our bearings, to catch our breath, and to wipe the sweat from our faces. It was hard for me to remember how many steps I was taking. I didn't know for sure because I kept falling, and I'd lose my temper.

It was hotter than a match head, no wind, just dead heavy air filled with humidity. We were hot, tired, aggravated, hungry, and thirsty. At about 4:00 P.M. we were sixteen hundred meters or so from the perimeter—a little over a klick and a half.

"We'll go another half hour, then we're setting up. This shit is just too thick, besides, you never go as far as they tell you on a SRP," Jim said.

After fifteen minutes, we found a small clearing with low brush at one end, which we set up behind.

The foliage was so thick above us that the sky was green. About four feet apart, we set up in a half circle, facing the clearing, trying to make as little noise as possible. I spread my C rations out on the ground next to me, unrolled my poncho and liner, laid my air mattress out (without blowing it up), and propped my pack up against a small tree as a backrest. Only an hour and a half remained before dark, so we chowed down. Jim leaned over and whispered that I would have third watch. Of course, I was the FNG, and third watch was from 1:00 A.M. to 3:30 A.M.—the worst watch, middle of the night.

As it grew closer to dusk, I became more and more nervous, not knowing what the night would bring, gooks or crawly things. I prayed to St. Jude, the patron saint of hopeless cases and impossible things, to protect us during the SRP.

I felt better after praying. I wasn't a Holy Roller, I just believed that in Nam you needed a little help from whoever. I prayed every day, probably because I was in danger.

As the final rays of the day disappeared and darkness covered Vietnam, it felt like you became part of the jungle, and you had to rely on your hearing because it became *so* dark that you just couldn't see. I sat, wondering what was out there, listening to the sounds of the darkness, pulling the poncho over my head to protect me from light rain, I drifted off to sleep.

Suddenly I was awakened by someone shaking my boot. It was Jim. He groped for my hand in the darkness to hand me the radio handset; it was my watch.

I had to check my eyes about every ten minutes to see if I was awake. The sitreps would come about every half hour, as the CP first called the LPs then the patrols. We were 1-2 and when the RTO (the command post's radiotelephone operator) called, I answered with two squeezes of the handset. I called for a time check once an hour to stay awake. There was nothing to look at, so I tried to occupy my time. I thought that using a radio with an earplug would keep me awake, but I didn't have one. I thought of songs, sang some in my head, home, girls (*don't* think about girls), baseball (Cubs) games I went to when I was a kid, and some outstanding games I played in Little League, Pony League, Colt League, and high school. Some bummers, like the time I broke my best friend's nose in Pony League playing for the American Legion. Louie Pontillo was my own catcher, my battery mate, my best friend all through grade school and until I was drafted. I broke his nose when I had slid into home under the tag and the ump called me out. I got up screaming, "He never touched me!" took my helmet off, and threw it as hard as I could. Louie was walking up to the plate, and I hit him square in the face. Everybody in the stands booed me, and I felt about a foot tall. I thought of football, playing Kiwanis and then high school.

Eventually my watch was over and, groping in the darkness, I crawled to where Ken was sleeping to wake him up. Then I drifted back to sleep under my poncho, clutching the M-16 to my chest the way I would a lover. It seemed like I'd been sleeping only a few minutes when somebody was shaking my foot again. I woke up foggy headed. It was just starting to get light, and dew was falling like rain from the trees. Ken said nervously in a whisper, "We hear something coming."

I sat up, pointing my M-16 from my left hip toward the clearing, my heart beating faster with every breath, my hands breaking into a clammy sweat. I listened to the bushes moving, twigs snapping. The movement was one hundred to two hundred meters to our front. Most sound doesn't travel far in the jungle, and you can only guess about how far it is. My head cleared quickly; the noise was real.

I clicked my M-16 off of safe to semiautomatic. I already

had a round chambered. A few minutes passed, and we sat silently, listening. The sounds of movement grew louder. Then we heard voices. I couldn't make out the language. The closer they got, the louder they were. I sat pointing my M-16 in the direction of the movement. My heart seemed to beat through my shirt, and I suddenly had to piss. The voices grew louder, but I still couldn't make out the words.

My finger moved to the trigger; the voices became singing, whistling, and laughing. As soon as I heard that, I knew the source wasn't Americans; they were having a good time. In an instant, they broke through the jungle at the edge of the clearing. I glanced over at the others, sitting like statues. Ken had his rifle pointed toward them; I glanced back. Standing at the edge of the clearing were two gooks in short pants and khaki shirts, ammo bandoliers crossing their chests, carrying AK-47s.

It seemed like we were frozen somewhere in the twilight zone. The one gook said something to the other, and then he turned and looked straight at us. In that split second, Jim yelled, "Shoot, shoot!" I pulled the trigger as fast as I could. Ken opened up at the same time. *Pow, pow, pow, pow.* I shot from my side, moving the barrel back and forth in a six-inch horizontal line. I emptied all eighteen rounds in the magazine. Ken emptied his magazine also.

The smoke from my M-16 barrel curled upwards in an eerie stream. There was complete silence for a moment. Then the silence was shattered by a bloodcurdling scream from one of the gooks. The other one was dead. The one screaming had to have about ten rounds in him. It was his death scream, but it scared the living shit out of us. Jim yelled, "Let's get out of here! Grab the radio and your ammo."

I grabbed my pack, my helmet, ammo, and started reaching for the C rations and poncho, Jim said, "Fuck that shit, leave it. Let's go! There's more of them. I heard them hitting the dirt."

There were no more screams when we took off running through the jungle. The CO was calling on the radio, "What happened, 1-2. Over?"

Jim grabbed the handset and tried to talk, breathing heavily into it, saying, "We made contact! Send artillery! Over!"

"Will do," the CO answered. "We'll have a marking round fired first; mark for HE [high explosives]." We were still running, stumbling, and falling. We heard the marking round fall in the distance. It wasn't even close to where we were, but who cared.

"Fire HE," Jim screamed into the handset. We kept on running. What confusion; my mind skimmed over what had just happened. Then I thought to myself, Shit, I just shot lefty from the side; I'm righty. It didn't matter, they were close enough. Then it dawned on me, where are we running?

I yelled up to Jim in front, "Jim, which way are we going?" We stopped, I took a fast leak; he took out his compass and pointed it to the direction we were heading.

A look of surprise came over his face and he said, "We made a complete circle! We're headed back to where we were."

We made an about-face. Now I was point, and I took off. The only sounds we heard were our own breathing and artillery barrages in the distance. Funny thing was, it took us about eight hours to get out to the position, it only took us about two hours to get back to our company perimeter. We were hauling ass.

There was a lot of commotion and confusion when we entered the perimeter. Guys came up to us, wanting to know what happened. We dropped our packs at the bunker, headed up to the CP, and reported to the CO. Jim told the CO that Ken and I had opened up on the gooks and that they seemed to be walking point for a larger force.

The CO told Lieutenant Murphy to get our platoon saddled up to sweep the area of contact. First Platoon left immediately, and a lot of guys came over to congratulate Ken and me, patting us on the back. The captain shook our hands and said, "Well done, boys." He then told us to go take it easy for a while, and he wanted us back up to the CP in a few hours to tell our story to a couple of reporters from *Ivy Leaf*, the 4th Infantry Division newspaper. At first I thought he was kidding, but he wasn't. I found out later that these were the first gooks our company had killed in four months. I shuffled down to our bunker. I felt drained; my legs were like rubber; my mind was reeling. Too much excitement. I sat down, thinking of what had happened. I'd never killed anyone before. I thought of the looks on their faces when we opened up. What if those two gooks had families, kids? I felt bad for an instant, but that changed to Better them than any one of us! Then I thought of how quickly your life could end in this miserable place, a split second, just the way we ended their lives. That patrol taught me that it was going to be a hell of a year; I'd have to keep control, never get lax. I sat there sipping on a canteen of water and staring off into the jungle toward Cambodia, wondering what next.

The "what next," was a giant black bird with an orange beak and a wing span of eight or ten feet. The bird flew like it was in slow motion, about one hundred meters from the perimeter. I could hear its wings break wind. It looked like something out of prehistoric times. The black UFO landed on a treetop, and the whole top of the tree swayed back and forth from its weight. We gave the bird a nickname, the HE (high explosive) bird.

Vietnam was strange—what were we doing there? I heard Happy Jack say, "It's a strange, strange world we live in, Master Jack." He couldn't sing, but I got the message and laughed.

About two hours went by before I heard a chopper in the distance. Someone yelled, "Hey, Leninger, get up here." I started up to the CP; at the same time, I saw the platoon coming through the wire from the sweep. Lieutenant Murphy was heading toward the CP.

I yelled, "Hey, Lt., did you find them." He shook his head, no.

I reached the command post, and about twenty people were standing around. I went and sat with Ken, Jim, and Doug. The chopper landed, and two Spec Fours got off, one carrying a briefcase. They were base-camp commandos: their uniforms were clean and starched, their boots were spit-shined. They started asking questions directed to Captain Burton, and he told them to ask the squad leader (Jim) what had happened.

Jim just said, "Two gooks walked up on us, and Ken and Jack blew them away! We took off because there were more of them. We could hear them hitting the brush behind the two we killed. We then called in artillery as we made it back to our perimeter."

Then they asked Jim, "Were they carrying weapons?"

"Yeah, AK-47s," Jim answered.

"Did you get their weapons?"

"What? Are you crazy?" Jim said. "I told you, these two guys were walking point to a platoon or company, or who knows what, and we're going to take time out to get their fucking weapons? My responsibility was the lives of three men, besides myself! We got our asses out of there, but quick. You base-camp commandos, what the fuck do you know?"

They both looked at each other and looked down to the ground, lost for words. So the captain said, "We sent out a platoon sweep led by Lieutenant Murphy of the 1st Platoon. What did you find, Lieutenant Murphy?"

"Sir, we found pools of blood and tracks where they dragged the bodies away."

Then I said, "What about our ponchos and food?"

He shook his head, no.

One of the reporters asked me, "How did you see it?"

I replied, "It's pretty much like Jim said. Those two gooks were singing and whistling, having a good time, and they happened to walk into the wrong spot. They ain't singing anymore."

The reporter wanted my full name and home. I told him, "Forest Park, Illinois, PFC John Leninger. But people call me Jack."

Then they asked Ken a couple of questions, got him to tell them his home town (Rayne, Louisiana). Jim's was Edmonton, Oklahoma.

According to division report recommendations:

(Operational Report 4th Infantry Division period ending Oct. 31, 1968)

During the reporting period the 4th Infantry Division made widespread use of a new patrolling technique called the Short Range Patrol (SRP) Screen. The concept involves the saturation of an area with a series of four men stationary teams equipped with radios and positioned for a 48 hour period astride likely enemy infiltration routes. The SRPs are located up to three kilometers from the patrol firebase. The mission of the SRPs is to adjust artillery and mortar fire and to call in air strikes and gunships on any enemy which it can observe or hear. The concept is designed generally to disrupt the enemy's activities and specifically to prevent the enemy from massing for an attack.

During the month of October the division maintained an average of 150 SRPs in position per day. Frequent contacts made by SRPs in the Ban Me Thuot area proved effectiveness of the technique and were largely responsible for thwarting the attack by the 66th NVA Regiment on Ban Me Thuot. On several occasions SRPs were successful in adjusting timely air/artillery fires on NVA forces of company and battalion size.

EMPLOYMENT OF SHORT RANGE PATROLS (SRPs)
ORLL Ending Oct 31, 1968

1. Observation: SRPs should not engage the enemy except to adjust indirect fire or air strikes.

   Evaluation: A recent violation of this principle resulted in the death of all four members of a SRP. A later sweep of the contact area revealed that the SRP had engaged a small NVA force which had withdrawn to a nearby heavily vegetated draw. The SRP pursued the enemy and was subsequently ambushed.

   Recommendation: That, in order to preclude the possibility of an ambush by a larger force, SRPs or any other small patrols with a similar mission should not intentionally engage any NVA force with small arms.

2. Observation: SRPs must move into position quietly and without being observed.

   Evaluation: Two SRPs in the vicinity of Kontum were attacked shortly after they had been observed moving into position by Montagnards in the area.

   Recommendation: That SRPs move into position at dusk or later to minimize the possibility of compromise.

3. Observation: SRPs should not leave their position except to return to the patrol/firebase or when the close proximity of air/artillery fire may necessitate relocation.

   Evaluation: Because of their small number, SRPs should make every effort to avoid unnecessary risks. On one occasion a SRP conducted a sweep after having adjusted artillery on an enemy element. The SRP was engaged by another enemy force and suffered several KIA.

   Recommendation: That SRPs remain stationary to reduce the possibility of being detected.

4. <u>Observation</u>: SRPs should not smoke, use scented soap, or wear shaving lotion prior to going into position.

<u>Evaluation</u>: A Hoi Chanh commented recently that the NVA were usually able to locate U.S. positions because of the odors emanating from burning cigarettes or lotion/soap recently used.

<u>Recommendation</u>: That SRPs refrain from smoking or from using scented soaps/lotions.

5. <u>Observation</u>: Only one member of a SRP should be permitted to sleep at any one time.

<u>Evaluation</u>: The primary function of the SRP is to detect without being detected. This also serves as the patrol's best defense. When only one SRP member is awake, the enemy has a better opportunity to approach the SRP position undetected. In one case, a tiger killed the only SRP member awake and dragged the body away undetected.

<u>Recommendation</u>: That only one member of a SRP be permitted to sleep at any one time.

After an hour, the reporters left. The captain again told us we did a fine job and he was proud of us. He also told Ken and me that we were being promoted to Spec Four and that we had a three-day in-country R & R to Vung Tau coming as soon as division approved it. I didn't know what to say. We just did our job, that's all; if we didn't, one, if not all of us, might have been killed. An instant promotion and an in-country R & R was our reward, kind of like getting a piece of candy when you were a good little boy. The thing that changed was the candy; the candy now was women.

We were the talk of the company for a few days, but that soon wore off, and it was back to the same routine of reinforcing our position, laying more wire, filling sandbags. I did notice that more guys were talking to me. It's surprising what killing a few gooks did for your image.

The end of October was about a week away. I went on another SRP, but we just sat for two days. I wrote a few letters, got some sleep during the day, taking turns with the others. I was nervous that something would happen again; it didn't.

In the distance, we could hear a couple of 155s firing across the border into Cambodia. We heard them whistling overhead, but all of a sudden, one went *shhhhhh, wham!* The short round had landed right outside the wire! When it hit, Ken and another guy popped out of the jungle, yelling, "Hey, what the fuck?" They had been pulling observation post (OP), and the round had just missed them.

Great, another thing to worry about. Our own artillery.

The last week of October arrived along with mail. Mail, contact with the World, was the only thing that kept up our hope and morale. Dean came back clutching a couple of packages under his arms; the letters were in his hands. We all gathered around, anxiously awaiting our names to be called. The packages were for Bill and Happy Jack. Happy Jack said, "Hey, Ma. Hot shit, pepperoni party." Then Dean passed out the letters. I made a decent haul: four letters, one from my parents; one from my brother; one from an old girlfriend, Mary Ann; and one from Mrs. Sortino (who was like a mother to me). My dad sent some race results; Mrs. S. sent a small St. Jude medal. I added it to my chain, which already had one Sacred Heart and one Virgin Mary on it. (I also wore an OD green rosary made from cloth, with a plastic blue cross). I read the letters. My mother told me that my ex-fiancée had married. I was glad I wasn't attached to any *one* girl; being in Vietnam, I had enough to worry about already. Let Jody have a field day; I didn't care.

Happy Jack came over with a hunk of pepperoni for me, and we sat around talking about what was in our letters. I handed two of my letters to Greg, and I read his mail. Then I let Happy Jack read the letter from Mary Ann. Reading each other's mail tightened the bond between the men in our squad. At night, on bunker guard, we always discussed home.

The next day we got paid, and I was called up to the CO's hootch. Top told me to get ready, an allocation had come down for an in-country R & R.

I went over to my pack and emptied my C rations on the ground. I had two cans of peaches, one fruit cocktail, two cans of beans and weenies, one pound cake, one beefsteak, and two chicken and noodles. I asked, "Who wants it?" Hands appeared from all over, grabbing. I said, "Wait a goddamned second. We've got to do this fair." So I thought of a number between one and ten, and whoever guessed the number got to choose one can. After my Cs were gone, I said, "Who needs water?" I gave all that I had away, except for two quarts of water and a couple of fudge bars. Then Dean said, "Give me five dollars MPC for our SPs (special privileges—beer and soda); the cigarettes and candy are free."

"I thought all of it was free?" I said.

"No way, if we didn't pay for beer and soda, we would never get it! The supply guys have to pay for it, also."

I gave in.

I still had to roll up my air mattress, poncho liner, and poncho, so I went into the bunker.

When I came out, Little George said, "Hey, Len, can I have your air mattress? You can get another one in Camp Enari. Mine has a few holes in it. The fucking termites bit the shit out of mine."

We exchanged air mattresses. Hell we were family; there was hardly any selfishness in our squad. Dean, Little George, and Wild Bill asked me to bring back film. Everybody else told me to bring back something, anything.

When somebody yelled, "Hey, Leninger, get over to the pad," I told everyone, "Don't get your asses blown away while I'm gone. Take care because the gooks may try something, knowing I'm not here!" Everybody just laughed.

I walked up to the pad and sat down. I could hear the sound of a chopper coming closer. I was excited and happy to get away for a few days. Who wouldn't have been?

Ken didn't go with me. Only one allocation had come down, and I was chosen to go first.

The Huey came in, kicked out a few cases of C rations and a water bladder, and I climbed on. As the chopper began to rise, the guys were standing around our bunker waving. I gave a thumbs-up sign, and we were off toward Pleiku and Camp Enari. By the time I reached the 1/12, it was already about 3:00 P.M. I checked in with the company clerk, and he told me I wouldn't leave until the next morning. I headed down the wooden sidewalk toward the weapons hootch to check my M-16 and ammo and then dropped my pack on a bunk in the transient barracks. I had some time to kill, so I headed up to the PX to browse around. I picked up the film for the guys and a few "raincoats" (rubbers) and went back to 1/12 for a shower before heading to the mess hall for some hot chow.

I could get used to this rear-area life real easy; being a base-camp commando beat the shit out of the bush. After chow, I ran into a couple of guys from C Company walking down the street. They were headed for the EM (enlisted men's) club so I went with them. The club was just a stage with a few gook broads go-go dancing, and a lot of small tables, with a bar at one end. We got a beer and sat down. We talked about B and C companies and the news. They were headed out of country on their R & Rs. I told them I was going on in-country to Vung Tau.

As I looked around, I noticed that the blacks sat all together at a couple of tables and the whites at other tables. No mixed tables. I asked one of the guys I was sitting with, "What gives here?"

"It's a different war here in base camp. An ethnic war," he said. "You know, whites against blacks, North against South. A lot of shit goes on here in base camp. Shootings, knifings. Guys fucked up on drugs or booze or both." Then he added, "One dude went down to Pleiku to see his girlfriend and found her with one of his buddies. He took his M-16 and blew both of them away! That's not the end of the story. This dude was married to a broad in the States! Can you beat that shit?"

Then one guy asked me how short I was. I told him I had a little over ten left in country.

"Ten days!" he said.

"No, ten months," I said. His mouth dropped open.

Watching the Vietnamese broads made me horny. Hell, the guys in base camp could go down to visit the women in Pleiku; I couldn't wait till I got to Vung Tau. While I was dreaming about women, a guy wandered over and sat down. He was drunk, and he started babbling about his wife, worried that she might be screwing around on him back home. Insane with jealousy, he hit the table a few times. We told him to calm down, but he only got worse.

Between the dancers and that guy, I had to get out of that EM club. Besides, the booze and the smoke were getting to me. When I got up to leave, so did the other guys, and we left. As we walked down the street, I said, "Boy, I'm sure glad I broke my engagement before I left the World. Being tied to one girl the way that guy is would have driven me nuts, man. I wonder how many guys will get themselves killed by doing something stupid over their girlfriends or wives."

One of the other guys said, "Plenty man, plenty. You got to keep your head in this fucking place."

The next day, someone came in about 6:00 A.M. and woke everyone up. I walked over to the mess hall, had scrambled eggs, bacon, toast, milk, and coffee. What a treat compared to C rations. We had a formation at 7:00 A.M. and, of course, everyone got in line and "policed" (picked up papers, cans, whatever) down the street. Typical army bullshit, even in Nam. At 9:00 A.M. a deuce-and-a-half (truck) pulled up to headquarters, and we piled on. There were about ten of us, four guys still drunk from the night before—they were going home, the lucky bastards. About three others were going to Vung Tau, and the rest were headed for out-of-country R & R. The deuce-and-a-half took us out of Camp Enari, through the stench of Pleiku, to the air force base. We got on a C-130 that took us to Vung Tau, about two hours away.

(Operational Report of the 4th Infantry Division Ending Oct 31, 1968)

Kontum Province

On October 27th and 28th, wheeled vehicle tracks were noted along the northern section of the Plei Trap Road, indicating the intention of the NVA to use this road once again. This is the first sign of vehicular use of the road since it was closed on April 6.

The C-130 landed at the air force base, and then a bus took us to an army billet located in the middle of Vung Tau, a town almost like Pleiku. The streets were packed with three-wheel taxis and bikes, small shops one after another, old mama-sans and papa-sans squatting, chewing betel nut on the side of the road. There were open markets selling vegetables, restaurants, bars, and tailors, and all the streets were littered with garbage. The billet was about four stories tall, surrounded by a wall about ten feet high with barbed wire on the top. There were two guards each at a front and a rear gate.

I signed in and went up to my room to drop off my gear. When I went back downstairs, I heard music. I followed it to a room with a bar, jukebox, and a few tables. Four guys were sitting around, having a beer. The song on the jukebox was "Hey Jude" by the Beatles. It was the first time I heard it. I liked it. I got a beer and walked over to the jukebox to see what jams were on it. "Whiter Shade of Pale" by Procol Harem was the next song that came on. I drank up my beer and headed into the streets of Vung Tau.

I asked an MP how to find the beach, and he told me just follow the street. As I walked little kids came up to me, tugging at my fatigues and offering me their sisters and mothers. I made sure my wallet was in the pocket my hand was in.

But I wanted to first check out the beach, women would come later. Besides, I had to melt away a few zits by swimming in saltwater and lying in the sun. After about ten sweaty minutes, walking in and out of a maze of people and traffic, I stumbled onto the beach. I couldn't believe my eyes: white sand, rolling waves, people basking in the sun, guys surfing, lifeguards. It was like any beach Stateside. I stood there for a minute. I turned around and looked back, thinking only a few miles away, guys are dying or getting maimed, and here, here was paradise.

I made a beeline for the men's changing house and got into my swimsuit, picked up my fatigues and boots, and trudged out onto the sand. The hot sand felt good on my white, wrinkled, cruddy feet. In fact, the sand started to burn the bottom of my feet.

I dropped everything and made for the water. Ahh, what a relief. The water was warm, like bath water. I swam away from the beach about thirty or forty yards, turned around, and gazed back. It was hard to realize such a place could be situated in the middle of a war. I thought about the guys in my company. I was lost in my own thoughts until someone swam past me and yelled, "Watch out for the jellyfish; they sting like a motherfucker!" Can't even swim in this crazy land without something fucking with you. That was the end of my swimming for now. It was the first time I had been in the ocean; back home the closest thing was Lake Michigan.

I went back and lay on my towel, but I started to sweat immediately. So much for laying in the sun. I walked over to a lifeguard sitting in his chair, looking real slick with his tints on, and asked him, "How in the fuck did you get a job like this?"

"This is the air force!" he answered. It figured. "In my spare time," he added, "I'm a mechanic." He smiled.

Guys in the bush would give a left arm to get a job like his. I walked back to my towel and fatigues, picked them up, changed, and headed for the streets in search of some boom-boom.

• • •

I woke up in the billets the next morning about 9:00 A.M. I guess I needed the sleep.

I went downstairs, had some chow, took a towel and my bathing suit, and went to the beach again. This time I stayed about three hours, then got horny and went and found a different woman. I went back to the billet, then to the bar to get drunk. I managed to do exactly that. Later, I went out on the town with four other guys I met in the bar.

The next day, my last in Vung Tau, I just hit the streets, walked around, and came upon an open cafe with a stage, some tables, and a bar with Vietnamese waitresses. I ordered two beers and sat down. A gook rock 'n' roll group came on, and they played American music. They did "Whiter Shade of Pale" by Procol Harem so well, I thought it was Procol Harem. I couldn't believe how good the group played American jams. I stayed there all day, met some other guys on R & R, and got loaded again, found another woman, and that was my stay in Vung Tau. I left the next morning for Pleiku.

It was Halloween, October 31, 1968. Once I reached Camp Enari, I went up to the PX and bought a Panasonic portable radio. I then went back to the 1/12 area. When the beer hootch opened up later that afternoon, I bought a case for the guys in my squad. If I hadn't, I would have been on everyone's shit list.

On October 31, President Johnson announced a complete halt in bombing of North Vietnam and the expansion of the Paris peace talks to include the National Liberation front and the backed South Vietnamese Government. The South Vietnamese Government did not agree to negotiate, however, until November 26, and four-way talks did not begin until 1969 because of disagreement over the shape of the conference table.

(Operational Report of the 4th Infantry Division Ending Oct 31, 1968)

The 4th reported at the end of October 1968 that the 18B Regiment as well as elements of the 101D Regiment posed a threat to Duc Co and other installations in western Pleiku Province at the end of the reporting period. Indications were that the enemy plans a major offensive effort against Duc

Co, possibly at the beginning of November. A contact with elements of the 18B Regiment at the end of October southwest of Thanh An-Oasis confirmed the probability of impending enemy operations in western Pleiku.

The decrease in enemy activity continued through the month of October. There has been no further identification or contact with the K-37, K-25, K-39 Bns, and the 66th, 320th, 95X and the 95th Regiments during the month of October. The E-301 LF Bn was identified on October 26th by PWs as having two companies operating west of Mewal Plantation vic AZ 8221. The C-2 Co, E-301 LF Bn has been identified by documents as located south of Ban Me Thuot. The 401 LF Bn was reported by PWs to be operating east of the Mewal Plantation. Also, the PWs stated that the H-5 District Headquarters is located in the Mewal Plantation. On October 18, a PW captured east of Ban Me Thuot from the 316th Trans Bn stated that his unit was subordinate to the 559th Trans Group.

A contact on October 27 southwest of Thanh An identified the 408th Sapper Bn along with the 18B Regiment, indicating that elements of the 40th Sapper Bn, which normally operate in or north of Pleiku City, have probably been attached to the 18B Regiment for support. In addition, at least two new sapper battalions have been formed. The K-25 and K-37 Sapper Bns have recently been identified near Ban Me Thuot.

Source: Operational Report Lessons Learned Period Ending October 31, 1968

Recapitulation of Enemy Battle Losses (1 Aug - 31 Oct)

(a) Personnel:	KIA (BC) BODY COUNT	472
	NVA CIA	8
	VC/VMC CIA	23
	TOTAL	503

CAPTURED

(b) Weapons:	S/A SMALL ARMS	163
	C/S CREW SERVED	21
	TOTAL	184

(c) Ammunition:

S/A rds	53,281
C/S rds	12,668
Grenades	352
Mines	106

(d) Miscellaneous captured items:

Explosives	427 lbs
Documents	56 inches
Rice	14.9 tons
Salt	5 lbs

4th Infantry Division
Casualties:

Unit	Kia Dead	Missing	Hostile Wounded	Dead	Non-Hostile Missing	Injured
1st Bde	51	1	95	2	0	34
2d Bde	34	2	184	2	0	24
3d Bde	46	0	133	4	0	49
DIVARTY	9	0	45	1	0	22
DISCOM	0	0	17	0	0	5
2-1 Cav	3	0	12	0	0	12
1-10 Cav	1	0	41	0	0	12
1-69 Armor	5	0	50	0	0	4
4th Engr	3	0	7	0	0	17
4th Avn	1	0	9	0	0	1
124th Sig Bn	0	0	0	0	0	0
HHC, 4th Inf Div	0	0	0	0	0	0
4th Mp Co	0	0	0	1	0	3
4th Admin Co	1	0	2	0	0	2
Scout Dog	0	0	0	0	0	5
E, 20th Inf	0	0	9	0	0	3
E, 58th Inf	0	0	3	0	0	2
4th MI	0	0	0	1	0	0
TOTAL	154	3	607	11	0	195

Est. Enemy Composition, Disposition and Strength on 31
Oct 68.

UNIT	CURRENT EST STR	LAST KNOWN LOCATION
B-3 Front Hq	500	CAMBODIA/KONTUM Border
1st NVA Inf Div (HQ & SPT)	1,450	Base Area 740 (Border west of Kontum)
66th NVA Inf Regt	1,800	CAMBODIA//DARLAC Border
320th NVA Inf Regt	1,400	Base Area 740
95C NVA Inf Regt	1,200	Base Area 740
18B NVA Inf Regt	1,800	Base Area 701 DUCCO
95th NVA Inf Regt	1,800	CAMBODIA/DARLAC Border
24th NVA Inf Regt	900	CAMBODIA/KONTUM Border
40th NVA Arty Regt	1,200	Tri-border Area
95B NVA Inf Regt	850	E. PLEIKU Province
304th VC LF Bn	150	North of KONTUM City
406th Sapper Bn	100	North of KONTUM City
X-45 VC LF Bn	200	W. PLEIKU Province
H-15 VC LF Bn	50	DAK AYUNH Valley
407th Sapper Bn	300	Unlocated
408th Sapper Bn	275	Northeast of PLEIKU City
301st VC LF Bn	250	BAN ME THUOT Area
401st VC LF Bn	300	BAN ME THUOT Area
K-39 NVA Inf Bn	300	Southwest of BAN ME THUOT
K-25 Sapper Bn	200	East of BAN ME THUOT
K-37 Sapper Bn	300	East of BAN ME THUOT

The following units were left out of this report but were added in for report ending January 31, 1968. They were located in the 4th Division A.O. (Area of Operation)

101D NVA Inf Regt	1,800	Base Area 702 (Border west of Kontum)
303D LOCAL Force	250	Eastern Darlac Province
966 NVA Inf	250	Western PLEIKU Province
LOCAL Guerrillas	3,000	(Est)
TOTAL COMBAT INFANTRY	20,625	

DIVISION AWARDS

	Aug	Sep	Oct
(1) Decorations Awarded			
Distinguished Service Cross	4	1	1
Silver Star	18	25	14
Legion of Merit	11	4	1
Distinguished Flying Cross	13	3	4
Soldier's Medal	2	9	0
Bronze Star (Valor)	119	162	99
Army Commendation (Valor)	142	154	134
Air Medal (Valor)	31	12	15
Bronze Star (Service)	255	290	94
Army Commendation (Service)	1,010	1,177	593
Air Medal (Service)	484	380	490
Purple Heart	99	113	65
Total	2,188	2,330	1,150

	Aug	Sep	Oct
(2) Badges			
Combat Infantryman Badge	333	1,313	1,204
Combat Medical Badge	60	37	23
Aircraft Crewman Badge	0	56	1
Miscellaneous Badge	91	41	0
Total	484	1,447	1,228

Task Organization as of 31 October 1968 with supporting artillery:

1st Bde, 4th Inf Div	3d Bde, 4th Inf Div
1-8 Inf	2-8 Inf (-)
3-12 Inf	3-8 Inf
C/2-1 Cav	1-14 Inf
6-29 Arty (-) DS	1-22 Inf
C/5-16 Arty CSR 6-29	1-35 Inf
D/5-16 Arty CSR 6-29	1-69 Armor (-)
A/1-92 Arty CSR 6-29*	A/1-10 Cav
B/6-14 Arty CS*	C/1-10 Cav
A/4 Engr	2-9 Arty (-) DS
TACP	C/4-42 Arty DS 1-22
	C/6-29 Arty CSR 2-9

2d Bde, 4th Inf Div
1-12 Inf
2-35 Inf
1-10 Cav (-)
4-42 Arty (-) DS
B/2-9 Arty DS 2-35
B/5-16 Arty CSR 4-42
C/1-92 Arty CS*
B/5-22 Arty CS*
B/4 Eng
TACP

A/5-16 Arty CSR 2-9
A/3-6 Arty DS 2-8*
B/1-92 Arty CSR 2-9*
A/6-14 Arty CS
C/6-14 Arty CS
C/7-15 Arty CS*
D/4 Engr
TACP

Division Troops
(BASECAMP)
C/2-8 Inf
2-1 Cav (-)
7-17 Cav (-) 7
A/5-22 Arty CS*
4 Engr (-)

TOTAL APPROX 5000 COMBAT INFANTRY
*NOT ASSIGNED TO 4TH INFANTRY PART OF FIELD
FORCE I SUPPORT ALSO USED FOR GENERAL
SUPPORT 4TH INF DIV

Each Infantry battalion had 4 Companies A,B,C,D and one recon platoon, approx strength, 100 per company, (Field) approx. 40 clerks and re-supply, 30-40 Recon, Platoon because of Rotation, R and R, Sick, ETC. This figure fluctuated mostly under 100 per line company and under 40 for recon platoon.

(Operational Report of the 4th Infantry Division Ending Oct. 31, 1968)

The NVA units in KONTUM Province used the majority of the month of October to refit and reposition; consequently, there was an almost complete halt of enemy activity during this period. The DAK PEK area was the scene of increased activity as a result of the enemy's resupply efforts; however, despite this activity, no significant contacts were made in this area.

In late October there were indications of increased enemy activity in the BEN HET area that culminated in several intense attacks by fire on FSB #29 just south of the BEN HET Special Forces Camp and one 122 MM rocket attack on BEN HET itself. This was the first rocket attack on the Special Forces Camp since 16 Feb, and indicates continued enemy interest in this area. The enemy involved were the 40th Arty Regt and possibly elements of the 24th Regt.

The company was still southwest of Duc Lap, and nothing had happened while I was getting my rocks off. I was anxious to tell everyone about my sexcapades in Vung Tau, so I passed out the beer and film and started telling my story. It got a lot of laughs.

When I was finished, Dean said, "I hate to bust your bubble, but you are going out on patrol tomorrow with Jack Shoppe."

"Well, I kinda expected it," I replied.

That night I pulled bunker guard with Double G, and after we talked for a while, he talked me into writing to a girl who was a friend of his girlfriend in Detroit. He wanted to see if I would "get over."

The next day after chow, I went over to the 2d Squad's bunker and headed out on SRP with Jack, Bud Kutchman, and Jay Click. Once we were far enough from the perimeter, Jack held us up, we waited about ten minutes until a patrol from the 2d Platoon came by; we hooked up, and eight of us headed out to one position.

I felt secure being with seven others, and I'm sure everybody else felt the same way; if we ran into anything, eight guys could put out a lot more lead than four. Linking up SRP patrols would become common practice when we knew the gooks were around. Total secrecy had to be vowed by all involved because if the CO or any of our cadre found out, the squad leaders' asses would be in a jam for not carrying out orders. The squad leaders didn't really disobey, they just stretched orders a bit for the safety of all.

We went out about two klicks to our squad's location, the other location was a phony one called in by the 2d Platoon's patrol leader. Hey, why not? That's all the army cared about, was for us to run into the gooks so they could call in air strikes and artillery on them. Everyone was an eight-digit number in a vast sea of US (i.e., draftee) and RA (volunteers and lifers) numbers, and that's it. And if the shit hit the fan while we were on SRP, we were on our own.

We set up and ate, and I started to write a couple of letters before it got dark. I rolled up my sleeve and found I had a leech on my arm, about the size of a fat match. It didn't hurt, it was just ugly.

We checked each other out and found a few more on legs, backs, and arms. To get them off we just sprayed some insect repellent on them and they fell off.

Bud told me that while I was in Vung Tau he found something on a SRP. He reached in his pocket and pulled out what looked like a diamond the size of a golf ball, that he got out of a Buddha's forehead. He was going to send it home and was probably rich. I told him if he was I was going to hit him up for a loan.

I pulled out writing paper that I had wrapped in plastic from a PRC-25 radio battery. My wallet was wrapped the same way.

(Operational Report 4th Inf. Division for period ending 31 January 1969, RCS CS for-65(RI))

2. (C) Intelligence.

a. General: In early November, division attention centered on the increased NVA use of the PLEI TRAP Road in southwest KONTUM Province. Operation DEADEND, conducted by CIDG elements and the 2d Brigade, 4th Infantry Division, successfully closed the road to vehicular traffic in late November, although foot traffic in the area has continued to date. During the same time period, a buildup of NVA forces was observed in Base Area 701 west of DUC CO, signifying that an enemy operation was possibly intended in the area. Occupation of FSB's (Mary 3/YA764326), Karen (YA815309), JEAN (YA806233), JOAN (YA842280) and VERA (YA835172) apparently frustrated enemy intentions concerning DUC CO, and the hostile forces dispersed in late November without initiating a major ground action.

(1) KONTUM: Since early November, there has been extremely limited enemy activity in KONTUM Province. The majority of contacts with the enemy have involved VIET CONG LOCAL FORCE/MAIN FORCE units rather than NVA Forces. During November, activity was concentrated in the BEN HET-DAK TO area. The BEN HET Special Forces Camp and Fire Support Base (29) came under intense attacks by fire during the first two weeks of the month, but after the evacuation of FSB 29, the attacks were reduced to minor ha-

rassing actions against BEN HET. During the attacks on FSB 29 (YB839223), the enemy employed 100mm and 105mm artillery from within their CAMBODIAN sanctuary.

Enemy transportation units used the PLEI TRAP Road extensively in early November. Reconnaissance aircraft detected vehicular movement on several occasions with the most significant being a convoy consisting of 21 trucks and four tanks. Foot traffic, at times heavy, has continued through the area.

(2) PLEIKU: In early November, NVA forces massed in Base Area 701, across the CAMBODIAN border from DUC CO. Units of the 4th Infantry Division's 3d Brigade occupied FSBs MARY S(YA764326) and KAREN (YA815309), north of DUC CO, and FSB's JEAN (YA806233) to the west, JOAN (YA842280) to the east, and VERA (YA835172) to the south of DUC CO. Occupation of this key terrain made DUC CO a difficult target for any ground effort by hostile forces. The enemy did, however, employ 105mm artillery fire against FSB's JEAN (YA806233), JOAN (YA8842280), and VERA (YA835172). In late November, the enemy abandoned his plans and apparently withdrew from Base Area 701.

VIET CONG local forces and NVA engineer units have harassed friendly units in the area west of PLEIKU City between Highways 509 and 19W throughout the reporting period. This harassment has consisted of small arms and RPG-2 fire, with some mining activity.

(3) DARLAC: Contacts with enemy forces in DARLAC Province were light during the month of November. Most enemy elements in the area of battalion size or smaller. The only indications of forces larger than battalion size are agent reports from the DUC LAP area in nearby QUANG DUC Province. These reports indicate the presence of as many as 8000 NVA, but corroborating information by other than agent sources has not been produced. Intelligence gained from prisoners and captured documents indicates that the 95C and 320th Regiment have moved to the III Corps Tactical Zone, leaving no known regimental or larger size force in the DUC LAP area.

During the entire period, the 155th Assault Helicopter Company, located at BAN ME THUOT City Field, was the subject of continual attacks by fire from 75mm recoilless rifles, 60mm and 82mm mortars. The units responsible for these attacks are believed to be the K-34 Artillery Battalion and the K-39 Infantry Battalion. Both of these units have been identified as a result of contacts approximately 35 kilometers south-southwest of BAN ME THUOT in late January.

Although it has not been positively identified, the K-25 Engineer Battalion is believed to be located east of BAN ME THUOT City, between Highways 14 and 21, with the mission of harassing and interdicting these highways.

The 301st LF Battalion also has not been identified but it is believed to be operating in an area approximately 21 kilometers north of BAN ME THUOT.

I thought I'd write my parents first, then Greg's girlfriend's girlfriend. I told my parents that I was on SRP and that I hated SRPs, but they gave me time to write. I told them about my R & R to Vung Tau—not everything of course—and mentioned that I'd been promoted to Spec Four, which I knew would make them proud. But I never told them why. I also asked for a care package containing Spaghetti-Os, tuna, etc. because Cs were already boring. Then I asked for sports clippings from the *Sun-Times* and a racing form so I could study it. (I loved the track.) I also told my dad to send me the results for the racing forms so I could see what I had done wrong in picking a loser and why a horse won. I told them not to worry, that I would be okay. I was with one of the best companies in the 4th Infantry Division.

The next letter I wrote was to a girl I didn't even know, but wanted to, and I used words from songs. After that, I was tired of writing, so I got out my radio and plugged in the earphone and listened to AFVN (Armed Forces Vietnam Network). AFVN played current hits and some oldies; I heard "Hooked on a Feeling" by B.J. Thomas, "Heard You're Getting Married" by Brooklyn Bridge, and "Time" by Chamber Brothers. Music always seemed to cheer me up when I was feeling low, especially after writing and thinking about the World (home).

I put the radio away until it was my watch. It would help me to keep awake and pass the time, because time just *stops* when it's your radio watch. With half an hour until dark, I opened up some peaches and a can of pound cake, mixed them together, opened up a can of crackers and cheddar cheese. I would be in heaven until I was through. I downed some water and had dessert—a chocolate fudge bar and a can of Del Monte orange pop. Jack leaned over and whispered that my watch would be from 9:30 until 10:45.

"An hour and fifteen minutes!" I said. He shook his head and smiled. Linking SRPs was great.

Darkness came quickly. I wasn't tired, so I just leaned back against my pack listening to the sounds of the jungle and the breeze through the trees. The ground was full of leaves that glowed in the dark, and the fireflies twinkled like blinking Christmas tree lights. Sometimes nature was beautiful, peaceful, I thought. Before I knew it, it was 9:30; my watch. Jack handed me the radio handset and whispered, "See you in the morning."

I turned on my radio and plugged it in to my left ear, then held the handset close to my right ear. Both were turned low enough so I could still hear something coming through the jungle. About every ten minutes, I took the ear plug out and listened for five minutes or so just to make sure. Buying that radio was the smartest thing I ever did. What a difference. I could also use it on bunker guard, LP, or whatever, but I had to make sure I didn't get careless. My radio watch was a snap, and I went to sleep after I said my prayers to the Big Guy and St. Jude.

The following day was spent sitting around. I played cards for a while with a couple of guys, took a nap, wrote a couple of letters and listened to AFVN (Cris Noel) in the morning. I had to take a dump in the afternoon, so I took some toilet paper (which we always carried in excess), and went away out about twenty meters. I didn't want to go too far, or I might get my moon shot off. I also worried about snakes, so I always made sure nothing was around before dropping my drawers.

I leaned on my M-16 with one hand and held up my drawers with the other hand, and crouched down, hurried as fast as I could, looking behind and all around to make sure nothing was coming. What I didn't notice is that I pissed all over the back of my pants. I wiped myself and went back to the guys and my AO.

As I passed by, two guys looked up and whispered, "What happened?" They started snickering.

I was embarrassed. I took a canteen of water, dropped my drawers, and poured water all over my pants and tried to semiwash them the best I could. Everybody was watching, trying not to laugh. I gave them all the finger and pulled up my pants. It was cold. I stood up for about fifteen minutes, letting the air dry my pants. That was the last time that would happen to me.

The next morning, we packed up and moved back to the perimeter. We split up on the outskirts. As with many SRPs, nothing had happened; we had a rest for two days. But one never knew on an SRP or sweep or anytime when Sir Charles would pop up or we would accidentally run into him.

I "only" had 310 days left in country. Unfortunately only 310 days in country would make me an "official" short-timer (fifty-five days); I was still an FNG, but learning every day, getting used to the heat, humidity, monsoons, living like a gopher, out in the day, and going underground at night.

A few days later, we were put on full alert; intelligence thought the NVA was going to launch a major attack on various objectives. We manned our positions all day and into the night on 100 percent alert, peering out into the darkness, nerves on edge, illumination flares popping in the cloudless sky, casting eerie shadows as they floated down. The moon was out, and it was quite light, and artillery barrages could be heard firing across the border into Cambodia. Puff the Magic Dragon (AC-47) (Spooky) circled the sky while a FAC recon plane, an 0-2, searched the ground for movement. Occasionally Puff would let loose with miniguns. The Dragon was a morale builder, just knowing it was around. It could piss lead; it had three miniguns and a searchlight and could fire in any direction.

If we were going to get hit, tonight was the night because the moon conditions were right. We heard small-arms fire a few miles away. It had to be one of our sister elements, A, C, or D Company, or maybe the recon platoon, E. Nobody knew.

First Battalion was spread out over about three thousand meters. Sometimes, we were further apart, which made us ineffective as a battalion because it would take hours for us to get to anybody to help and vice versa. In addition, if the battalion had too much space to cover, it would be easy for small units to penetrate its lines. I often wondered why the gooks would attack a dug-in infantry company. What would they gain? Casualties is about all, unless we were blocking their way. But this time we were in the middle of nowhere as it turned out.

We stayed awake for nothing; there was no attack. I had a feeling intelligence reports really weren't worth much, but there was no way of telling when they would be right. We

were being used as a blocking force to protect Duc Lap, I
guess, or to aid Ban Me Thout if necessary. We enlisted folk
did not know what our objective was, but we stayed in that perimeter for over a month, and nothing happened except the
contact made on my first SRP. I was anxious to leave the area,
but division kept us in the same position. We still improved
our position every day, sent out SRPs, sat around, played poker
or bid whisk, and tried to figure out what to do with C rations
to make them better to eat. Turkey loaf, we couldn't do much
with; to Beans and weenies, my favorite, we could add cheese
or hot sauce if someone was holding the sauce. Beefsteak, we
could fry over a C-4 fire by holding it with a stick. And we
could put cheese on that too. Ham and lima beans . . . forget
it, nothing could save that. The best thing to do was chuck it
into the sump. To ham and eggs we could add catsup, but it
still had a greenish tint.

Some of the C rations were from the Korean War; some
were probably from World War II. Chicken and noodles,
wasn't too bad, but I didn't know that chickens had so much
fat or gristle. The noodles were okay, but it wasn't anything
near my ma's soup. That's why I wrote home for care packages. Anything beat C rations. Even the rats in our perimeter
just ate the cans for half the meals we threw away.

The days that followed brought nothing but an occasional
heavy downpour, followed by blistering heat. Our daily routines
were a bore. The only excitement we had was to listen to AFVN
radio and sing songs like, "Suzy Q" (CCR), "Sunshine of Your
Love" (Cream) "People Got to be Free" (Rascals), "Heard it
Through the Grapevine" (Marvin Gaye), "Hello, I Love You"
(Doors), "Baby, Now That I Found You" (Foundations), and
dancing a few steps while doing our duties. Our perimeter
smelled pretty bad from the food we threw away and the human
waste we couldn't easily move far away. That's probably why
the gooks never attacked. The smell would have wiped them out.

About 10 November, we got mail again. It seemed to come
every two to three weeks when we were set up. Some guys
wouldn't get any mail, and it demoralized them. A letter was
always the single most important morale booster unless it was
a Dear John letter. I thought any woman mean enough to send
one to a guy in the field should be shot.

After mail call, Jim L. came over with an *Ivy Leaf* (the 4th
Division paper) and said to me, "Hey, Len, read this on the
back page." He was excited.

VC Sings Very Sad Song

BAN ME THUOT—Two Viet Cong were strolling through the jungle, talking loudly and singing to themselves. Their voices alerted a 4th Division patrol and the VC have not said a word since.

A Short Range Patrol (SRP) team from the 2nd Brigade's 1st Battalion, 12th Infantry, commanded by Lieutenant Colonel Joseph T. Palastra Jr., of Salina, Kan., had spent a quiet night in the jungle near the small Vietnamese hamlet of Duc Lap.

Enemy troops had been reported in the area, and the patrol was sent to investigate.

The first rays of the morning sun were filtering through the dense Central Highland foliage as Private First Class Kenneth D. Comeaux of Rayne, La., stood guard over his sleeping team mates.

After the long cold night, the warm sun was a welcome sight to the Ivy pointman.

The trees had cast menacing shadows in the night. Now they swayed peacefully in the morning breeze.

As the Ivyman scanned the terrain, he detected the faint sound of voices heading toward the team.

Cautiously, PFC Comeaux woke his team leader, Specialist 4 James M. Leonard of Edmond, Okla.

The voices were growing louder.

"They were singing, talking and laughing all at the same time," the team leader recalled. "They were really happy about something."

With the entire team now awake, the Ivymen prepared for any event.

"Whoever they were, they were heading straight for us," explained Private First Class John Leninger of Forest Park, Ill.

Apparently, the strangers were not aware of the team and continued walking toward the hidden Red Warriors.

With the possibility of more enemy in the area, the team pulled back to higher ground.

From their vantage point, they guided the artillery, then moved out for the fire base.

After I read it, I said to Jim, "What is this bullshit?"

"I know, can you beat that?" he said. "In the first place, those two gooks you and Ken blew away were NVA!"

"They had khaki shirts and pith helmets, not pajamas," I added.

Then Jim said, "Maybe this is what division wanted the reporters to write."

"Could be," I said, "but why didn't they put in here that there were more of them? Those two were walking point."

"Well, we told the truth and that's all that matters, I guess. Maybe they were reinforcements for a VC unit. Who knows? They never made it to wherever they were going."

Chapter IV

THE MOVE NORTH

Another week passed before, early one morning, we finally heard the call to saddle up. A rush of excitement ran through me. "Where we going," I yelled over to Dean while rolling up my air mattress, poncho liner, and poncho.

"Who knows? But at least we're getting out of here. We're flying to a place where a convoy is picking us up. Word has it we're going north to Pleiku for a three-day stand-down."

"Hot shit," I said.

Laughing, Little George said, "It's party time."

Happy Jack replied, "Gee, I wish I had some pepperoni left! Hey, Ma, send some real quick."

According to 4th Division policy, we were supposed to get a stand-down once every three months. Everybody's morale shot sky-high. Not knowing this was the last time we would be this far south again, we tore apart our bunker the best we could. As the choppers came in and took out squads, one by one, we said adios to Duc Lap, not knowing where we would end up, but it sure beat the dense jungle we'd been in for over a month. My mind went back to the SRP when Ken and I blew away two gooks. I hoped that the future would bring luck in our new AO.

We were taken by chopper to an airstrip north of Ban Me Thuot. That night, the partying began. We were popping whatever beer was left from our SPs. Some guys also had bottles that had come from the States in care packages; some smoked hootch. Some guys popped hand-held flares, and one shot at the CP, going right through somebody's tent. Fortunately, nobody was in it. Everybody was having a good time. For most of the half-timers (six months) and old-timers, it was their first stand-down also. Things finally calmed down around 2:00 A.M.

I'm sure things were the same at A, C, and D companies and the recon platoon. The whole battalion was being convoyed up to Camp Enari, and there were a lot of guys around at once. Let Charlie come now! No way he'd attack us when we were strong. It was one of the few times we felt cocky.

The next morning came too quickly for everyone. We ate chow and shuffled over to Highway 14 to board the open deuce-and-a-halves along the road, two squads per truck. Our squad took the back.

The convoy started snaking through a rubber plantation, and I took pictures for the first time. In the front of the convoy was a Duster (a truck with two 40mm cannons) and one quad-.50 (truck with four .50-caliber machine guns). A couple of Huey gunships flanked the convoy. The road was dirt in the open areas, and the dust was gagging us in the back of the truck. The convoy stretched for a couple of miles, winding through villages, along open rolling hills where light green and dark green vegetation mixed against a background of blue skies dotted with white fluffy clouds. A countryside like a picture postcard.

We bumped along, sometimes slowing down as we went through small villages. Kids ran alongside the road yelling, "Chop-chop GI." Some of us threw them a few cans of food we didn't want or candy from our SPs.

The convoy reached Camp Enari around 12:30 in the afternoon. It had taken us about three hours from Ban Me Thuot. We got off the trucks slowly. My whole body was sore from being bounced around on the back of the truck. I looked around and started laughing my ass off. All the black guys were white from the grayish dust, and all the white guys looked black. We all started laughing. I took out my camera and took a couple of pictures.

Then Greg said laughingly, "Hey, blood, you should see your ass, your ugly black!"

Then I started singing, "I'm a soul man . . ."

Harris, Little Joe, Bill, and Ken came over, yelling "Get it, bro."

Laughing, Little George said, "You are crazy, man, you really crazy."

I said, "Thanks, honky. Right on, right on." Then we started laughing again.

After we got our gear together, we still had to put up hootches. I paired up with Greg, and we built a hootch, using some steel slats that were around on the ground. Then we went to the shower tent to wash off the grime.

First Battalion had been down near the small airstrip on the northwest corner of Camp Enari. Far away from the PX and EM club, so we wouldn't screw anything up. That night we just sat around, drank beer that we had to pay for, and had a few slugs of booze. I got screwed up quickly and crashed early. The next day, after eating chow at the mess tent, a few of us went up to the PX to shop. I wanted to go swimming, so I found a couple of guys going to the pool, bought a swimsuit at the PX, some extra radio batteries for my box, some film and writing paper, and that's all I needed.

We spent most of the day at the pool, hoping the sun and water would cure the jungle rot on our arms and legs. Our feet were a mess from being inside boots for so long; mine weren't as bad as some of the others. The red-and-white wrinkled skin stood out, like wearing socks with swim trunks. We made it back to our AO in time for hot chow. That was one of the best things about stand-down, not having to eat C rats. That night, some guys went up to the EM and NCO club. Others just stayed in our area, most of our squad and myself. We drank and sat around toasting marshmallows from the chow hall. A regular camp-fire party, big deal—they should have let us go into Pleiku to get a piece of ass. You can't build up morale with just beer and hot chow. They must have thought we were grown-up Boy Scouts or something. Even so, it was still better than the bush.

The following morning after chow, we were told to saddle up; the battalion was moving out. We were headed for Kontum. It was November 19. We had only a two-day stand-down, one day short.

We loaded onto troop transport trucks (cattle cars), one platoon per truck. I hadn't seen those type of trucks since basic and AIT. They moved the battalion convoy the same way: gunships, Dusters, quad-.50s, and two tanks, toward Kontum. Our battalion would operate northwest of Kontum City and set up defensive positions to stop NVA, the main enemy units operating in Kontum Province, from attacking Kontum City. The convoy rolled along on the blacktop of Highway 14; the ground was mostly flat and open until we neared Kontum City, then, suddenly, mountains rose northeast and northwest of the city, dark and mysterious. After seeing nothing but jungle for over two months, the mountains seemed strange to me.

The convoy stopped at LZ Marylou, which was also called Trains. It was the 2d Brigade's logistics support area for operations around Kontum Province. We unloaded off the trucks, formed up, and humped out. Northwest of Kontum, the battalion split as usual, and B Company again was headed on its own to points unknown. We humped the rest of the day. The sun was setting somewhere behind the trees, bamboo, and jungle vegetation when we reached some hilltop a few miles northwest of Kontum City. There was only enough light left to form a perimeter, put out a couple LPs and eat some cold Cs, which turned my stomach; they were bad enough hot. I had cheese and crackers and some fruit cocktail. The following day we started to dig in.

A platoon of engineers came in to blow the vegetation off the hilltop, using bangalore torpedoes and C-4. When they yelled, "Fire in the hole," we moved down the ridgeline and held our ears. *Wa-whoom.* Our ears would ring for a few minutes, and the smell of blown-up wood and vegetation along with C-4 lingered in the air, making it hard to breath.

Little George and I were digging our fighting bunker; the others were chopping jungle, and cutting trees. We still had about another foot to dig when two engineers came over and told everybody another fire-in-the-hole was going off on the other side of the perimeter in about three minutes. Little George and I both said, "Shit," at the same time and crawled out of the hole and went down the ridgeline again. *Wah-whoom.* The ground shook. The explosions scared the shit out of me even though I knew they were coming. I just didn't like loud explosions. We all headed back up the hill to resume what we were doing. Little George and I went back to our fighting bunker where we were digging. We'd only been digging a couple of minutes when Little George screamed and high stepped it out of our hole. He moved so fast, he was out of sight before I looked up.

I said, "What?"

Little George said, "Get your ass out of there!"

I did but quick. I still didn't know why.

He said excitedly, "Look, man; step-and-a-half," and pointed to the hole. There on the wall of the bunker where we were digging was a bright green snake, about three feet long, a bamboo viper. We called them a "step-and-a-half" because rumor had it that if one bit you, that's how far you'd get before you died.

By this time, a few guys came over wondering what all the commotion was about.

We yelled, "Look," and pointed.

Jerry, Ken, and Bill said, "Kill it!"

We both said, "Fuck you, you kill it!"

Just then, LT came over with a machete and, in one swing, chopped its head off and then went into the hole to pick up the head and rest of the body. The skin on a step-and-a-half was a bright green; it looked like it would glow in the dark. LT took the head and opened the mouth with a knife; the two fangs on it were about the length of a small finger nail. I didn't know if the medics carried any snakebite serum.

We cleared that hill for two days with the engineers. At night, we watched the twinkling lights of Kontum City in the distance. It was the only thing to look at besides the stars. On the third night, we were told a B-52 strike (codenamed Arc Light) would occur to our east, about three klicks away. When it happened, the first thing we saw was the giant fireballs rising hundreds of feet in a straight line, along the ridgelines and mountains across the valley. Then the sound and ground vibration almost shook our asses off the bunker. What a sight, pure devastation. Intelligence must have thought they'd found a staging area for the gooks. Whether or not the gooks were there during the Arc Light, one night later they were, and we watched 122mm rockets being shot at Kontum City from where the Arc Light had dropped. The gooks fired about twenty rockets into Kontum. After the rocket show, artillery pounded the general vicinity, but they waited about half an hour before opening up, too long. We were sure the gooks were long gone. Then Spooky arrived at the scene, with its 0-2 spotter, and pissed lead for about forty-five minutes. The platoon leaders were called up to the CP, and we all guessed why.

"Bet you we hump out tomorrow morning, first light," Jerry said.

"To check out the area for any bodies," Bill said.

"Bet we don't find any," Ken said.

When Dean returned from the CP, he said, "We're leaving in the morning at first light, so you guys better get some sleep."

"Bunker guard starts now!"

We humped out at first light. My heart started to pump, and adrenalin was flowing through my body. So much for clearing that hilltop we'd never see again. We reached the ridgeline across the valley in the afternoon. We found the spot from where the gooks had launched the 122mm rockets, and the spent canisters. We searched the area, but they were gone, thank God, and St. Jude, too.

Things got loose, and we joked around as usual. We broke for chow, and spent two hours sitting around while division thought of what to do with us next. I guess they figured as long as we'd humped to this area, we could hump a few more days and sweep the area north and east of Kontum; we did. Our squad got stuck on flank. Flank was a bitch! We hacked through all the underbrush while the rest of the company took the winding paths or open areas. Also, we relearned that whoever said not to make noise while you're humping couldn't have tried to follow his own advice. It was impossible: getting tripped by vines, stepping in holes, and getting cut. I'm sure we sounded like a herd of elephants.

We humped for a couple of days and made no contact. The only news we heard was that malaria reached its highest level in 1968. There were 251 cases, including 89 cases of vivax, reported throughout the division, and the medics were watching to see if we took the daily white pill and the weekly orange one.

On the third day, we were supplied with C rations and told that we would be airlifted the next day. The next morning, we were told to hurry and saddle up. Then we waited four hours before the choppers came in to pick us up. This would become the normal practice. The choppers finally came to transport us to the mountainous region northwest of Kontum, south of Dak To, to a hilltop that was already cut and had bunkers. We replaced one company that loaded on the choppers as we stepped off. We nodded at one another as we passed. Another company had already taken one-half of the perimeter. I think it was our battalion's A Company. When the dust cleared, I noticed a few 4.2 mortar pits and a water trailer. Not bad, a ready-made perimeter for two companies. Maybe we would catch a break for a few days.

The squads were told to go down to the bunker line and pick one, so our squad hurried down. Bill and Jerry ran ahead, checking out the bunkers until they came across one that was large enough for all of us. They dropped their packs on top and sat down to wait for the rest of us. We got the largest bunker on the perimeter. It was cut into the mountain and had a steep drop to our front and a ridgeline running down to our right into the dense trees and jungle. The position was on Hill 1570, the highest peak for miles. In every direction, we could see dark green, rolling hills, above the valleys. In the distance, toward the border, puffs of white smoke were rising from the ground where Phantom jets dropped their payloads on suspected enemy areas of operation. We sat on the bunker, turned on my radio, and watched the air strike in the distance. A Huey gunship flew by. There was a lot of activity in the valley, about ten klicks away, and I hoped it would stay there. We goofed off for a few days, just pulling bunker guard at night, playing cards during the day. One day it rained like hell, and lightning hit a tree right outside the wire and almost killed Bill Butler and Dill Bailey who were out on OP.

About the fifth day, the company sent out four SRPs. I got nabbed again from our squad. The patrol leader again was Sgt. Jack Shoppe. I'd been out with him when we hooked up patrols in Duc Lap. I naturally figured we would hook up again once outside the perimeter. But it was not to be.

"Not this time," he said. He wasn't too happy.

"Why?" I asked.

Jack looked around and whispered, "The patrols are all going different directions—north, south, east, and west—so there's no way we can hook up. It would take us a couple of hours to hump to them, and we might be detected by our own guys or by A Company and get shot at. It just won't work this time." He shrugged his shoulders, "Let's go."

My legs suddenly felt weak. One of the other two guys was Bud Kutchman. Glen Mong carried the radio. We headed out of the perimeter, north, down a ridgeline.

A small footpath snaked through a maze of tall trees and vegetation. We moved cautiously, eyes shifting back and forth, looking for anything unusual. Always looking for a place to hit the dirt in case something happened suddenly. My heart pounded; sweat poured down my face. We followed the path for about an hour, then ran into another path which cut up another ridgeline.

All of a sudden, I heard a loud noise in back of me and whipped around. It was Glen. He'd tripped and fallen. Jack told him to be quiet. Well, if there were any gooks around, they probably heard us coming. We started off up another ridgeline until we reached a small hilltop with leaves all over the ground. Jack whispered to me, "Let's set up over there," and pointed to a few trees and some bushes growing down the side of the hilltop.

"If someone's coming, we should hear them because of all these leaves," he added. We set up while he called in our location. It was about noon, so we quietly ate some chow, all the while looking and listening. After we ate, I lay back against my pack and closed my eyes to catch a short nap. The others were reading or writing. Glen was reading a dirty paperback, and I had dibs on it after him.

After about an hour, Glen shook my shoulder and said softly, "Something's coming." I clicked my M-16 off safety, thinking, "Oh God, not again". All of us were laying on the ground, with our rifles pointed to our left front. Leaves were being crushed and twigs breaking about forty meters away. I started silently praying to St. Jude. The sounds grew louder and closer. There was more than one, but we still couldn't see any figures approaching. My finger was on the trigger, ready to open up. I glanced over at the others. In an instant, we were charged by ten to twenty shrieking monkeys. It startled us, and we looked at each other, then burst out laughing, relieved. "Jesus Christ," Glen muttered out loud. We were still laughing but trying not to make too much noise doing it.

Jack got the radio and told the CO, "Negative movement. It was just monkeys."

The rest of the time on SRP, nothing happened. Shit, the monkeys were enough to make a young man old.

When we got back to the perimeter and the word got around, everyone was calling us the "Monkey Patrol." We stayed on that hilltop for about ten days. We had two platoon sweeps around the area but made no significant contacts.

One morning, our platoon leader, Lieutenant Murphy, called us over to his bunker and told us we were going on a one-day sweep of the Ho Chi Minh trail. The Ho Chi Minh trail had many branches, one of which was called the Plei Trap Road. The road entered Vietnam in our area, ran through the Plei Trap Valley, south of Ben Het, which was west of where we were, close to the tri-border (Vietnam, Laos, Cambodia) area. He told us to pack light, that we would hump the trail for one or two klicks, which would take us inside the Cambodian border.

What was going on? We weren't supposed to go into Cambodia, especially with just a platoon. All of the enemy sanctuaries we knew were on the other side of the border. We packed up and waited for the choppers. Nobody liked the idea at all. We boarded the four choppers that came in and took us west to the border, about ten or twelve klicks away.

I wondered what the mission was all about: to search, probe, or make contact. I hoped it wasn't the latter. As usual, I said a prayer to St. Jude. The choppers left us a few feet from a dirt road. I wasn't expecting a dirt road ten to thirty feet wide. We spread out—about ten meters in between each man, staggered on both sides of the road. After about five hundred meters, the terrain changed to low hills and thick forest. The road wound around craters that were about thirty or forty feet in diameter and about ten feet deep (from B-52 strikes). The trees were blown apart, no leaves, no foliage anywhere. The ground was covered with a grayish powder, and the smell of cordite filled the air. It was like the moon, but the map said we were in Cambodia. *Chieu hoi* leaflets and propaganda were scattered everywhere.

After following the road for a couple of hours, we got off the road and humped, tripping over the fallen twigs and brush. When we stopped to rest, my mouth and nose were dry from the gagging dust. We sat around, trying to recover from the heat when I noticed small white bags laying around, some under twigs, some laying out in the open. I picked one up, squeezed it, and smelled it. It was like a pitcher's resin bags. Hell, I was a pitcher. I thought, what are these doing here? We were baffled.

Then I said, "Maybe this used to be a baseball diamond; we can play the gooks. I'll pitch grenades, and they can try to hit 'em."

Happy Jack replied, "I'm not catching."

We laughed. Just then we heard a loud explosion, *barroom*! We all crouched behind the fallen trees, waiting for something else. Word was passed up, nobody move! Somebody stepped on one of those small bags. "Holy shit!" I still had one in my hand. I threw it as far as I could, but nothing happened. We learned the small bags were antipersonnel mines dropped by the air force. The guy that stepped on it blew out the sides of his boot and shattered the bones in his foot, swelling the foot up like a balloon. The bag had a small glass tube that contained a chemical. When the tube broke, the chemical made contact with the powder that surrounded it, and it blew up.

About fifteen minutes after we found out about the mines,

this black guy from the 3d Squad, who was about fifteen feet from us, said, "I'm going home!"

We all laughed, and Bill said, "What you going to do, walk home?"

The brother said, "Watch me, motherfucker." He got up, picked up two of the small bags, put them on top of each other on the ground, got up on a log, and jumped on the two bags. *Baboom!* We couldn't believe what he did. He just lay on the ground smiling, his boots blown raggedy. LT, the platoon sergeant, and the medic came over after the explosion. Lieutenant Murphy was furious. "I told you people not to move. What happened here?" Nobody said anything. He got on the radio and called for a medevac to meet us back down the road about five hundred meters. We had two guys fucked up; one intentionally, one accidentally, but two casualties none the less. The Lieutenant had to explain what happened to battalion on the horn, and the mission was aborted. So much for our Cambodian excursion. The two guys had to be carried by makeshift stretchers. I was glad they weren't in our squad.

We humped back to where we were supposed to meet the medevac chopper. We then waited an hour for the choppers to pick us up and take us back to our company.

One day, I asked Little George to teach me some dance steps. We danced on top of our bunker to AFVN radio. Anything to kill time. Rumors leaked through about the rest of the division, and some units were making contact almost daily. It was a matter of being in the wrong place at the wrong time. We just happened to be in the right place at the right time. Artillery and air strikes could be seen from our location but nothing happened around our immediate area.

Significant activities "Operation Binh Tay-MacArthur" (Operational Report of the 4th Infantry Division Ending Jan 31, 1969)

2 November. Shortly before 0655H, near ZA056224, a tiger attacked and killed one member of a SRP from Company A, 2d Battalion (Mechanized), 8th Infantry. The victim had been on watch while the other members of his team slept.

At 1340H, a patrol from Company D, 3d Battalion, 12th Infantry exchanged small arms fire with five NVA near

YB826285. The patrol killed one NVA as he fled from a bunker. Two platoons of D/3-12 attempted to sweep the area but came under heavy fire from automatic weapons. The platoons withdrew and artillery bombarded the area with unknown results. US losses were 2 KIA and 8 WIA.

3 November. At 1212H, Company D, 1st Battalion, 35th Infantry exchanged small arms fire with an enemy force in bunkers near ZA018100. Artillery supported Company D. Results were one NVA KIA, one AK47 CIA, two US KIA and two US WIA.

4 November. At 0921H, Company D, 2d Battalion, 35th Infantry found one decomposed NVA body near YU864787. At 1410H, while moving to its night location, a SRP from Company A, 1st Battalion, 35th Infantry encountered an enemy force of unknown size near YA801162. In the exchange of small arms fire three US personnel were wounded; one M16 and one pack were lost. With artillery support, the SRP broke contact at 1420H.

10 November. Standoff attacks on Fire Support Base 29, YB839223, held by Company C, 1st Battalion, 8th Infantry, resulted in four US WIA. One attack, at 1115H, consisted of nine 82mm mortar rounds; the other, at 1307H, consisted of thirteen 75mm recoilless rifle rounds.

At 1720H, while moving to its night location, a SRP from Company A, 1st Battalion, 35th Infantry made contact with approximately ten NVA near YA809173. The enemy broke contact at 1724H, leaving one US KIA and two US WIA.

11 November. At 0700H, near YA780223, a SRP from Company D, 1st Battalion, 35th Infantry was ambushed by approximately 10 NVA using automatic weapons and claymores. Three US soldiers were killed and one escaped unharmed.

At 2330H, an unknown number of sappers attacked LZ OASIS, ZA114275. The enemy employed 30 to 40 hand grenades, satchel charges, B40 and B41 rockets. Third Brigade employed small arms, automatic weapons, tanks, artillery and Spooky against the sappers. Results were nine NVA

KIA, 10 US WIA, a ¼ ton truck destroyed, a ¼ ton truck damaged, three enemy small arms and miscellaneous grenades and explosives CIA.

13 November. From 0040 to 0235H, Fire Support Base VERA, YA834178, held by Company A, 1st Battalion, 35th Infantry and Company B, 3d Battalion, 8th Infantry, received approximately 40 rounds of 60mm mortar and ground probe from an NVA force of unknown size employing small arms and hand grenades. Results were six NVA KIA, four AK47's and one B-40 rocket launcher CIA. From 0710H to 1645H, FSB VERA received in excess of 200 rounds of 82mm mortar and four 122mm rockets. US losses were five KIA, 38 WIA, one truck destroyed and one truck damaged.

Between 0726 and 1837H, Fire Support Base JEAN, YA808233, held by Companies C and D, 1st Battalion, 35th Infantry, received an intense attack by fire. The enemy employed 75mm recoilless rifles, 82mm mortar and twenty-four 122mm rockets. Gunships, tactical air and artillery fired on enemy mortar and troop positions with unknown results. US losses were one killed and three wounded.

Between 1720 and 1830H, Fire Support Base VERA, YA833178, received approximately 25 rounds suspected to be 100mm artillery, and 16 rounds of 82mm mortar. Nine US personnel were wounded. Artillery fired on suspected enemy locations with unknown results.

Between 1800 and 1855H, Fire Support Base JEAN, YA808233, received 15 to 20 rounds of 82mm mortar and 10 rounds of 75mm recoilless rifle. One US soldier was wounded. Artillery fired on suspected enemy locations with unknown results.

26 November. At 0100H, four B-40 rounds impacted in the vicinity of the 3d Platoon, Company C, 2d Battalion (Mechanized), 8th Infantry, ZA166399. Two rounds hit an APC, causing heavy damage and wounding five US personnel. The platoon returned fire with caliber .50 and M60 machineguns, then swept the area with negative findings.

At 1712H, a platoon of Company C, 1st Battalion, 22d Infantry, operating near ZA043221, came under automatic weapons fire. One US soldier was killed. The platoon returned fire and swept the area, capturing ten packs but finding no enemy.

30 November. At 1755H, a squad size Bushmaster ambush, posted by Company I, 2d Battalion, 35th Infantry at YU835790, made contact with an estimated company of NVA. Mortars and artillery supported the Bushmaster. Contact broke at 1835H, with seven NVA KIA, two US KIA and two US WIA.

The law of averages had to change sooner or later, but most of us wished for later. Way later. Our easy duty ended with the old words, "Saddle up, we're moving out." We were going to hump for a while, how long, nobody knew. The column moved out down the ridgeline, never to see that hilltop 1570 again. Humping made everybody nervous because it took us out of a defensive position and put us on the offensive, not knowing what our objective really was. Up and down ridgelines, trying to follow paths that crisscrossed in different directions, losing all sense of direction. We couldn't see the sky because of the double and triple canopy of trees and jungle. Only the squad leaders had maps and a compass. We would trudge along, sometimes stopping, other times almost double timing to close the gap of fifteen or twenty meters that separated you and whoever was in front of you. Occasionally, someone would trip and fall, and you would have to wait until he picked himself up. If we were going up hill, it was a real bitch, our legs felt like they were made of lead, and we would huff and puff trying to catch up, especially if we were with the rear element, which we were for this day.

Platoons generally switched every day from point to rear; the company commander and the rest of the CP (command post) would hump in the middle of the column. Flank duty was the worst because you had to hack your way through the bush.

We humped all day, and we were lucky if we made a klick (1000 meters). We set up on the high ground or on ridgelines. No fires, so we had to eat cold C rations; most of the time, we were too tired to eat. On LP (listening post) it was almost impossible to stay awake because of the beating we took on the trail. Our muscles would tighten up, and our bodies cried out for sleep. Perimeter watch was just as hard, and everybody had to be wakened at one time or another during his watch. When a new day dawned, we ate and then moved out again. I tried to chew gum all day to keep my mouth moist. Hilltops like 840, 735, 1140, and 640 came and went. We spent only a night on each. Morale was at the lowest while we were humping; we didn't get enough sleep; we didn't eat well; our bodies went through some of the most draining physical torture imaginable.

Water was the most important thing we carried, and we never got any mail while humping. I tried to think of different songs in my head to pass time, I kept on thinking back to that song by Edwin Star "25 miles." Some guys ripped their pants so badly (inner knee to inner knee) that their family jewels were swinging in the breeze. We were filthy, stinky, and the cuts we got turned into jungle rot within a day. A few *monstrous* zits broke out on my face. They turned purple and hurt like hell from the dirt, sweat, and not being able to shave. Bugs became a real pain—mosquitoes, gnats and black bugs that flew like they were drunk. They would get in your eyes, nose, and if you had it open, your mouth. The humidity and heat were unbearable. Everyone was pissed off, wondering how long would we be humping. Of course, we were all afraid that if we humped long enough, we were bound to run into something.

Activities Cont. "Operation Binh Tay-MacArthur" (Operational Report of the 4th Infantry Division Ending Jan 31, 1969)

1 December. At 8020H, a squad of 3d Platoon, Company B, 2d Battalion, 35th Infantry, patrolling near YU827769, exchanged small arms fire with an enemy force of unknown size. Contact broke immediately. Results were one US KIA, enemy casualties unknown. Artillery and 4.2 inch mortars (employing CS munitions) fired in support of the US squad.

At 1100H, an armored personnel carrier belonging to Troop B, 2d Squadron, 1st Cavalry hit a mine buried in the side of the road at BR007508. Eight US and eight ARVN personnel were wounded. The APC's track and hull were damaged.

At 1145H, LRP 2G, operating near YB738054, made contact with three NVA armed with AK-47's. The LRP killed two NVA, then evaded to the south and called in artillery on the contact area.

2 December. At 1420H, as tanks of Company B, 1st Battalion, 69th Armor were conducting a sweep near ZA 5372, a booby trap grenade fell from a tree and exploded on top of a tank, wounding the tank commander. At 1755H, near ZA003369, the explosion of a B-40 rocket wounded another man from B/1-69. The company then came under small arms fire. Contact continued until 1845H, with B/1-69 employing 90mm main guns as well as tank machineguns. At 2000H, with Spooky on station employing flares, A and B/1-69 swept the area with negative findings.

3 December. At 0630H, Company B, 3d Battalion, 12th Infantry, while conducting a sweep near YB966178, found 10 foxholes, fresh drag marks, and the remains of one NVA.

5 December. At 1340H, Company A, 2d Battalion, 35th Infantry found three badly decomposed NVA bodies near YU815770.

10 December. At 1304H, the 1st and 2d Platoons, Company A, 1st Battalion, 22d Infantry, operating near AR923741, exchanged small arms fire with three or four enemy. One US soldier was wounded. At 1320H, the Platoons again made contact, wounding and capturing one NVA who died before he could be evacuated. At 1350H, near AR929728, the same two platoons made contact with an enemy force of unknown size. Gunships expended in the area. A sweep revealed nine NVA KIA. At 1610H, as A/1-22 was closing to a pickup zone, three NVA fired on the company and fled, leaving one US KIA.

At 1403H, Company A, 1st Battalion, 69th Armor, and the Scout Section, 1-69, received B-40 rocket fire from the vicinity of YA962367 and small arms fire from the village of PLEI YA PON (YA956367). An APC hit by a B-40, sustained moderate damage and one US soldier was slightly wounded. The armor returned fire, then cordoned the village. A search revealed five villagers slightly wounded and one VMC KIA.

December 1, 1968, the division changed command from Major General Stone to Major General Pepke, which really didn't mean a thing; we still were humping. We humped day after day, from first light until late afternoon. More guys were writing FTA (fuck the army) on their helmets, along with month calenders for guys who still had more than five months, and day calenders for the short-timers who were less than 90 days. I noticed that the short-timers were jumpy, uneasy, and sometimes overcautious. Morale was lower than a leech.

Muscles in our legs, shoulders, and backs were so sore that it hurt to rest; nobody wanted to rest. We pushed on. Every once in a while, we had to stop because somebody would develop cramps. We never were told what our mission was, our objective or where we were heading. Upper cadre didn't inform us lowlifes of anything; we just pounded the ground, grunting and groaning. The terrain would change from ridgelines with anthills and huge mahogany trees, fifteen to twenty feet in diameter, to double- and triple-canopy jungle. Some ridgelines were so steep, we had to hold on to small trees to pull ourselves up and down. We filled our canteens from blue lines (rivers, because they were blue on maps) that we crossed. Supply helicopters kicked out boxes of C rats as they hovered above the trees.

A few times, boxes of Cs ended up in a steep draw or down at the bottom of a ridgeline, which took us extra time and energy to get them. It's a good thing those choppers didn't stick around because a lot of guys had a hell of a time retrieving their Cs. We pushed ourselves onward, exhausted, fatigued, sometimes too tired to eat or to talk.

Some of the terrain had been virgin for hundreds of years. Days came and went when we never saw the sun through the triple-canopy jungle and trees. Some idiots took the C-4 out of the claymores to use for heating C rats when we could. So they were carrying empty claymores, which was pretty dumb because if we needed them around our perimeter at night, we would be in deep trouble. This grind went on for three weeks.

Dec 14. The U.S. Vietnam death toll passed 30,000. U.S. forces in Vietnam were about at their peak of 550,000 men.

Activities Cont. Operation Binh Tay-MacArthur (Operational Report of the 4th Infantry Division Ending Jan 31, 1969)

Activity throughout KONTUM Province during the month of December was extremely light. Enemy units were content to continue their mining activity along Highway 14 and to harass friendly installations in the KONTUM City area. The major enemy effort was directed toward gathering freshly harvested rice and resupplying their depleted supply caches. This activity was pre-empted by the seizure of over 15 tons of rice, in an area 20 kilometers north of KONTUM City, by units of the 4th Infantry Division.

20 December. At 1100H, Company A, 3d Battalion, 8th Infantry found several natural caves and a cooking area near BR178294. A sweep of the area disclosed caches of ammunition, weapons and rice. During the sweep the company came under small arms fire from an estimated 20 to 25 NVA. One US soldier was killed and three were wounded. The Company returned fire, then withdrew while gunships, 81mm mortars and an airstrike hit the area. The company returned, swept the area, and determined that the enemy had fled. Captured enemy caches contained one AK-47, six SKS, 72 rounds of 82mm mortar, 102 rounds B-40, 29 rounds .75mm recoilless rifle, 155 small Chicom grenades, 40 sticks of Chicom TNT, 7 reels of commo wire and 50 bushels of rice.

21 December. At 1030H, near BR178292, Company A, 3d Battalion, 8th Infantry found a cooking and sleeping area consisting of 35 huts and several bunkers with overhead cover. In the same area they found one complete 82mm mortar and a wounded NVA. The Company destroyed the huts and bunkers and evacuated the prisoner and mortar.

22 December. At 1420H, near BC014352, an armored personnel carrier of Troop C, 1st Squadron, 10th Cavalry, providing convoy security from PLEIKU to BAN ME THUOT, received one round of B-40 rocket fire resulting in moderate damage to the APC and two US KIA. The convoy returned fire and gunships expended in the area with unknown results.

23 December. At 0235H, the Reconnaissance Platoon, 1st Battalion, 12th Infantry, located at ZA029933, received eight to ten rounds of 60mm mortar fire. Two US troops were

wounded. Artillery fired on suspected enemy locations with unknown effect.

With no sign of the enemy, the division decided to CA (combat airlift) us out of the area. The choppers landed at LZ Blackhawk, east of Pleiku along Highway 19, about twelve miles. A flat, open plateau with boot-high yellow grass and not a tree for miles. We finally got resupplied, clean clothes, mail, and SPs (special privileges). Everybody made quite a haul on care packages from the World. It was Christmas Eve, and we started partying early. After mail call, we were standing around ripping open letters and packages, etc., when Top yelled out, "Listen up, the CO wants to say something."

We all stood quietly. The CO, Captain Burton, said, "Well you guys, it's been a hell of a time, but good things must come to an end sometime. Division is rotating myself and Lieutenant Ranger; it's that time. We've been pretty lucky; keep your heads and asses down. Your new CO and lieutenant will be here tomorrow, and Merry Christmas."

We stood there, some of us in shock; I didn't know division rotated officers every six months. That didn't make any sense to me, but others knew it was coming. Everybody broke up and went back to their positions. Shit, what is going to happen now? Who will be the new CO and the lieutenant for 1st Platoon? It worried me, and I was sure it worried others. You get used to your cadre, you respect them. Now you have to get used to new ones all over again. And what if they were assholes? "Merry Christmas, you're getting new cadre," what kinda shit is that? Six months in a line company, six months in the rear somewhere unless you get somebody pissed off, that's what I was told how the cadre rotated within the division. I sat down to read my mail and looked through the letters to see who they were from, when my eyes hit a letter from a Yolanda Wilson. I thought who is this; it was from Detroit, Michigan.

I yelled, "Hey, Double G, I got a letter from that girl you told me to write."

"No shit, man! Let's take a look-see," he said.

I opened the letter, and we both read it together. It started off Dearest Jack, and she went on and on about how she wanted to meet me when I got home, etc., etc.

Laughing, Double G said, "You got over! I knew it! You fucking got over; she digs your ass."

A picture was enclosed. She wasn't bad at all, cute. The rest of the letters were from my parents; brother; a friend's mother, Mrs. Sortino who sent me my St. Jude medal; a girl I dated a few times (Mary Ann); a friend who was in country with the engineers, and a care package loaded with goodies.

Little George got a small Christmas tree. We decorated it with beer and pop cans, and pop tops. Someone took a picture of us standing around the tree. For dinner on Christmas Day, we had turkey, mashed potatoes, gravy, stuffing, etc. It was a treat, but still everyone was down, thinking about home, opening presents, being with our families, our girlfriends.

It was the first time I hadn't been home for Christmas. I'm sure it was a first for a lot of us. We tried to cheer each other up, but we sat around in a circle bullshitting about home, which got us more depressed. We tried singing a few Christmas songs. That didn't work either. Instead of admiring Christmas lights, we watched flares flickering in the clear evening sky. Everyone turned in early, but I lay awake for two hours, with my head out of the hootch, watching the stars, thinking. Then I prayed, "Oh God, protect us from what the future holds. St. Jude watch over us," then fell fast asleep.

The next morning word came down that our new CO and lieutenant had arrived. Our new CO, Captain Patrick, wasn't from the 4th Infantry Division, he was from the Big Red One (1st Infantry Division). The new Lieutenant was straight from OCS (Officer Candidate School) in the States; and he was younger than I was. His name was Lieutenant Scurr. This didn't sit too well with everyone.

We were told to saddle up; we were moving out again to points east of LZ Blackhawk, humping, of course. We were part of Task Force Winner, which was organized using four infantry battalions, one ARVN infantry battalion, one Mobile Strike Force (MSF) battalion, and a cavalry squadron. And we began search-and-clear operations in Dak Payou Valley ("VC Valley") and Dak Doa Valley, home of the 408th Sapper Battalion.*

We humped out east, not knowing what our objective was and not having seen a map of the area. Most of the terrain was flat until we reached the mountains of Chu Drou, which jetted

*Since the French Indochina war, these two regions have harbored many insurgent forces. Dak Payou Valley was home to the 95B (NVA) regiment for years.

upwards some thirteen hundred meters above a valley floor of dense jungle.

According to intelligence reports, the area had caves with hidden food and weapons caches. Occasionally, we heard small-arms fire a few clicks away, but all we ran into was steep ridgelines with double- and triple-canopy jungle. I didn't know which was worse, dense jungle or walking uphill; they both kicked ass. We humped the expressway footpaths that the gooks used. There were steps cut into steep ridgelines to make the climb easier. Some of the trees were marked with Vietnamese writing and some with red arrows; it was spooky to use their trails. We knew they were somewhere around, so we humped cautiously, eyes darting all around looking for anything out of the ordinary.

One day, when we stopped for a chow break, I found a curved knife engraved with pictures and writing. It was old, and you could pull a blade that was about nine inches long out of the wooden handle. I wondered how long the knife had lain by the tree. Maybe it was from a battle long ago. I put the antique into my pistol belt. A few days later, word came down from the CP that the French lost a battalion of men in the area we were humping, back in the fifties. We were in the mountains above the Mang Yang Pass.

It was a deathly silent area, and I couldn't stop thinking about a whole battalion of French getting wiped out twelve or thirteen years previously. (That battalion was the elite French Mobile Group 100, destroyed by Viet Minh.) We had been told about the Viet Minh before; they were the experienced fighters. About the only thing they knew was war and guerilla tactics from when they fought against the Japanese in World War II and the French after that. I was definitely scared of those guys. They were hard-core old-timers; half of us were twenty and under. The Viet Minh were experts in avoiding contact when they wanted to, as well as in hit-and-run tactics. According to division intelligence, when we started into the valley, the enemy fled southward out the lower end and east into Binh Dinh Province to somewhere south of An Khe.

The only thing we found was a small cache consisting of ten one hundred-pound bags of rice and some medical supplies that were "Donated by the people of Portland, Oregon," according to the print on the packages. That was a real bummer. We humped north of Mang Yang Pass, along the border that separated Binh Dinh Province and Kontum Province. We ended up getting lost, and nobody knew where we were. Division and battalion tried to shoot illumination rounds at night so the CO could get his bearings, but we never even heard the pop. The second day of being lost, we just humped up and down ridgelines with thick dense bamboo and foliage. We were trying to find a landmark that would be on the map. We did this to no avail, and finally ran out of food. I had two cans of crackers and one can of fruit left.

The following day, the CO really got a case of the ass, I'm sure battalion and division were ticked off, too. We didn't think too highly of our new CO, and everybody wondered what was going on. If we ran into anything, we would be on our own, no support artillery or gunships because nobody knew where we were.

The third day of being lost, the CO decided we would hump a blue line, to follow it out of what we were in. We humped all right, right down the middle of that blue line (river), water up to our chests; boy, were we pissed off.

The CO was so mad that he went up and walked with the point, Jack Shoppe's squad, which was unheard of. The point did hit something when they went up on shore—a swarm of bees. Smitty and another guy, were stung so badly that their faces and arms swelled up with welts the size of large marbles. All day, we slithered down the river. Late in the afternoon, we finally broke out of the mountains, and the CO knew where we were at. A medevac was called in for the two guys who'd been stung because they were in shock.

The CO explained to battalion that strong magnetic fields made the compass give inaccurate readings. At the time we all thought, "*right.*"

Activities Cont. "Operation Binh Tay-MacArthur" (Operational Report of the 4th Infantry Division Ending Jan 31, 1969)

27 December. Between 1000 and 1500H, Companies B, C and D and the reconnaissance Platoon, 2d Battalion, 35th Infantry, and the National Police cordoned and searched the New Life Hamlet of QUANG NHIDU, AQ835175. Results were 25 HOI CHANHS (all on the Black List) and 59 detainees (37 on the Black List) evacuated to BAN ME THUOT.

29 December. At 1045H, a SRP from Company B, 3d Battalion, 12th Infantry, in position at AR954688, observed two VC closing on the SRP's location. The team opened fire, killing both VC and capturing their SKS rifles.

At 1120H, LRP 41, Company E, 20th Infantry (LRP), operating near BR033202, observed from nine to twelve individuals with AK-47's moving toward their position. The LRP opened fire at a distance of five meters. Gunships arrived on station and expended with unknown results. At 1155H, the enemy broke contact and fled. The 1st Platoon, Company A, 3d Battalion, 8th Infantry swept the area with negative findings. Results were one NVA KIA and three US (LRP) WIA.

At 1610H, LRP 43, located at BR091181, exchanged fire with three NVA, killing one. Gunships expended in the area, accidentally wounding two team members. The LRP was extracted at 1700H.

At 1620H, LRP 2D, operating near BR003933, reported movement near their location and requested air support. Fighter aircraft, Headhunters and gunships all received ground-to-air fire from the area, but took no hits. Three airstrikes and three sets of gunships hit suspected enemy locations. During the strikes four members of the LRP were wounded, apparently when a rocket fell short of its target. The Aero Rifle Platoon of Troop D, 1st Squadron, 10th Cavalry was inserted to evacuate the LRP. At 2205H, extraction was complete.

1 January. At 0115H, an element of Company A, 2d Battalion, 35th Infantry, in position near AQ878212, ambushed an estimated seven individuals. The ambush employed claymores, M-60 machineguns, M-79 grenade launchers and M-16's. They then remained in position after movement ceased. At 0345H, the patrol detected movement and again executed its ambush. A sweep at dawn revealed four VC KIA, three AK-47's, one M2 carbine, six packs and two sets of US dog tags. A tracker team followed a blood trail out of the area, and at 1210H, near AQ880211, captured one lightly-wounded suspect.

At 1145H, Jan 1, 1969 an element of Company A, 3d Battalion, 8th Infantry, patrolling near BR174389, observed four individuals to their rear and engaged them with small arms fire. Gunships of Troop C, 7th Squadron, 17th Cavalry provided support. Contact broke at 1210H, when the enemy fled. Results were one NVA KIA, two US WIA (slight), one AK-47 and one Soviet RPD light machinegun CIA.

Task Force Winner was terminated on Jan 3rd and netted 29NVA/VC KIA and units captured 22 tons of rice, 400 pounds of medical supplies, some weapons and ammo.

What effect this operation had on the enemy, who really knew? Division seemed happy about it. *We* weren't too happy; we had humped our asses off. We moved to a clearing with an old perimeter, and we were airlifted out to Polei Kleng.

The war turned back to the north and west of Kontum and Pleiku. Polei Kleng was almost directly west of Kontum about ten miles. The fire base had a battery of 155mm and an airstrip to handle C-130s.

We headed from the landing strip, past a few Huey helicopters, and set up a makeshift perimeter. As soon as we set up and grabbed a meal, it was off to the swimming hole, which was really a river. Everybody stripped down and dove in. The water was dark green, but it felt great. I swam in my boxers to wash them out; they were funky. After I had been swimming about an hour or so, somebody yelled out "Hey, Len, come here!" I got out and went over by some trees where about ten guys were sitting around, a few from each platoon. A few took out bags of grass and put some in pipes they had. At first, I was reluctant; I had never smoked pot before. But the bowls were passed around, the smoke was sweet, and tasted good. Before I knew it, we all were screwed up, laughing and making no sense. One guy opened up his M-16 and put a bowl into the barrel and gave everyone shotguns. There was smoke everywhere, and I got a little paranoid about something happening, but everyone assured me it was cool, that we were entitled to it. Why not, it was safe; the gooks were nowhere around. Maybe. They probably were right; the gooks weren't about to hit Polei Kleng in the daytime, with a Special Forces camp nearby and four infantry companies. There were also 155s and some gunships sitting on the airstrip.

We partied all day, drinking beer, smoking hootch, and

swimming. We had a lot of laughs that day. We felt secure for the second time since I came in country, a whopping almost four months. My "Magical Mystery Tour" was really just beginning. That night, we had no bunker guard, and I don't think there were too many of us who could see very straight after partying all day.

The new day brought a few things besides a hangover. As I was heating some water for coffee, Dean told me I would be carrying the M-79 for a few weeks. I bitched about it; I didn't want to carry it, but I had no choice. I had only fired the M-79 once, and that was in AIT. I wasn't familiar with it, and hoped I wouldn't have to use it. The FNG 2d lieutenant giving orders didn't cut it in a lot of our minds, and a lot of unhappy talk went through the platoon. Nobody knew anything about what our CO had done before. Since he got us lost on his first mission, nobody trusted or respected his ability. We'd lost Captain Burton and Lieutenant Ranger, two topflight leaders, who were well liked. We all felt like our luck ran out.

After our briefing, we saddled up and waited on the airstrip to be picked up. Destination unknown, as usual. We waited about an hour in the midmorning sun. We were soaking wet from sweat. A dip in the river would have been just what the medic ordered, but it wasn't meant to be. The *thump, thump, thump* of the choppers could be heard a couple of miles away. The choppers came in, kicking up dirt and clouds of dust so thick you could hardly see through them. We got on and, feet and legs dangling in the wind, we were headed south. The choppers dropped us in an open, elephant-grass field. We humped about a klick and set up for the night. We were told that the next day we would cordon and search a Montagnard village called Plei Broch, which was about fifteen miles west of Pleiku, between Pleiku and Plei Djerang. A few ARVNs would be flown out to question villagers.

At first light, we moved out, and each platoon split up. First platoon went to the village, and we set up a blocking force in a position stretched out along one side. The 2d Platoon blocked the other side, and the 3d Platoon set up an ambush along a footpath that ran out of the village into the jungle.

The ARVNs, about six of them, went into the village of about twenty thatch huts that were raised off the ground on poles. The morning sun filtered through the jungle growth, and the different shades of green leaves moved lazily in the gentle warm breeze. At times the jungle was so peaceful that it would almost lull you into sleep. We'd been sitting around for about a half hour when rifle fire erupted from the jungle. No one knew what had happened, and we were all pointing our rifles toward the village. Word came down that the 3d Platoon had seen about eight gooks with weapons enter the Montagnard village. They shot and hit a couple of them. Then there was an eerie silence. We anticipated a firefight but were told not to fire into the village while the ARVNs were still in there. All of a sudden, an armed Vietnamese with a pistol ran out of the village; he must have been spooked by something. He ran right into one of our guys, who shot him almost point-blank with an M-79 shotgun round; the gook went down right away, like he hit a brick wall. This all happened about thirty feet from Happy Jack and me. After about ten minutes, I ran over to see what had happened; so did a few others.

I was expecting to find the guy's head blown off, but I couldn't believe what I saw—his nose was blown off and part of one ear, that was all. He was dazed, moving his head back and forth. He got up, stark terror written on his face, but he didn't make a sound. Our medic patched him up, and a medevac was called in. The 3d Platoon had one wounded NVA or VC or whatever. They had also killed one, but the others had fled and could not be found. We returned to our positions, I had lost faith in the M-79 buckshot round and reloaded with HE (high explosive). Hit him with that, and it would blow that gook into the following day.

I didn't like my chances of getting off one, or maybe two, M-79 rounds at a charging gook who was firing an AK at me, and I prayed this wouldn't happen while I was carrying the sawed-off SOB.

Activities cont. "Operation Binh Tay-MacArthur" (Operational Report of the 4th Infantry Division Ending Jan 31, 1969)

7 January. At 0655H, during a cordon and search of PLEI BROCH, ZA078477, men of the 3d Platoon, Company B, 1st Battalion, 12th Infantry observed five to ten individuals with weapons enter the village. The Platoon fired on the enemy who fled. Results were one NVA KIA, two NVA WIA/CIA, one M2 carbine, one 7.62mm pistol and miscellaneous NVA and US equipment CIA.

Montagnards looked different from Vietnamese; they were darker and their facial features were different. We saw a few milling around. The excitement died down, and word came down to saddle up; we were moving out. I looked up as a puppy ran out of the jungle right to me. It was white and had fluffy hair; it almost looked like a husky, a real cute dog. So I picked it up and put it in my side pocket. I'd always loved dogs since I was a kid. I named it Tootsie and took care of it, sharing my C rations and water with it. She was no trouble and seemed content to peer out of my pocket. At night she cried and whimpered because she was only a few weeks old. We had a lot of fun playing with her when we stopped to set up for the night. She took our thoughts away from the war. But, as usual, the hump produced nothing, and we were picked up by helicopters that flew us to Fire Base Mile High, the 1/12 Battalion headquarters, located about ten klicks due west of Polei Kleng.

Life at the fire base was really quite different from a regular LZ. A battery of 105 howitzers from the 4/4 Arty and about six pits of four-deuce (4.2) mortars and some 81mm mortars made up the fire base. Battalion headquarters was located in the center of the perimeter. In front was a pole, on it a human skull. Hair wrapped in plastic hung from the pole. The skull and hair had been taken in different contacts.

There also was a sign shaped like a large feather with the words RED WARRIORS printed on it. There was also a mess tent.

Activities Cont. "Operation Binh Tay-MacArthur" (Operational Report of the 4th Infantry Division Ending Jan 31, 1969)

9 January. At 0910H, LRP 3A and the 2d Platoon, Company B, 1st Battalion, 35th Infantry, sweeping an area where LRP 3A had had contact on 8 January (YA854650), received small arms fire from approximately 10 enemy. The US troops returned fire and gunships expended. Contact broke at 0915. Results were two US KIA and three US WIA.

At 0955H, LRP 11, operating near AR929143, observed approximately 10 NVA and engaged them with small arms. The team evaded to high ground. At 1140H, the Reconnaissance Platoon, 3d Battalion, 12th Infantry was inserted and swept the area, finding one NVA KIA, one SKS, one rucksack containing documents, and one wounded NVA whom they took prisoner. The platoon also found and destroyed a ton of rice. At 1650H, LRP 11 and the reaction force were extracted.

We had hot chow daily, and while we were at FB Mile High, we had to wear flak jackets and steel pots because the gooks popped mortars and recoilless rifle at the fire base from the surrounding hills. At about four in the afternoon, the fire base was hit with about five rounds of recoilless, one landing in a mortar pit and wounding one guy.

Activities Cont. (Operational Report of the 4th Infantry Division Ending Jan 31, 1969)

10 January. At 0930H, as Company D, 1st Battalion, 12th Infantry was conducting a combat assault into an LZ at YA935585, a man stepped on a cluster bomb unit (CBU) planted in the LZ as a booby trap. He and another man were wounded. An explosive ordnance disposal team swept the LZ and found five more CBUs emplaced as mines.

At 1915H, the perimeter of the 1st Battalion, 12th Infantry, YA934578, held by Companies B and D, came under 75mm recoilless rifle fire followed by a ground probe. Contact broke at 1940H. One US soldier was wounded.

At 1400H, LRP 32, operating near BR021113, exchanged small arms fire with three or four individuals 25 meters from their position. They killed one VC, then evaded. Gunships expended in the area and at 1518H, the team was extracted.

11 January. At 1055H, elements of Company B, 1st Battalion, 8th Infantry, operating near AS832064, shot and killed one VMC, then recovered one SKS, a stethoscope, a syringe and personal letters from the body.

Part of our squad, Happy Jack, Ken, Bill, me, and two RTOs from our platoon, Monkey and Jay, were assigned to the command bunker, which had a .50-caliber machine gun mounted above it with a forty-thousand-dollar Starlight Scope. I had never seen one that big, about two feet in diameter, about four feet high, mounted on a tripod. We split up bunker guard between us to sit with the .50 caliber on top. I pulled guard with Monkey (Glen Mong), and we talked about who would fire the .50 caliber if something happened.

That night while we were sleeping after our bunker guard, the 105 battery opened up, and it seemed like they were shooting right over our bunker. The whole place shook, and dirt fell from the sandbags. It's a good thing my mouth hadn't been open because I caught a face full of dirt. I heard Monkey say, "Jesus Christ," and I fell back to sleep on my stomach. The next morning after we went through the chow line, the CO told me and Monkey to clean the .50 caliber and straighten out the top of the bunker. We were collecting the claymore mine detonators that were scattered on the top of the sandbags when I tripped and fell onto the forty-thousand-dollar Starlight Scope. My heart stopped as I watched it roll right to the edge. The CO and Top Page saw what happened. Then the CO said, "Leninger, if you broke that Starlight Scope, your salary will pay for it for the next ten years!"

I picked it up, flicked on the switch, and heard it warm up. I was relieved. The CO then told us to lay some more barbed wire in front of the bunker after we cleaned the .50-caliber machine gun. After we cleaned the .50 and brushed off the ammo, we had to walk up to the chopper pad and pick up the barbed wire. It was about noon, and we were sweating heavily, the sun burning our already darkened skin. It was over one hundred degrees. The flak jackets and pots made the work almost unbearable as we were walking back to the bunker carrying the wire.

We got back to the bunker, then down the slope of the ridgeline, and dropped the roll of wire. We headed back up to the pad to get another one. By the last time, we were dripping sweat as if we'd just stepped out of a shower. The air was still and heavy; we could hardly breathe because of humidity. I couldn't take it anymore, ripped off my flak jacket, threw down my steel pot; I didn't have a shirt on, or I would have ripped that off too.

"Fuck it, fuck this fuckin' place," I yelled.

Monkey said, "Jumpin' Jack, calm down!"

"I can't take this heat," I yelled. "It fries me like a hard-boiled egg, and my head is pounding."

"Then leave your shit off for a while, be cool," Monkey said.

"That's a rodge," I replied.

We bent over to pick up the wire when we heard what sounded like a gunshot in the distance. We stopped and looked at each other, and I said, "What was that?" Monkey shrugged his shoulders. We bent back down then heard *ssh-barroom*; a mortar round landed not six feet from us. We went diving into a fighting bunker, landing on our heads. We got up to our feet coughing and gagging from the dirt we caught in our mouths while diving into the bunker.

"Holy shit, that was close," I said.

Monkey was laughing and said, "How did both of us fit through that opening at the same time?" The opening was only big enough for one to fit through. Then I started laughing. He picked up his steel pot and put it on; my eyes got as wide as an owl at night.

"Look at your helmet," I said. He had a hole in it the size of a dime in the front right side, and when he took it off, there was a hole the same size in the back of the helmet.

I said, "You are one lucky fucker, Monkey." He just shook his head in disbelief. The piece of shrapnel tore through the front, around the curvature of the helmet and liner inside and out the back. He could have been killed in an instant! Then I thought, I was right next to him without my helmet or flak jacket on, I could have been killed. Then we both thought out loud, "The .50!"

I was the first one out of the bunker and ran my ass off to the command bunker with the .50-caliber machine gun on it. Monkey was right behind me; I got behind the .50 and let the bolt go, chambering a round, and started firing, *pop, pop, pop*, in the direction we heard the sound. The red tracers lazily floating out and bouncing off of the hills and ridgelines about a mile or two out.

Then Monkey said, "Let me do it, *Let me do it*!"

I did. Hell, it was fun; it was a change from the everyday shit. The CO came down and told us to cease fire and put an end to our fun. All of this happening in a span of about twenty minutes. We stayed at FB Mile High for three days, occasionally taking mortar rounds and recoilless-rifle fire; one round landed inside a parapet, wounding all four guys. I hated being at fire base because there was too much bullshit, and besides you never knew where a round would fall. I did learn that if it was from a recoilless rifle you would hear the crack, and the round would be there almost at the same instance.

After three days, we humped out south, not knowing that we would pull security for fire base only once more, although according to battalion SOP, each company was to rotate periodically, sort of a ministand-down, once a month.

Activities Cont. "Operation Binh Tay-MacArthur" (Operational Report of the 4th Infantry Division Ending Jan 31, 1969)

January 15, 1969. At 0300H, a Shadow aircraft observed a Russian Yak-24 medium transportation helicopter. It was flying at an altitude of 300 feet at grid YA6654. Upon being sighted, the aircraft dropped to treetop level and disappeared.

At 1150H, Troop A, 7th Squadron, 17th Cavalry observed 15 individuals in black pajamas near BR195225. Gunships expended and the ARP of Troop C, 7th Squadron, 17th Cavalry was inserted. They found 9 VC KIA.

At 1225H, a platoon from Company D, 1st Battalion, 12th Infantry observed several individuals moving on a trail at YA939596. The platoon set up an ambush and killed two VC.

At 1625H, a Cobra gunship of Troop C, 7th Squadron, 17th Cavalry received ground-to-air fire, crashed and burned. The ARP of Troop C was inserted to secure the downed Cobra. At 1800H, the ARP made contact with a force of unknown size. Three platoons of Troop D were inserted and fighting continued. Spooky and artillery hit suspected enemy locations during the night.

16 January. At 0950H, three platoons from the 1st Battalion, 14th Infantry combat assaulted into the area of contact to reinforce C/7-17. A sweep after contact broke revealed hasty fortifications and pools of blood. Friendly casualties were five KIA and 21 WIA. Known enemy losses were six NVA KIA.

At 1158H, an APC from troop B, 1st Squadron, 10th Cavalry hit a mine buried on the side of the road at ZA148472.

The explosion blew a road wheel off the APC and wounded one US soldier.

17 January. At 1215H, Company A, 2d Battalion (Mechanized), 8th Infantry, operating near AR48705, exchanged small arms fire with 7 to 8 individuals. Airstrikes hit suspected enemy positions. Results were two US WIA and enemy casualties unknown.

18 January. At 0213H, elements of Company B, 1st Battalion, 8th Infantry, located at AS835118, observed two individuals west of their perimeter who employed grenades and B-41 fire. Perimeter guards returned the fire. The individual carrying the RPG was hit. A round in his launcher exploded, killing him and the other VC. Friendly casualties were one US KIA and seven WIA.

At 1000H, near YA999219, a B-40 rocket hit a tank of the 1st Platoon, Company B, 1st Battalion, 69th Armor, wounding four US soldiers.

We left Fire Base Mile High and humped footpaths the gooks used. We saw the same thing we saw in Mang Yang Pass—a lot of red-paint markings on the trees. They were around, which kept everybody alert, not only humping but at night while on guard, so a couple of hours of sleep were in order. We humped all day and set up at night without digging in. We couldn't have any fires, so we ate cold C rations again, which turned my stomach inside out. We tried to be as quiet as possible, although I'm sure they knew where we were; what they probably didn't know was where we would end up, in what we called the Punch Bowl, an area southwest of LZ Brillo Pad. It was a wide open plain, surrounded by mountains and ridgelines, a punch bowl. We couldn't believe we were setting up in a place so vulnerable. We were all uneasy while we were building bunkers.

"The gooks are probably up in those mountains laughing their asses off at us," Jerry said.

"They (division or battalion) must want the gooks to hit us," Ken replied.

It was so open, there wasn't a tree for more than one hundred yards in any direction, just some elephant grass and a few small bushes. There was nowhere to go to get out of the blistering sun. We built a fighting bunker and part of a sleeper and laid a few bails of barbed wire that day. At night we were all nervous on bunker guard. The CO must have been nervous, too, because we were on full alert until about midnight. Luckily, nothing happened that night.

The following day we spent laying barbed wire and building our sleeping bunker until midafternoon. Then LT came down to the bunkers and yelled out, "First Platoon, gather up!" We stopped what we were doing and crowded around LT. His eyes were gleaming, and he had a big grin on his face, which I felt like wiping off with a right cross. He told us to pack up light for a day sweep and night ambush, and hopefully, we would get some gooks. He was just itching to kill gooks so he could move up the promotion ladder of the army. What your achievements were in the field directly affected your future in the army as far as cadre were concerned. Contacts and body count were a faster way up. In a way, I was glad to get out of the perimeter; we felt like sitting ducks. We swept the mountain ridgelines south and southwest and followed a footpath to a small, clear blue line, filled our canteens, and moved out. We humped a while and then stopped while LT tried to figure out a good ambush position for the night. We ended up returning to the blue line. We set up on one side.

On the other side of the stream there were two large rocks to block their escape, and a footpath ran in front of the rocks. We lay still, in two-man positions in a straight-line ambush, until it grew dark, just waiting and listening. About 8:00 P.M., we heard explosions and small-arms fire coming from our company perimeter, about one klick away, followed by the pop of illumination flares, which lit up the whole area. Nothing happened around us, but there was sure a lot happening back at the company perimeter. The gooks must have watched us hump out and not return. Our company was in a bad position. After about an hour, things quieted down, although an occasional illumination flare popped.

I fell asleep, waking up whenever a flare would pop, which was about every hour through the night. The ambush had been a waste.

At first light, anxious to find out what happened, we headed back to our perimeter. When we got back to the perimeter, a few of us went over to the machine-gun squad of the 2d Platoon to find out what happened. It turned out that the perimeter had been hit by a few mortar rounds and some small-arms fire.

It was just a probe. Nobody got hurt, but everybody was on full alert all night, so nobody got any sleep. The men were shook up—you could tell by the puffy glazed eyes. They were also pissed off, saying, "If we stay here we will get hit again." We all agreed.

After another very nervous night, during which nothing happened, we were told to saddle up. For once, we were glad to saddle up. We were leaving a shooting gallery in which we were the ducks. We were lucky nobody got hurt. It would be the last time we took low ground for a perimeter. A few days later they made the Punch Bowl a fire base.

(Operational Report-Lesson Learned 4th Infantry Division Ending 31 Jan 1969)

During January there has been a large buildup of forces in the CHU PA Mountain Region. The 24th NVA Regiment has moved from Base Area 702 and is now in contact with US and ARVN forces in the CHU PA Mountains. A HOI CHANH, who rallied January, stated that elements of the K-6 Battalion, B-3 Front (also known as the 966 Battalion) and the K-31 Artillery Battalion are supporting the 24th Regiment. The CHU PA has historically been a large supply area, and many large food and weapons caches have been uncovered.

VIET CONG activity increased during the month of January in the TANH CANH area and in the area approximately 20 kilometers north and northeast of KONTUM City. In the TANH CANH area the 304th Local Force Battalion conducted harassing attacks against hamlets and continued to assume a more aggressive role. Division units operating in the area approximately 20 kilometers north and northeast of KONTUM City made light, sporadic contact during the month, uncovering numerous food caches and bunker complexes. Captured documents identified this region as a base area of the 304th Local Force Battalion.

In the CHU PA Mountain region, troops of the ARVN 24th Special Tactical Zone, in coordination with the 4th Infantry Division, began operations on 5 January 1969. The 24th NVA Regiment began infiltrating into the CHU PA area from across the CAMBODIAN Border with the intention of protecting the caches which had been laboriously built up over the preceding months. Their mission was to attack PLEIKU and KONTUM Cities, attack villages and hamlets to disrupt the GVN Pacification Program, and interdict Highway 14W between PLEIKU and KONTUM Cities. The ARVN battalion made contact with elements of this unit almost daily as they moved through the area.

Seizing the opportunity to trap this newly arrived enemy force, the 4th Infantry Division, after coordination with the ARVN 24th Special Tactical Zone, combat assaulted into the CHU PA region. While the ARVN blocked to the west, 4th Infantry Division troops attempted to drive the enemy from their strongholds and trap them against the blocking forces.

Activities Cont. "Operation Binh Tay-MacArthur" (ORLL Ending 31 Jan 1969)

18 January. At 1130H, Company C, 1st Battalion, 12th Infantry, located at YA959607, received fire from the northwest of their position. The company returned fire and the enemy fled. Results were 2 US WIA and enemy casualties unknown. At 1250H, a platoon from Company B, 2d Battalion (Mechanized), 8th Infantry while on convoy escort, received small arms fire and one B-40 rocket. The platoon returned fire and the enemy fled in an unknown direction. Friendly casualties were one US KIA and two US WIA. Enemy casualties are unknown.

19 January. The 2d Battalion, 9th Field Artillery radar at LZ Charmaine sighted numerous unidentified flying objects. A circling UFO was seen at grids ZA100271 to ZA079222 to ZA009231. A blinking red light could be seen, but no engine noises were heard. At 0500H, a UFO landed at YA975267. Artillery was employed. At 0615H the UFO took off and then landed at YA964276. Artillery was employed again. A sweep of the area produced nothing.

At 1010H, the 2d Platoon, Company B, 1st Battalion, 14th Infantry made contact with an estimated five to ten individuals at ZA140167. Contact broke immediately. Results were one US KIA, three US WIA and enemy casualties unknown.

CHAPTER V

THE 400 METER LP

We humped south along the far western ridgelines of the Chu Prong, ass-kicking terrain. Ridgelines with trees 100 to 150 feet high. Gulleys and ridgelines that dropped sixty degrees in places, some on the map, others that weren't. Trying to set up on high ground, if we couldn't make it, we at least set up on ridgelines five hundred or six hundred meters high. The nights got down to the fifties, but with the high humidity, it seemed a lot colder. At times, the nighttime temperature dropped forty or so degrees from the daytime. Before Christmas, I wrote a letter to my parents to send a navy blue stocking hat and a navy blue hooded sweatshirt. From humping in November, I knew it got cold in the mountains; sometimes at night, I could see my breath. My head, ears, and neck were cold.

We humped for five days. Our position grew closer to the Chu Pa Mountain with each passing day. Before we crossed the Ya Krong Bolah river, we set up for the night on a five-hundred-meter ridgeline. We still had about an hour and a half of sunlight left. We had enough time to eat and unroll our sleeping gear. LT came over to Dean and told him he needed somebody to go on LP.

"Hey, Len, it's your turn," Dean yelled over.

"Shit," I replied with disgust. "What a bummer."

The last thing in the world I wanted after humping all fuckin' day, pushing my body to the extreme, was to go on a listening post. Dean told me to report up to the CP to get the radio and instructions. Not knowing who I was going out with, I dragged myself up to the CP. At the CP, Lieutenant Nathan from the 3d platoon stood with two guys, one from our platoon, the CO, and 1st Sergeant Page. The CO said, "You'll be going out with Bill Butler. Lieutenant Nathan and a guard will show you where to set up." I thought what's this shit, a lieutenant and a guard are taking us out? Bill Butler was a scrawny guy with glasses, about five feet seven and 130 pounds. I didn't know him very well.

We set out up the ridgeline. Normally an LP was set up fifty to one hundred meters outside the perimeter. We went two hundred, then three hundred, then four hundred meters; I kept pace count. We were on a hilltop which had some huge mahogany trees, all about twenty feet in diameter. It was starting to get dark when Lieutenant Nathan whispered to us to set up. Boy, was I pissed off. Lieutenant Nathan and the guard left us; they had just enough time to get back to the perimeter before it got completely dark. As soon as we could see them no more, I turned to Bill and whispered "If something happens, we'll never get back to the perimeter, let's pull back down the ridgeline about one hundred meters."

We cautiously moved back down the ridgeline and set up behind a large mahogany tree with three-foot-high fans extending from the base of the trunk. It was dark, and the sounds of darkness engulfed the area. We whispered to each other about what a bunch of shit the LP was, then we talked about other things, neither of us was tired; we were too scared. We were just too far away from the rest of the company. That LP was almost like being on a short-range patrol with one other guy, and God help us if we had to get back; our own guys would probably kill us if the enemy didn't. Every few minutes, we stopped whispering to listen for anything out of the ordinary. Light from a half-moon shone through the trees, and it cast spooky shadows throughout the area. About every half hour we had to answer sitreps requests that the CP called to us and two other LPs. It was about 9:30 when we heard something to our left front, a few hundred meters away. We listened closely; it sounded like twigs being broken and a few cans rattling. "Movement!" I grabbed the radio handset and called into the CP that we had movement about three hundred or four hundred meters away. The RTO asked me if I was sure; I replied, "Affirmative." The CO got on the radio and told me he'd get some artillery out there.

I told Bill, "Let me handle this."

He replied, "Go ahead."

About ten minutes later, the CO called me on the radio. "Okay, Fire Base Nicole is shooting an illumination round. Shoot an azimuth with your compass, and let me know if it's okay to shoot HE (high explosive)."

"Roger!" I answered.

We heard the 155mm howitzer in the distance fire, then within seconds heard a pop in the sky and saw the illumination flare round floating in the air. I told him the azimuth and about how far it was from us. He came back about a minute later saying, "They are going to fire a volley [six guns]."

We heard in the distance the firing of six guns then a *ssshh-boom-boom-boom*. It sounded way off. Although the rounds landed in a deep draw on the other side of the hilltop, and the sound was cushioned by the ground and rock, how close they were never dawned on me; I made a very critical mistake; I called in on the horn to the CO "Right one hundred, drop one hundred." I did this two times. The second time he asked me if I was sure; I said "Yeah." After five minutes, we heard the distant sound of the battery firing, then a whistling shriek, *sshhh baboom*!

The rounds landed all around us, and a few exploded in the trees. I never heard anything so deafening. My ear drums popped and shit was flying all over. I tried to push myself into the tree while screaming on the radio "Stop, stop you're going to kill us. Stop!" I couldn't hear through the high-pitched ringing in my ears. My heart was pounding, and Bill and I were both screaming. I thought we were going to die by our own guns. Just then I felt a sharp pain in the back of my thigh. I screamed, "I'm hit, I'm hit," into the handset.

I was scared senseless, but when I put my hand down slowly to my leg, expecting to feel warm blood oozing out of it, to my surprise it was dry; the pain was a muscle cramp from being so tense. My ears were still ringing, and I couldn't hear anything. I felt sick to my stomach. I looked over at Bill; the light from the illumination flare danced across his face. He was white as a ghost, shaking like a leaf. I'm sure he saw the same thing, looking at me. The smoke choked us as we tried to breathe, and the smell of gunpowder was everywhere. We were covered with wood splinters and dirt.

About ten minutes had gone by since my last radio transmission, I was still shaking, my nerves were shot, and my voice cracked. I yelled, "Tiger 1, this is Tiger 2. Over."

"Tiger 2, what is your status?" came the reply.

"We're pretty shaken up, scared to death. We almost got killed. Permission to return to perimeter."

"That's a negative, Tiger 2. Remain in your position."

"You will hear about this in the A.M. Fucking Out!" I replied.

I asked Bill if he was all right. He shook his head yes; then I said, "Can you believe those assholes? We almost get killed, and we still have to stay out here!"

Without warning, something went *rrrrrrrr whoom*. A tree fell about thirty meters away. I said "Great! If the 155s didn't kill us, a tree will!"

I felt like screaming; you can take so much before you're ready to break. Neither of us slept. Debris was falling all night. At first light, we gathered up our shit and looked over the area around the tree. In front of the tree we'd been behind was a crater about three feet deep and fifteen feet in diameter. Shrapnel had ripped the front of the tree open. Ten feet over, and we'd have been dead, blown to bits by our own artillery. Trees, branches, and foliage were blown all around. My hands were still shaking. The area still had that gunpowder-splintered-wood smell. I said to Bill, "Let's *di di mau* [get out of here]!" We headed back to the perimeter.

We went up to the CP. The captain and all the cadre were sitting around for their daily meeting. I took my helmet off and threw it to the ground, then ripped off my pack, saying, "I ain't never going on LP again; we were almost killed out there!" I lifted my arm to show my hand, "Look at my hand; I'm still shaking; we weren't supposed to be that far away. We were about four hundred meters away when we are only supposed to be one hundred meters at the most. I should report this!"

I was bullshitting, but I wanted to put my point across to the CO and the others standing around just watching me carry on. The CO told me to calm down.

"It's hard to calm down when you're almost blown away by our own shit," I said. I picked up my helmet and pack and walked down to where my squad was. Fuck talking anymore. I was emotionally drained, tired, and hungry.

Everybody asked what happened; I told them, then cooked some chow. After eating, I fell asleep for about an hour before I was awakened by someone shouting, "Saddle up." We moved out down the ridgeline and crossed the Ya Krong Bolah river up the far western ridgelines of the Chu Pa.

(Operational Report of the 4th Infantry Division Ending Jan 31, 1969)

Operations.

(1) In the latter part of January, the 4th Infantry Division was disposed as follows:

(a) The 1st Brigade, having transferred its command post from DAK TO (ZB004217) to SOUI DOI (BR023522) on 20 January, continued operations in the vicinity of the DAK PAYOU Valley and the MANG YANG Pass. In anticipation of renewed enemy offensive operations, the 1st Brigade remained alert for deployment as required within the II Corps Tactical Zone. The first element to be committed would be the 3d Battalion, 12th Infantry.

(b) The 2d Brigade, in an economy of force role with two battalions, occupied blocking positions in KONTUM Province. The 2d Battalion (Mechanized), 8th Infantry conducted reconnaissance in force and pacification operations in the region between KONTUM City and PLEI MRONG. The 1st Battalion, 22d Infantry occupied fire bases in the vicinity of DAK TO and BEN HET.

(c) The 3d Brigade continued operations in conjunction with the ARVN 24th Special Tactical Zone in the CHU PA Mountain (YA9567) region northwest of PLEIKU City. While ARVN rangers and infantry blocked west of CHU PA and the 1st Battalion, 12th Infantry blocked to the south, the 1st Battalion, 35th Infantry combat assaulted onto the mountain and attempted to drive the enemy from their stronghold and trap them against the blocking force. When Airborne Personnel Detector sensings indicated that the enemy was attempting to flee northward across the YA KRONG BOLAH River, three companies combat assaulted into the area between the river and CHU PA to cut off the enemy withdrawal, Companies of the 1st Battalion, 35th Infantry then swept northward across the CHU PA, encountering heavy resistance from entrenched enemy forces. Plagued by heavy ground-to-air fire that prevented dustoff helicopters from evacuating the wounded, the companies withdrew to link up with companies of the 1st Battalion, 14th Infantry, which had combat assaulted onto CHU PA. The 1st of the 14th then relieved the 1st of the 35th and continued offensive operations on CHU PA.

(2) Approximately 20 January, while the CHU PA battle was in full swing, a large enemy force, believed to be a regiment, entered the region 15 kilometers north of CHU PA, beginning the campaign that was to develop into the Winter-Spring Offensive. From their staging area they threatened POLEI KLENG, PLEI MRONG, and KONTUM City. On the night of 24–25 January, the 3d Battalion, 12th Infantry conducted a tactical road march from SOUI DOI to KONTUM in order to seize the high ground to the southwest of POLEI KLENG the following morning. Occupying LZ's BUNKER HILL (YA995826), BRILLO PAD (YA962855), ALAMO (YA950880), and ROUND BOTTOM (YA937852), the 3d of the 12th made sightings and small contacts that indicated the enemy was attempting to slide northward around the battalion's blocking positions.

It was January 20, and I was hoping we would set up so I could celebrate my twenty-first birthday the next morning. We set up for the night among the trees, and I told the guys in my squad about my birthday being the next day. They wanted to celebrate as much as I did. Morning came too quickly, as it always did when we were humping. January 21, my twenty-first birthday, everyone wished me a happy birthday, but right after we ate some Cs I was greeted with a "Saddle up." I was really pissed off; I felt like I was pissed on. I yelled out "Bullshit, man, I'm staying right here!" Nobody said anything, and as they packed up, I just sat there watching. Everybody put on their packs and started to trudge up the ridgeline. I yelled out, "Son of a bitch!" I had to hurry up and pack, then run my ass off to catch up to my squad. What a birthday! My ass got kicked by humping that whole day until dusk, and everyone was too pooped to celebrate. In fact, we had to eat cold C rations because it was too late to have any fires. So much for my birthday. It came and went like any other day. I knew other guys had been and would be less fortunate. At least I got to see my twenty-first birthday. I was angry and grateful at the same time.

Activities Cont. "Operation Binh Tay-MacArthur" (Operational Report of the 4th Infantry Division Ending Jan 31, 1969)

21 January. At 1045H, a platoon from Troop B, 1st Squadron, 10th Cavalry made contact with a VC squad near

YA810505. A B-40 round detonated on the antenna of an APC, wounding six US soldiers. The enemy evaded with no known casualties.

Also at 1045H, Company D, 1st Battalion, 35th Infantry, operating near YA939685, made contact with an enemy force of unknown size. Gunships expended on enemy positions. At 1140H, the enemy employed 60mm mortars. Sporadic small arms fire continued all afternoon. Results of the action were two US KIA, 14 US WIA and one NVA KIA.

We humped another two days and ended up on a ridgeline southwest of Chu Pa about five klicks, with the Ya Krong Bolah river bordering our position to the west. We were told to dig in and clear the trees for an LZ, which became LZ Emery. Our humping was finally ended for the time being. We cleared that ridgeline for a few days and built only fighting bunkers. We were supposed to be a blocking force to keep the enemy from getting to the Chu Pa, so we were told.

(Operational Report of the 4th Infantry Division Ending Jan 31, 1969)

23 January. At 1820H, a Dustoff helicopter, extracting wounded of Companies A and D, 1st Battalion, 35th Infantry from an LZ at YA948678, was hit by a B-40 rocket. The helicopter crashed and burned, killing seven US soldiers.

The third day on Emery, we had to pull off the ridgeline and head east about one klick because the air force made a B-52 strike on the other side of the river. When we returned, artillery was shooting white phosphorous shells on the hilltop across the river. Clouds of white smoke were followed by pieces of reddish orange dirt flying lazily in different patterns. The gooks were around the area, and small-arms fire could be made out among artillery and air strikes. Something big was going on. We received mail, and I finally got a package from home with a stocking cap and hooded sweatshirt, which I immediately put on. I went out on two SRPs; the first one was with Jim Leonard, Monkey, Claiborne, and myself. We used a large footpath south of our perimeter and set up in a fairly open area behind a large mahogany tree.

That night, it was pitch-black. About eight we heard something coming. We figured it was an animal because gooks weren't going to walk around at night when they couldn't see where they were going. The sound of crushing leaves came closer and closer; we heard low muffled growls. It was a tiger on the prowl. I clicked my rifle off safety and pointed it in the direction of the sound. The tiger came so close we could hear it breathing with muffled growls. He must not have been hungry because he kept on walking.

We didn't get much sleep because, worried that fucking tiger might come back, we kept two awake at all times. It didn't. When it got light out, we checked around our position, nothing.

I was talking to Monkey when I saw something out of the corner of my eye. On the tree, not two feet from us, was a black scorpion about six inches long. I had never seen one that size, not even in the zoo. I pointed to the tree and said, "Look at that!" Monkey looked and moved slowly back, saying, "Jesus Christ." We were mesmerized by it. Jim stood up and stomped it against the tree. It fell to the ground, and red fire ants came from all over and engulfed it in a matter of minutes. I thought, it really *is* a fight for survival in the jungle. After another night of our SRP, we headed back to the perimeter.

(Operational Report of the 4th Infantry Division Ending Jan 31, 1969)

28 January. At 1230H a SRP from Company C, 3-12 Infantry, located near ZA022764, received small arms fire from six to eight individuals 75 meters south of their location. The team returned fire and the enemy fled. Two team members were killed and two wounded.

At 1550H near YA955162, the Reconnaissance Platoon, 1st Battalion, 12th Infantry exchanged fire with an enemy force of unknown size. Results were one US KIA and one US WIA.

I spent two days back inside the perimeter and went back out on SRP, this time with Ken Comeaux, Jack Shoppe, and Jim Claiborne. We humped out of the perimeter and down the footpath away from view. Jack said we were supposed to head west across the river and set up on the other side. Then he said, "Bullshit. No way are we going to cross the river, for sure we would hit something. We'll go half as far and stay on this side of the river." He took out the map and looked it over, then said, "Let's go, we'll set up on the ridgeline this side of the river."

We cut due west, off of the footpath. After a while, we came upon a steep drop off of about sixty degrees. We could hear the river, fifty or so meters below but could not see it. Then Jack said, "Okay, this is as far as we're going. Let's set up about halfway down this ridgeline."

I thought he was kidding. "How are we going to set up?"

"We'll tie ourselves to the trees," he said.

Holding onto the small trees so we wouldn't fall, we started down the ridgeline. About halfway down was a large tree where the ground leveled somewhat. We set up, tying our ponchos to the small trees that dotted the steep slope, then putting our feet into the ponchos so we wouldn't slide down. After I thought about it, I decided that this wasn't a bad idea at all—no gook in his right mind would try to come up or go down this slope. After an hour or so, the midafternoon silence was broken by small-arms fire—AKs and M-16s, both coming from across the river, about five hundred meters to our right front. Jack listened intently to the PRC-25. His eyes widened, then excitedly he whispered to us, "Another SRP from the 1st platoon hit some shit on the other side of the river. "That's Joe Fegan's SRP," he added.

"That could have been us!" I replied.

He shook his head. I wondered how many gooks were across the river. I was glad that Jack took no chances when he took out a SRP. We spent the night and, surprisingly, didn't sleep too badly. The next morning, the company ordered us to pull back to the perimeter. Something was up. When we got back to the perimeter, I found out that Little George, Jerry, and Dean had all gone in from the field (Dean had to have a hernia operation). And the other squads all had guys that went into base camp and Trains (Kontum), too, so we were short on manpower.

I wasn't back twenty minutes before Bill came over—he was in charge when Dean wasn't there—and told me, "Jack, you have to pull LP with Eddie; sorry, but we have no choice."

"It figures. Why me?" I said.

"Why me" was a very frequent refrain; everyone thought that if you didn't complain, you would get stuck more.

The few hours of daylight that were left went quickly as the sun disappeared behind the mountains to the west. I took my pack to sleep against, poncho to sit on, poncho liner to wrap up in, my pistol belt with four grenades, two bandoliers, my stocking hat, and my hooded sweatshirt. We picked up the radio from the CP and headed down the ridgeline. We went about twenty meters from our bunker and set up on a ledge because there was a steep drop. Although we couldn't see it, the moon was out, and enough light pierced the trees to make it possible to see about thirty meters. About ten o'clock, we heard on the radio that Bill Butler's SRP, located down the ridgeline, had spotted a lot of gooks walking single file toward our perimeter. He estimated a hundred or so, and asked the CP what to do.

The CP told them to stay put and keep down. Each LP was alerted, and the perimeter was put on full alert. My heart started pumping faster; my hands started to sweat as my ears and eyes strained to see or hear anything other than the wind blowing through the trees. After twenty minutes, the silence was broken by a short burst from an M-16 on the other side of the perimeter. After about five minutes, we heard on the radio that a gook had walked right up to the perimeter and some guy blew him away. We were told to be on the alert because the gooks had scattered in all directions. Then we heard movement to our front, going away from us. I was going to throw a grenade down the hill, but I thought better of it because it might hit a tree and blow back at us. Butler's SRP reported that the gooks had scattered down the ridgeline. Nothing else happened that night.

At first light, an air strike was called in. All of the LPs were called back. We took the radio back to the CP, then went over by the 3d platoon to see the dead gook. He was dead all right, shot in the head; bugs and flies covered his half-blown-off head.

Activities Cont. 4th Inf. Div. (Operational Report Lessons Learned Period Ending 31 Jan 1969)

31 January. Between 0035 and 0120H, radar of the 2d Battalion, 9th Field Artillery, at LZ Charmaine, detected four unidentified flying objects. A blinking white beacon was visible.

At 0200H, Company B, 1st Battalion, 12th Infantry at 0200 detected approximately 100 NVA moving southeast up a draw in the vicinity of YA902658. The company engaged the enemy force with small arms. The enemy dispersed and fled without returning fire. SRPs in the area adjusted artillery on suspected routes of withdrawal. Company B swept the area at dawn and found one NVA KIA.

In late January, division and ARVN units made contact with the 24th NVA Regiment, supported by elements of the K-6 (also known as the 966) Battalion and K-31 Artillery Battalion, in the CHU PA Mountains area of western PLEIKU Province. Allied operations to date have resulted in significant enemy casualties, plus the discovery of large food and weapons caches in the area.

During late January, in an area approximately 20 kilometers southwest of the POLEI KLENG Special Forces Camp, activity increased due to the infiltration of a unit of unknown size. Friendly forces have thus far failed to identify this unit.

a. General. In late January a large enemy force, later confirmed to be the 66th NVA Regiment with supporting artillery and engineer units, infiltrated southwestern KONTUM Province in preparation for an offensive. From the region 25 kilometers southwest of POLEI KLENG two battalions of the 66th plus elements of the 40th Artillery Regiment moved northwest attempting to flank blocking forces deployed by the 4th Infantry Division. In the PLEI TRAP Valley of western KONTUM Province, the NVA expanded their road network. Truck traffic throughout the PLEI TRAP supported the enemy buildup. Material introduced into the PLEI TRAP included 105mm towed artillery.

a. On 1 February 1969, the beginning of this reporting period, the 4th Infantry Division initiated Operation DAN QUYEN—HINES.

d. Mission.

(1) During the first two and a half months of Operation HINES, the Division's general mission remained essentially the same as in the later stages of Operation MACARTHUR: conduct sustained, coordinated, and combined offensive operations to destroy enemy main and local force units, destroy or neutralize enemy base areas, interdict high-speed infiltration routes, assist in the protection of urban areas, and support pacification efforts and civil programs of the Government of VIETNAM.

(Operational Report of the 4th Infantry Division for Period Ending 31 January 1969, ECS CSFOR-65 (N1))

b. Estimated Enemy Composition, Strength, and Disposition as of 31 January 1969:

UNIT	STRENGTH	DISPOSITION
B3 Front HQ	500	Base Area 702
66th NVA Inf Regt	2000	Base Area 702
24th NVA Inf Regt	1800	NW PLEIKU Province
101D NVA Inf Regt	1800	Base Area 702
95B NVA Inf Regt	1600	PLEIKU-BINH DINH
1st NVA Inf Regt	2000	Border Area
*40th NVA Arty Regt	1200	Tri-border Area
E-301 Local Force Bn	300	Vic MEWAL Plantation
303d Local Force Bn	250	Eastern DARLAC Province
304th Local Force Bn	300	North of KONTUM City
401st Local Force Bn	300	Base Area 238
H-15 Local Force Bn	100	DAK AYUNH River Area
X45 Local Force Bn	150	West of PLEIKU City
406th Sapper Bn	150	NE of KONTUM City
408th Sapper Bn	350	NE of PLEIKU City
K25 Sapper Bn	100	NE of BAN ME THUOT
K25B Sapper Bn	100	IA DRANG Valley
K37 Sapper Bn	200	CAMBODIA
K39 NVA Inf Bn	300	SW of BAN ME THUOT
966th NVA Inf Bn	250	Western PLEIKU Province
Local Guerrillas	3000 (est)	
TOTAL	11750	
	8000	Left out this report last counted October 31, 1968
	19750	Total

*The 40th Arty Regt has four battalions with elements dispersed throughout the AO.

Left out this report
Last Est. count
OR-LL Ending Oct. 31, 1968
(Tabulated By Author)

320th NVA Inf Regt	1400	**Not in report Oct 31,	1968
1st NVA Inf Regt	1500	**101D NVA Inf Regt	1800
95C NVA Inf Regt	1200	**303D Local Force Bn	250
18B NVA Inf Regt	1800	**966 NVA Inf Bn	250
95th NVA Inf Regt	1800		2300
407th Sapper Bn	300		
	8000		

c. Significant Enemy Tactics, Techniques and Capabilities:

(1) General.

(a) Although NVA units appeared to be massing along the CAMBODIAN border in November, probably in preparation for a large scale attack in the DUC CO area, the enemy has generally adhered to the terror and harassment tactics which he reverted to in September and October. This regression to guerrilla warfare, conducted primarily by VC local force units, is probably the result of the severe punishment inflicted on NVA units when they attempted to engage in conventional warfare with Allied forces this summer.

(b) Numerous sightings were made of unidentified aircraft near LZ's JOAN (YA842230), CHARMAINE (YA998217), and LAMETTA (YA852457) by both visual and electronic means. No tactical significance can be attached to the sightings at the present time. On specific occasions the aircraft sighted were identified as a Soviet K-18 (Hog) helicopter, a Yak 24 medium helicopter, and a Czech HC-2 trainer.

(3) Recapitulation of Enemy Battle Losses (1 Nov–31 Jan)

(a) Personnel:	KIA (BC)	218
	NVA CIA	7
	VC/VMC CIA	35
	TOTAL	260

(b) Weapons:	S/A	116
	C/S	1
	Total	117

(c) Ammunition:

S/A rds	46989
C/S rds	151
Grenades	456
Mines	143

(d) Miscellaneous captured items:

Explosives	720 lbs
Documents	158 inches
Rice	123.9 tons
Salt	311 lbs

(e) Enemy facilities destroyed:

Structures	640
Fortifications	1751

d. Enemy Capabilities, Vulnerabilities, and Probable Courses of Action:

(1) Enemy Capabilities:

(a) The 32d and 33d Battalions of the 40th Artillery Regiment, and field artillery units of the B3 Front are capable of conducting attacks by fire in the Dak To, Ben Het and Dak Seang areas using 100/105mm artillery, 122mm rockets, mortar and recoilless rifle fire.

(b) The 304th and 406th LF Battalions are capable of conducting mining operation along Highway 14 and small scale attacks and probes of villages and friendly installations in the KONTUM City area.

(c) The enemy is capable of improving the PLEI TRAP Road and using it to infiltrate regimental size units into the area west of POLEI KLENG and across the province to the KONTUM City area.

(d) The 24th NVA Regiment is capable of sustaining contacts in the CHU PA Mountain area, and appears capable of governing the time and place of contact. Upon withdrawal of friendly units from this area, the 24th NVA Regiment has the capability to regroup its forces and stage attacks against PLEIKU City.

(e) In the PLEIKU City area, the K-31 Artillery Battalion, supported by the 408th Sapper Battalion, can conduct attacks by fire, employing 122mm rockets.

(f) The 95B NVA Regiment, supported by the X-17 and X-18 Engineer Companies and other local force units, is capable of harassing vehicular traffic along Highway 19E, and can conduct attacks by fire and ground probes on friendly installations from SOUI DOI to AN KHE.

(g) In DARLAC Province, the enemy is capable of employing local force and NVA units in multi-battalion strength against BAN ME THUOT City and Allied installations. The enemy forces are capable of conducting attacks by fire employing 60mm mortars, 82mm mortars, 75mm recoilless rifles, and 122mm rockets.

(h) In QUANG DUC Province, agent reports continue to indicate the presence of large enemy forces in MAN LYR base area in CAMBODIA, approximately 10 kilometers west of DUC LAP. Attacks during TET have been predicted by several sources, but the validity of these reports cannot be determined. It is highly probable, however, that enemy elements are present in the area and will eventually move into III Corps. Although the threat of attack against DUC LAP still exists, enemy action will probably be limited to attacks by fire, and probes by small ground forces.

4th Inf Div. OR-LL Ending Jan 31, 1969

d. (C) Casualties:

Unit	Hostile			Non-Hostile		
	Dead	Missing	Wounded	Dead	Missing	Injured
1st Bde	17	0	146	3	0	61
2d Bde	7	0	66	2	0	51
3d Bde	23	8	149	2	0	38
DIVARTY	1	0	16	2	0	33
DISCOM	1	0	5	1	0	12
2-1st Cav	1	0	32	4	0	20
1-10th Cav	1	0	28	2	0	17
1-69th Armor	2	0	38	3	0	13
4th Engr	2	0	8	1	0	14
4th Avn	0	0	2	1	0	2

124th Sig Bn	0	0	0	0	0	4
HHC 4th Inf Div	1	0	0	0	0	5
4th MP Co	1	0	2	0	0	3
4th Admin Co	0	0	1	0	0	1
Scout Dog	0	0	0	0	0	1
E, 58th	0	0	1	0	0	6
4th MI	0	0	0	0	0	0
TOTAL	57	8	494	21	0	281

e. (U) Morale and Personnel Services:

(1) Decorations Awarded	NOV	DEC	JAN
Distinguished Service Cross	0	1	2
Silver Star	14	11	17
Legion of Merit	4	5	3
Distinguished Flying Cross	5	3	1
Soldier's Medal	1	3	11
Bronze Star (Valor)	85	62	68
Army Commendation (Valor)	76	94	23
Air Medal (Valor)	25	4	1
Bronze Star (Service)	144	133	186
Army Commendation (Service)	913	519	1267
Purple Heart	56	155	163
TOTAL	1820	1511	2218

(2) Badges	NOV	DEC	JAN
Combat Infantryman Badge	909	559	1474
Combat Medical Badge	71	71	80
Aircraft Crewman Badge	2	84	15
Miscellaneous Badges	19	26	21
TOTAL	1001	740	1590

We were told to saddle up. We were moving out. We headed back to our bunker to pack our gear.

LT came over and asked, "Who wants to carry the radio? We need a RTO."

At first nobody said anything. Who wants to carry an extra twenty-five pounds? I thought a second and asked, "Do RTOs have to go on SRP or pull LP?"

"No," LT replied.

"Give me the radio," I said.

I had been looking to get out of SRPs and LPs and to get rid of the M-79. I gave the M-79 and all the rounds to Ken Thomas and got back my trusty M-16. I put the radio in my pack and packed my other gear around it. Then Steve Turzilli from the CP came over and threw down batteries for the PRC-25 and said, "Change one and hump the other."

The battery weighed about three pounds.

I put the PRC 25 battery in the bottom of the pack, put the radio on top, and repacked everything around it. I closed the top flap up and put my two-quart bladders on D-rings on each side of the pack then put my two one-quart canteens on each D-ring. I also put two bandoliers of M-16 ammo on top of the radio and tied them to the frame. I looked at the pack. It was big. I wondered if I had made a mistake. I put two more bandoliers around my waist and tied the straps around my back. Two bandoliers I put my arms through and across my chest. In addition to the six bandoliers, I carried a pistol belt with two ammo pouches with six mags and four grenades, two on each. I tried to pick the pack up and almost dropped my nuts. The pack weighed between eighty and ninety pounds. I said out loud, "This fucking pack is going to kick my ass!"

Everybody laughed. "No shit, Sherlock. Who gave you the clue?" Happy Jack said.

Shaking my head, I looked at the pack, then I said, "Boy, my shit is weak." I sat down and put my arms through the shoulder straps, then held up my M-16 and said, "Which one of you sorry asses is going to help me up?" Ken grabbed my rifle and pulled. I got to my knees, then one foot, then the other, and stood up, wobbling, until I got my balance. "Let's go, before I tilt," I said.

As usual, we started out in single file. We walked right by the dead gook and caught a whiff of the horrible stench. Maggots were crawling over the gook's face. It sent a shiver up my spine.

I took the whip antenna, bent it down, and put it through the ring on my shoulder strap. The handset I covered with the towel I had around my shoulders, so gook snipers couldn't see I was a radio operator. We first humped south down the ridge-line path we had used for SRP, then we cut east, then north, sweeping the area. No gooks to be seen.

I wasn't used to the extra 28 pounds from the radio, and I felt as if I was going to pass out from the extra exertion. The third day into the hump, I was sore and almost completely exhausted when we headed up a ridgeline to set up for the night. I had to reach down for some extra strength to make it up the steep slope. Our platoon was in the rear, and my squad was rear security. Just a little farther I thought, a few more minutes and then rest. Most of the company was already resting on top.

I pulled myself up the ridgeline, grabbing on to small trees so I wouldn't fall. I was near the top, with only three or four more steps to go, pushing, puffing, sweating. I saw our platoon unpacking; some of the men were eating, some laying against their packs, a few watching me bust my ass. I had just one more step to go, but I made a stupid move—I crossed my legs to get up and instantly lost my balance because the weight of the pack pulled me backwards.

I fell head over heels. My rifle went one way, my helmet another. I was knocked out instantly, which probably saved me from breaking my neck. I woke up with water rushing through my right ear. I couldn't feel anything—my body was numb, my head groggy, I couldn't move. After a few minutes, my senses started to come around. I felt my pack on the left side of my head. A thought immediately entered my mind: I have to have something broken—a leg, an arm, I hope not my back, but I hope something to get out of the bush. The feeling started to come back to my neck, then to my back and arms, right down my body. I wiggled out from underneath my pack and out of my shoulder straps and sat up. I was dizzy, and felt the back of my head with my right hand. At the base of my skull was a knot the size of half a golf ball.

Someone yelled down, "Hey, Leninger, you okay?"

"I don't know yet," I yelled back up.

A few guys were laughing; but I wasn't. I rose to my feet, giving the finger to the guys watching. I then bent over to splash water on my face. The only thing I got from the fall was a knot on the head and a bruised ego. I looked back up the ridgeline, wondering how I could fall head over heels down a ridgeline, about fifty meters, and not break anything. What a rip-off.

I had to climb back up, with everyone watching and cracking jokes. I went over to my pack, picked it up out of the stream, sat down to put it on, then pulled myself up with the help of a small tree. I looked around for my helmet and rifle. I yelled, "Where's my fucking helmet and rifle!"

"Up here," came the reply; at least somebody had helped by getting my helmet and rifle. Disgusted, I started back up the ridgeline. I had to do it again. When I finally reached the top, my squad clapped. Happy Jack and Ken both said words to the effect that, "Man when you fall, you fall. We thought you broke your neck. You should have seen yourself." They handed me back my helmet and rifle, and I thanked them. A few of the others—Bill, Jerry, Little George—were smiling and trying to hold back the laughter. Then I said, "Couldn't even break anything, what a pisser." That busted everyone up. "Next time you're falling," Happy Jack exclaimed, "yell something so we can get out of the way."

We humped out the next morning. I strapped my helmet to my pack. My head was throbbing. The sound of small-arms fire could be heard in the direction we were heading, about a klick away. Word came down that C Company had met some snipers and for us to keep on our toes. We stopped for chow about 1:00 PM. We heard periodic bursts of rifle fire, then artillery, then F-4 (Phantom) jets dropping bombs that made the ground shake. We all thought C Company had hit something big. We waited two hours or so before things quieted down. Choppers came in and left quickly, they must have been medevacs. We moved out, following a footpath.

It took us about an hour to reach the contact area. We slowed to a stop, sat down, and took a breather for about ten minutes. As fast as we'd stopped, we started again without warning. We filed past two dead bodies. Everybody stopped to take a look. We couldn't believe our eyes; the two guys had been fat with round faces. They wore hats with red stars on them. They were Chinese. We were shocked. Not only because they were Chinese, but all of the artillery that was called in besides an air strike for two guys? We surveyed the area and figured out the two snipers had been holed up in the rocks off of the footpath about thirty meters away, and then word filtered down that C Company had taken four KIAs and about five WIAs. All because of two snipers with good cover and concealment.

We humped on by the two dead Chinese. I took a picture of them laying side by side. Then we saw pools of blood where somebody got greased. Just seeing the blood, I felt sick to my stomach. As we got farther away, I felt better and tried to concentrate on the hump.

We ended up somewhere north of Chu Pa. As usual, only the CO and the cadre knew for sure. Why we were always kept in the dark about it, we never knew. Most of us didn't care, we were tired, worn out, and pissed off. Some guys wanted things to happen just to break the monotony and pain of the humping, setting up, digging in, and humping out.

After we dug in, another day went by. The next morning, LT came back from the CP wearing his famous big grin and a stupid red scarf around his neck. "First Platoon, saddle up," he yelled. We just looked at each other, dumbfounded.

"Where are we going?" I asked.

With a twinkle in his eyes he replied, "We are going approximately two and a half klicks to a hilltop that two companies couldn't take a week ago."

I yelled out, "What! Two companies couldn't take a hilltop, so now they are sending a platoon to the same place? What kinda shit is this?"

"Leninger, just pack up and shut up," Lieutenant Scurr snapped back at me.

I glared at him; I hated the smart-ass punk lieutenant. I wanted to slap him around then punch the shit out of him. I couldn't do it because I would have wound up in LBJ (Long Binh Jail), and *that* tore me up.

We shuffled out of the perimeter, down a ridgeline. About one hundred meters outside the perimeter, we stopped, and the squad leaders gathered around LT to ask him not to try to go all the way to that hilltop.

"Lets move it out, we're going," LT replied.

Everybody was pissed off. The lieutenant wanted the glory of war, killing gooks so he could get the promotions along with the body count. We just wanted to get home in one piece. We were firm believers that you don't do what the division or battalion wanted you to do, to go as far as they tell you to. It was asking for trouble. Don't fuck with Charlie, and he won't fuck with you. It was that simple. Shit, we all were scared, and half of the guys in our platoon had only three or four months left in country. So why take risks?

We humped a couple of hours. LT used my radio to call back our location about every half hour. LT and I were in the middle of the platoon as we snaked through the trees and undergrowth. I was praying to myself, to St. Jude, make the gooks be gone; let us get through this.

My thoughts were interrupted by Monkey; he was carrying the radio with the point. "One-Three, One-Three, this is One-Two. Over."

"One-Two, this is One-Three," I replied. "Go ahead."

"One-Three, the point has reached some bunkers. Over."

"I roger that, you have bunkers to your front." I gave the handset to LT, and he told One-Two to hold up. He relayed the situation to the company. We were told to cautiously check the bunkers out. LT relayed the message to One-Two. "Proceed cautiously, One-Two. We're coming up to your rear."

We ascended the steep slope. The point was about fifty meters away from us.

"One-Three, bunkers appear to be unoccupied, about two weeks old. Seem to be a hundred or so. Over."

The first bunker was a fighting bunker, large enough to hold four or five, and if there were a hundred bunkers, there were four or five hundred gooks around somewhere. We all breathed easier knowing the gooks had left. We found some equipment scattered around but nothing of great importance—a few pith helmets, some empty pouches, a few empty mags for an AK-47. LT radioed back to our company to tell the CO our situation. LT's disappointment was written on his face. We rested for a half hour before starting back to the company perimeter. If the gooks had been in those bunkers, we would have been torn up, just like the two companies that had tried two weeks earlier.

When we reached the perimeter, LT headed up to the CO to report. The rest of us just gathered around our squad's bunker and talked about how little we liked LT's gung ho attitude.

"Maybe we should frag his ass," one guy said.

We all looked at each other. Nobody said anything. Then another guy broke the silence, "Shit, man, we're surrounded by incompetents—our CO gets us lost, LT wants combat so bad he's creaming in his pants! We're humping a lot more than we ever did before. Why? They want us to get in contact! We're sacrificial lambs, and they don't give a flying fuck who gets killed and how many of us! Well I do, and if it means doing something about LT to save us from a suicide mission where we all might get killed, I'll do it." He threw down his helmet and kicked it about ten feet. "I'm not going home alive, I know it."

"Don't talk like that, man!" someone said. "We're all going home."

But we all agreed with the sentiments about LT. Things had changed drastically, and we didn't trust our leaders anymore. The only LT we trusted was Lieutenant Murphy who was now at 2d Platoon. The rest were new. It also seemed to us that battalion, brigade, and the division wanted us to get in the shit so they could report to whoever on how we were kicking ass.

(Operational Reports Lessons Learned 4th Inf. Division Period Ending April 30, 1969.)

a. On 1 February 1969, the beginning of this reporting Period, the 4th Infantry Division initiated operation DAN QUYEN-HINES.

Division's general mission remained essentially the same as in the later stages of Operation MACARTHUR: conduct sustained, coordinated, and combined offensive operations to destroy enemy main and local force units, destroy or neutralize enemy base areas, interdict high-speed infiltration routes, assist in the protection of urban areas, and support pacification efforts and civil programs of the Government of VIETNAM.

On 3 February, a PW captured in I Corps revealed that he was a member of the 19th Medical Company, 28th NVA Regiment, and that the regiment was to continue to B-3 Front.

On 7 February the 1st Battalion, 8th Infantry, released by the 1st Brigade, moved by truck to POLEI KLENG and then combat assaulted to occupy the high ground in an arc north and west of LZ MILE HIGH (YA936930) to again block the enemy force. The 1st Battalion, 22d Infantry combat assaulted south from DAK TO to protect the 2d Brigade's northern flank from infiltration.

(3) After 7 February, when the last ARVN battalions withdrew to protect the cities during the approaching TET holidays, the 1st Battalion, 12th Infantry and 1st Battalion, 14th Infantry continued their operations in the CHU PA region. They proceeded deliberately through the mountain area, working downward from the heights and relying on artillery and air support to soften the enemy positions. The 1st Brigade, with its one remaining battalion, terminated operations in eastern PLEIKU Province and joined forces confronting the threat in KONTUM Province.

In early February, we received a couple of E-6s, Sergeant Revels and Sergeant Cribb, and Sergeant Cribb was assigned to our platoon as platoon sergeant. At the time, Sergeant Cribb was in his forties. He was about five feet seven, with a well-rounded face and belly. With a red suit and a beard, he would have made a lot of kids happy at Christmas. When we first saw him, we made jokes because we thought that if we had to hump, he'd be in trouble—he was already carrying an extra pack up front. Sergeant Cribb was from South Carolina, and it was encouraging that he was older because we all figured that the older a sergeant was the more experienced he'd be.

We stayed on the hilltop for a couple of weeks, sending out SRPs from each platoon, and I was really glad I didn't have to go out on SRPs or LP anymore when we were set up. I grew closer to the other RTOs. The head RTO was Steve Turzilli, an Italian from New York, whom everybody called Ginzo, Wop, or Dago, whichever came to mind. Steve was about six feet and about two hundred pounds, with dark hair, moustache, and bushy dark eyebrows. He was mild mannered, and he took ribbing in fun, but you wouldn't want to get him pissed off. Steve carried one of the X-mode radios (for communication with battalion headquarters) for the CP, along with Ken Comeaux, Bill Sewell, Jay Click, and Parish. Steve talked with everybody and came over to our bunker every day to rap. Steve was a true New Yorker, and just then he was in heaven because the Jets had won the Super Bowl a couple of weeks prior. But Steve even thought that the Mets were going to win the pennant. He'd been in the machine-gun squad before becoming head RTO, and was one of the strong figures in the company. We had a few others—Dean Johnson, Jack Shoppe, and Joe Fegan. Almost all of the squad leaders were looked to for strength.

Ken Comeaux also came down to our bunker almost every day, and since that first SRP, when we shot the two gooks, our friendship had grown. But, in fact, the longer you were in country the tighter you got with the men in your company. During the day, after cleaning weapons or eating chow, guys walked to different bunkers to talk, play cards, or just visit.

(Operational Report Lessons Learned 4th Inf. Division, Period Ending April 30, 1969)

(4) With the enemy effectively blocked, the Division elected to realign its forces, thereby creating a more respon-

sive reserve. On 16 and 17 February, the 1st Battalion, 12th Infantry and the 1st Battalion, 14th Infantry, after terminating their operations in the CHU PA region, moved to the 2d Brigade's area of operation. While the 1st of the 12th occupied the east bank of the NA KRONG BOLAH to prevent infiltration toward KONTUM City, the 1st of the 14th relieved the 3d Battalion, 12th Infantry in place. The 3d of the 12th combat assaulted to the high ground west of PLEI MRONG, thus extending the Division's defensive screen southward across the YA KRONG BOLAH.

About the middle of February, we saddled up again and moved to another hilltop, a few klicks away but still east of the Ya Krong Bolah River. As I stumbled along carrying the radio for Sergeant Cribb, I was surprised how he kept up. His face was red, but he never complained. When we stopped to take ten, all he did was say, "Damn," in a Carolina drawl.

After resting a while, we cooked up some C rats for lunch. About an hour later, I had terrible stomach cramps, as if somebody reached inside of me, grabbed my stomach, and squeezed. I thought I might have stomach flu, but the medic had nothing for a flu, and for the next couple of days my stomach got worse. No matter what I ate or when I drank water, almost instantaneously it ran through me. The medic checked to see if I could go in with the CO, but there was no way, so I had to grin and bear it.

The next morning, February 23, we were told again to saddle up, that we were going to CA northwest of Polei Kleng to relieve some other company.

AVDDH-GC-MH
SUBJECT: Operational Report of the 4th Infantry Division for Period Ending 30 April 1969, RCS CSFOR-65 (R1)

On 23 February the 1st of the 12th and 1st of the 8th exchanged positions and returned to the operational control of their parent brigades. The realignment proved to have been effective when, on 23 February, the NVA Spring Offensive began, since it freed the entire 1st Brigade to once again become the Division's reserve, alert for commitment anywhere in the area of operations. The Division was now aligned with the 2d Brigade, controlling three battalions, west of the

YA KRONG BOLAH River blocking the enemy's advance and the 1st Brigade east of the YA KRONG BOLAH, protecting the approaches to KONTUM City and being prepared to combat assault to smash the enemy or cut him off from his sanctuaries.

(5) As part of their Spring Offensive, the NVA attempted to interdict Highway 14 North between PLEIKU and KONTUM Cities. On 24 February the 3d ARVN Cavalry smashed two attempted ambushes along the highway, killing 63 NVA and taking four prisoners. While these actions were in progress, a new threat developed in the BEN HET area with heavy attacks by fire against the CIDG Camp. To counter these threats the 4th Infantry Division deployed elements of the 1st Battalion, 69th Armor to BEN HET and DAK TO and sent the 2d Battalion, 35th Infantry, just returned from seven months of operations in DARLAC and QUANG DUC Province, into the CHU PRONG Mountain complex east of Highway 14. In a month of reconnaissance in force and denial operations, the 2d of the 35th killed 69 NVA; captured large amounts of ammunition, medical supplies, communications equipment, and documents; and saturated an enemy regimental command post and hospital complex with crystalline CS.

In mid-February the enemy commenced extensive reconnaissance efforts against friendly positions and became more overt in his movements. On 23 February, the enemy Spring Campaign began with attacks by fire against PLEIKU City, KONTUM City, and US fire support bases. The 24th NVA Regiment, despite its defeat in the CHU PA Mountain complex in early February, attempted to interdict Highway 14 North and harass the PLEI MRONG area. The 66th NVA Regiment infiltrated elements of two battalions to the vicinity of POLEI KLENG but withdrew after a series of small contacts. Although the enemy failed to take and hold any population center, local units in KONTUM and PLEIKU Provinces achieved some success in limited attacks against undefended villages. Pressed by the 4th Infantry Division's vertical envelopment operations, the enemy began to withdraw, covering his movement with harassing attacks. In late March and early April the bulk of the enemy forces successfully exfiltrated to base areas along the CAMBODIAN Border.

Elsewhere in KONTUM Province, enemy forces avoided military installations but launched attacks, up to battalion-sized, against lightly defended villages along Highway 14 southeast of DAK TO. Hardest hit was KON NORING (ZB125160), attacked by the 304th Local Force Battalion on 23 and 25 February. In spite of reinforcement by the 1st Battalion, 42d ARVN Regiment and support from gunships and tactical air, the village suffered 52 civilians killed, 36 civilians wounded, five civilians missing, and 132 houses destroyed. Kon HOKONG (ZB143149), DIEN BINH (ZB0918), and TANH CANH (ZB0622) were also attacked during February and March. Mining and ambushes along Highway 14 ten to fifteen kilometers north-northwest of KONTUM City were probably the work of the 304th Local Force Battalion; the 5th Battalion, 24th Regiment; and possibly the K25B Engineer Battalion.

After defending its caches in CHU PA Mountain (YA9537) in January and early February, the 24th NVA Regiment exfiltrated across the YA KRONG BOLAH River to regroup in the southern PLEI TRAP Valley. After receiving supplies and replacements, the regiment, less its 5th Battalion, moved east across northern PLEIKU Province into positions east and west of Highway 14. The 5th Battalion infiltrated northward into KONTUM Province.

The thought crossed my mind, Relieve another company? What does that mean? Couldn't they cut it? No, that couldn't be it; did they catch some shit? Most likely! We were never told if it would be a hot LZ, (that is, contact before your feet hit the ground) or a cold LZ. I was nervous about going to a new location, and that didn't help my stomach at all.

The choppers were on their way as we shuffled to the LZ. The choppers came in one by one, picked up a load of guys, and took off, barely clearing the treetops. As we flew along, we sat, looking down, with our legs dangling in the wind. Sometimes we flew over a village, otherwise we just stared into the mysterious green below or at the other twelve or so choppers flying in formation.

We were in the air about forty minutes, passing over mountain ranges and ridgelines that formed the eastern side of Plei Trap Valley. Then the chopper made a sudden turn and descended. We could see yellow smoke coming from a hilltop, and the closer we got, the easier it was to see guys waiting for the choppers to land.

Holding our helmets as if they were going to blow off, we landed, then got off and passed the guys getting on. They seemed drained, and they didn't even look at us. A few of us walked over to some guys sitting on one of the bunkers, waiting to leave.

"Hey, man, what's up?" Bill asked one of them.

Just then a helicopter with loudspeakers flew over, saying, "If you can hear this, pop a flare."

Then the guy replied, "*That's* what's up. We got two guys lost out there somewhere; they got in contact and the SRP was split up. Who knows if they are alive or whatever. We had a few SRPs get in contact off this hill; the gooks are definitely around. Shit, not far from here, two companies were wiped out—don't know who they were with, but that's what we heard. Keep your asses down. The fuckin gooks shoot a recoilless rifle up here."

The guy got up and headed toward the pad. He yelled out, "Good luck. You'll need it."

We silently looked at each other. If he was trying to scare us, he did a hell of a job, but I thought he was just being truthful. The first platoon was sent to the far side of the perimeter, and we set up in the bunkers among the tall trees.

(ORLL Ending 30 April 1969)

On 24 February, the 24th Regiment sprang two abortive ambushes on Highway 14 between PLEIKU and KONTUM. Elements of the 3d ARVN Cavalry dispersed the ambushers, killing 63. The 24th Regiment remained in the vicinity of CHU PRONG Mountain (AR7764), attempting to interdict Highway 14. The 2d Battalion, 35th Infantry, sent into the CHU PRONG to destroy the 24th, met a well-disciplined, aggressive enemy who initiated numerous sharp fire fights at close range, employing small arms, RPG-2, and RPG-7 (Rocket Launchers).

The company before us built only fighting bunkers, no sleepers, so we had to set up hootches (tents made with two ponchos and a couple of sticks). I paired off with Monkey again, and we set up close to my old squad, 1/3. I was thirsty, so I drank down some water. Almost immediately the cramps came. I grabbed the shovel and my rifle and ran toward the bushes, but I didn't make it. After I was through, I went over to Doc Pelky and told him how bad it was. He went to the CP and told the captain. About fifteen minutes later, Doc Pelky told me that I was going to take a supply chopper in about an hour to the Trains area, Kontum. I thanked him, packed up, went to the CP, and waited. I had only been there about ten minutes when a call came on Steve Turzilli's radio that the two guys had been picked up who were lost from the 1/8 company that had left two hours earlier.

Then Steve said, "Boy, what smells like shit around here?"

"It's me, man," I told him.

He just laughed, then said, "While you're in Kontum make sure you get a new pair of shorts with a cork attached."

"Real funny, Ginzo." Then I asked him, "Does this hill have a name?"

"Yea. It's 1018, [Chu Kram Lo], on the map."

I pointed to a rock wall four or five hundred meters northeast from the hill and about five hundred meters higher, and said, "That SOB scares me. If there are any gooks up there, they could lob mortar rounds at us all day long or snipe at us."

Just then I heard the chopper in the distance, and yellow smoke was popped on the pad.

At the 1/12th area near Kontum, I went straight to the hospital tent and checked in. I told the doctor my problem, and he asked me for a stool sample. After that he gave me a cup of some brown syrup that tasted like coke syrup. When I asked him what it was for, he told me, "To kill stomach worms."

Then I asked, "Are you sure this won't make them get bigger?"

He laughed and gave me a small bottle of the syrup saying, "Drink half of this about four hours from now and the rest four hours later. By tomorrow you'll be okay. We'll keep you in here for two days just to make sure."

He told me I'd probably got the worms from the water. Then I asked him if I could see a dentist.

He said, "As long as you're in here you might as well." He also told me to get some clean fatigues.

It was almost chow time, so I would have the next day to see the dentist and to report back to the doctor. Reluctant to eat for fear of the reaction, I went to the mess tent. When I saw the hot chow, I couldn't resist. They had steak, mashed potatoes, gravy, corn—and ice cream for dessert. I hadn't really eaten for the two weeks since I'd contracted the stomach worms, so I chowed down like a hungry dog, making a pig of myself and hoping the worms wouldn't know what hit them. Halfway through I stopped to see what my stomach would do. My stomach was fine. I jumped back into my grub. After I finished, I went up for seconds and told the cooks, that, next to my mom's cooking, it was the best meal I had ever eaten. I lied.

After chow, I went to supply to get clean fatigues and underwear, then I visited the outdoor shower fed by cold water from a fifty-five gallon drum. Who cared? I was getting the jungle scum off. After the shower, I felt great. I was clean, and I had a full stomach, with no cramps. I returned to the transient barracks where I found out that it was a good thing I was taking a shower because some sergeant had come by and taken all but two guys for bunker guard. I took full advantage of the extra time to sleep. I woke up in the middle of the night anyway and took my medicine, then drifted back to a sound sleep.

I was up at dawn and could smell the scrambled eggs from the mess tent, so I promptly followed my nose. Scrambled eggs, bacon, coffee, and milk! Boy, the guys in Trains area ate great, just like in a base camp. It *was* a mini-base camp. After breakfast, I had to pitch a loaf, which came out almost normal. The wonders of medicine, which I promptly finished like a good trooper.

During my visit to the dentist, he promptly pulled two teeth, gave me a no-duty slip, a couple of codeine painkillers and told me to take it easy for the rest of the day. It was close to lunchtime. I couldn't eat, so I went to the tent and lay down to listen to AFVN on my radio. I heard songs like "Beautiful Morning" by the Rascals, "Cry Like a Baby," by the Box Tops, "Jumpin Jack Flash" by the Stones, "Time of the Season" by the Zombies, "Unknown Soldier" by the Doors. Then I heard "We Gotta Get Out of this Place" by the Animals, which couldn't have been more appropriate. They were all songs that made me think of home, which sometimes was good, other times it built up loneliness. New songs like "Rock Me Baby" by Steppenwolf, "Crimson and Clover" by Tommy James and the Shondells, "Who's Making Love" by Johnny Taylor, "Start All Over Again" by Tyronne Davis, "Can't Get

Next to You" by the Temptations, "Papa Was A Rolling Stone" by the Temptations, "Time" by the Chamber Brothers, "Down On The Corner" by CCR, "Honkey Tonk" by the Stones, "Laughing" by The Guess Who all became symbolic in Vietnam. After a while, the novocaine had worn off, and my jaw hurt as if somebody had coldcocked me. I took one of the pain pills and soon felt fine. I fell asleep. I was awakened by somebody kicking the bunk. I woke up. An asshole E-6 was glaring at me.

I got up and he said, "What do you think you're doing?"

"Catching some sleep," I replied.

"You're coming with me."

"For what?" I said.

"You're going on bunker guard tonight. Get your shit."

"No, Sarge, I'm not." I pulled out my no-duty slip, signed by the dentist, and handed it to him.

He read it and handed it back. "You lucked out, soldier." He turned and left. No wonder nobody else was around. My fellow "transients" were hiding somewhere. Then I thought, what an asshole. No wonder we were hearing more and more about fraggings and shootings. Some assholes didn't understand grunts.

Still high from the pain killer, I shuffled over to the mess tent. I only ate a little because I couldn't chew. I popped the other pain pill right before dark and slept like a log.

The next day, my third, my sham was over, and I caught a supply chopper that was headed out to my company in the Plei Trap Valley. The Plei Trap Valley stretched from just south of Ben Het in Kontum Province to just west of Plei Djerang in Pleiku Province. The valley stretched approximately forty-five miles along the Cambodian border. The Plei Trap Valley area was generally rugged, and the mountainous regions rose to heights over seven thousand feet and were covered with double-, sometimes triple-canopy jungle (the trees were 100 to 150 feet high). Ass-kicking terrain. Hill 1018 was about fifteen kilometers from the Cambodian border and twelve kilometers northwest of Polei Kleng. As the chopper flew over all of that ass-kicking terrain, I again prayed to St. Jude—first, to watch over the helicopter ride (which I did each time I went into the air), and, second, to protect me when I got back to the company.

Before I knew it, the chopper banked to the right and descended towards hill 1018. I was glad to be back with my friends. Shamming ain't no fun alone anyway! I could see Ken on the pad, bringing the chopper in. When the dust cleared, he came over and asked me how Kontum was; I told him "Great chow!" Then headed through the middle of the perimeter, passing a few 3d Platoon bunkers. I had to pass by the CP.

I saw Steve out of the corner of my eye; he yelled over at me, "Hey, Len, hope you brought some beer!"

"No chance," was my reply.

"Hope they at least put a plug in your ass."

I just gave him the finger and headed to my hootch to put down my pack. Monkey was sitting in front of the hootch, writing a letter.

He turned and said, "Did you bring any beer?"

"Do I look like a liquor store or something? I brought a couple cans of pop. I didn't have but three days."

I gave him a rare can of Pepsi, and Monkey filled me in on the little that had been going on—the gooks had fired a few rounds of recoilless at our hilltop. Nobody was hurt. Soon we'd be going on a platoon sweep. For now, the CO was just sending out SRPs. Just as he finished telling me what had been happening, we heard what sounded like a rifle shot. Monkey said, "Shit," but didn't even get up before we heard *ssshh-boom*! The shell had exploded up by the chopper pad. We ran and slid into the fighting bunker, which was about ten meters away.

Once in the bunker, I said to Monkey, "Man, that was quick."

He answered, "That's the trouble with recoilless; it's already here by the time you hear the sound of them firing it. The gooks will fire a few more before they stop for a while; they're just fucking with us."

He was right. Three more rounds came zooming in within ten minutes. Two hit up in the trees, the other sailed over our hilltop. We stayed in the bunker while artillery pounded the approximate area it came from for about twenty minutes. Of course, since it took fifteen minutes to get in the artillery, we were sure the gooks were gone. But not far. About 5:00 PM, the gooks fired a few more rounds, which sent us scrambling into the bunkers. The same pattern was repeated for the next couple of days—the gooks fired at us twice day from the same area about noon and at 5:00 PM. One guy from the 3d Platoon got hit with shrapnel while using the shitter outside the perimeter. He was medevaced out. I wondered if he would tell the truth about how he got his Purple Heart. We all laughed about his "contact" even though it wasn't funny; he could have been killed. That's how February ended, and I scratched off another month on my camouflage cover. The ides of March were coming.

SUBJECT: Operational Report of the 4th Infantry Division for Period Ending 30 April 1969, RCS CSFOR-65 (R1)

On 1 March, the 1st Brigade composed of the 1st Battalion, 8th Infantry; the 3d Battalion, 8th Infantry; and the 3d Battalion, 12th Infantry, combat assaulted west of the 66th NVA Regiment to effect a vertical envelopment and cut the enemy off from his lines of communication. Heavy fighting began as soon as the lift ships reached their LZs. The 3d Battalion, 12th Infantry drove an NVA platoon off LZ SWINGER (YA837965), killing 30 while losing only one man of their own.

In the PLEI TRAP Valley, the K25A and K25B Engineer Battalions constructed roads, fortifications, and weapons positions. Logistical elements, using the road system, attempted to establish a supply base in the region 20 to 25 kilometers west-northwest of POLEI KLENG. Elements of the 40th Artillery Regiment infiltrated through the PLEI TRAP road system to shell US fire bases with 105mm howitzers. Antiaircraft guns, some as large as 37mm, fired on aircraft flying over the PLEI TRAP. On 2 March, Company C, 1st Battalion, 8th Infantry discovered two Soviet one and a half ton GAZ trucks abandoned 30 kilometers northwest of POLEI KLENG. One truck was evacuated.

Chapter VI

THE BATTLE FOR HILL 994

March had erupted with the NVA launching attacks and harassment throughout most of Kontum Province. We continued to get hit by incoming recoilless-rifle fire and once in a while a mortar round or two. Everyone wondered which platoon would be chosen to sweep to the north where the incoming was coming from. I prayed every night to St. Jude that it would not be the 1st Platoon.

On March 2, the platoon sweeps started. Second Platoon went first. The men packed up and headed south out of the patrol base with smiles on their faces. First Platoon's chances of being chosen went up to 50 percent. Nobody said anything, but everyone was thinking about it.

About an hour after the 2d Platoon left, Lieutenant Scurr came down to the bunker line and said, "Squad 1/3, pack up light, you're going on a water patrol. Leninger, get your radio; you go with them."

We gathered up a few five-gallon plastic bladders, and our empty canteens. Seven of us were going—Ken, Little George, Happy Jack, Ray, Eddie, Bill, and myself. In a way I was glad to get out of the perimeter; it got our minds off of worrying about going north on a sweep. Besides, there were seven of us, and we weren't going too far, five or six hundred meters east. Bill showed us the map, a small blue line (a river or a stream) started somewhere down the ridgeline.

Humping, light, downhill, was easy. I only had the radio in my pack, plus two bandoliers of M-16 ammo. I also had my regular two bandoliers across my chest, two around my waist, and my pistol belt. I felt I could hump a few thousand meters, no problem. After about four hundred meters, we found a small stream flowing out of the rocks into a pool about three feet in diameter. The water was clear and cool. It was the best water I ever tasted in Nam. We spread out about ten meters and took turns filling up canteens and the five-gallon plastic bladders. I radioed back about our find.

We sat around, shamming for about an hour. At about noon, we heard the recoilless shells hit up the hill toward our patrol base, but one landed about fifty meters from us. We laughed about it because the gook was so far off. After the firing stopped, we headed back to the patrol base.

When we got back, we learned that there had been a fight while we were gone. Around noon, one of our best squad leaders Joe Fegan got in a beef with Lieutenant Scurr about taking out a SRP made up of FNGs. Joe Fegan argued that it was too late to go out. LT got smart, and Joe hit him. The captain jumped in, and he got popped. A chopper was called to take the squad leader back to LZ Mary Lou in Kontum.

Joe Fegan had done what we all wanted to do, and we all sided with him. SRPs did always go out early, seven or eight in the morning. Starting late and sending three FNGs was a stupid idea. Besides, like most of our squad leaders, he was short, under three months.

The 2d Platoon returned from its sweep. They hadn't seen anything.

The next day, March 3, the 1st Platoon was told to saddle up. We were going on a sweep. As we packed up, I kept an eye on Lieutenant Scurr. When he came back to the bunker line from the CP, he wasn't happy, which we thought was good news.

"Which way LT?" I asked.

"West," he answered.

We were relieved. We left the patrol base at about 0830, southwest down the ridgeline, following a footpath. We made a thousand meters in an hour, then we heard small-arms fire coming from the north, a few klicks away. I radioed back to the company to find out what was happening. I was told by Johnny, who was on the radio at the time, that we should hold in place, that he'd get back to me. I told LT, he put out flankers, and we rested for about half an hour.

We heard artillery exploding about two klicks to our north; we had figured one of our short-range patrols must have made contact. Johnny radioed back to confirm what we already thought.

Radio Log (DAILY) S-3 1/12 March 3, 1969 (Call Signs O Div. or Bde. 21-'A' Co.; 22-'B' Co.; 23-'C' Co.; 24-'D' Co.; 75-Recon; 72 Battalion)

Time	From	To	Message
0930	22	72	One of our subs in contact further word will follow.
0940	22	72	2283A exchanged fire with undetermined size force at 916985 neg. casualties employing red leg and small organic.
0955	22	72	Patrol spotted 1 dink moving down trail, the point man opened up on him, the dink ran about 20 meters then turned and fired on them. He was wearing khakis, pack and carried AK-47. Employed small organic are sweeping area now. Dink fled north.

We continued on our sweep but with more caution than we had used when we left the patrol base. The contact by an SRP from the 3d Platoon brought us back to reality. We swept another klick or so, then we headed back to our perimeter. We saw nothing. When we got back to our perimeter, mail was waiting for us. Mail, we loved it. It took our minds off what lay to the north of our hilltop. The gooks were there; the question was how many? After the patrol from the 3d Platoon fired on the gook they saw, a sweep of the area produced nothing.

Everybody was reading mail and cooking up goodies we got from home. Spirits were up, and AFVN radio could be heard coming from a few radios besides mine around the perimeter. "Crimson and Clover" by Tommy James and the Shondells came on.

Somebody up by the CP (command post) yelled "Turn that fucking song off, I hate that song." I looked at Monkey and turned my radio down. "If I hear that song again," the captain said, "I don't care whose radio, that person will be on LP tonight." About a minute went by, and somebody turned the radio back on. From up by the CP, the song blared across the perimeter. By then, everybody was standing on bunkers looking toward the CP and wondering what was going on. Then we heard the captain yell above the music, "That's it, mister. You've got LP tonight!"

We all laughed, but we still didn't know who did it. It was funny, but then again, it wasn't funny at all. We all were wondering what kind of leader we'd been stuck with. First, he gets us lost for three days in January; yesterday he gets into a fight with one of the squad leaders, (although I've got to admit that I didn't know the whole story), and now this.

Later, we saw Steve walking toward our bunker. He was laughing and shaking his head.

"Who was it?" Bill asked.

"Johnny P," Steve replied.

"That ain't right, man," Ray said. We all agreed.

The sun was setting; another day had ended.

(Operational Report of the 4th Infantry Division Ending April 30, 1969)

On 3 March, Company A, 3d Battalion, 8th Infantry intruded into the base of an enemy battalion, suffering heavy casualties in the ensuing battle. From 4 through 8 March other companies of the 3d Battalion, 8th Infantry combed the area of contact, destroying remaining enemy forces. Confirmed enemy losses in the fighting with 3d of the 8th were 189 NVA killed.

AVDDH-CS
SUBJECT: Combat Operations After Action Report (RCS: NACV J3-J2)

a. Company A sustained 20 infantry KIA, one artillery man KIA, and one engineer KIA. One infantryman remains MIA. Fifty-two men were wounded, and three originally missing in action managed to evade to friendly positions. In addition, one man captured by the NVA was recovered on 6 March by Company D, 3d Battalion, 8th Infantry.

b. Enemy confirmed losses are 50 KIA by body count in the contact area. Further, the soldier captured by the NVA and subsequently recovered reported seeing a large number of NVA wounded along the top of the north-south ridgeline of the scene of action. During the night our battalion received a report on the radio from Division, or Brigade.

Radio Log (DAILY) S-3 1/12th March 4, 1969 (Call signs—0, Div. or Brigade, 21 (A Co.), 22 (B Co.), 23 (C Co.), 24 (D Co.), 75 (E-Recon), 72 (Batt.)

Time	From	To	Message
0215	0	72	Ben Het under attack. 15 enemy PT-76 tanks and vehicles were used for support. Friendly forces knocked out, one enemy tank and two or three vehicles. Also hit by a ground attack by estimated Battalion size enemy force on west hill and at main camp. Taking incoming 85mm, some larger, and B-40 rockets. B 1/69 is on location at this time. 1 friendly tank has been knocked out. Employed air strikes, still taking incoming at this time.
0310	0	72	LZ Bass receiving incoming B-40 and mortars. A 75rr hitting in close also a 60mm mortar not doing any damage.
0330	0	72	Ground attack at LZ Bass requesting firecracker. 122mm rockets coming into LZ Bass also receiving gas.

By the time the sun came up on March 4, one of our sister units whose call sign was Recon (75), was getting a ground probe by an enemy force, of unknown size. Recon was a reinforced platoon, of thirty-odd men. They were commanded by Lt. Mike Ranger, who was our 2d Platoon leader until he was transferred in December.

Recon was on a hilltop called LZ Roberts, about five klicks southwest of our location and about three klicks west of our battalion fire base, LZ Mile High. LZ Mile High, a C-Company-secured fire base, was nine klicks west of Polei

Kleng. A Company was located two klicks south of the fire base, and D Company was two klicks north of us. Our company RTOs kept us informed on what was going on by coming down to the bunker line after their radio watch.

Radio Log March 4, 1969 cont.

Time	From	To	Message
0615	75	72	2 or 3 dinks came up to the bunker line on the SW side of the perimeter. Lost commo with all my elements radio being jammed. We threw frags and fired at them. Working up redleg.
0645	75	72	We had 4 more dinks come out of the woods from the S we threw a few frags and opened up with M-16s, then employed large organics.
0715	75	72	We checked out the area found 4 sets of sandle tracks.
0808	75	72	75F sp'd to sweep area.
0821	75	72	We have contact on ridgeline details later.
0845	75	72	Still receiving incoming, and small arms fire, have 2 wounded and my 75F is pinned down. Send gunships and LOH. Employ firecracker rounds now.
0850	bde	72	Gunships are in the air will be to my location shortly, also there is no LOH available when there is you will get it.
0915	75	DO	Dust off called for recon 2 WIA frag wounds.

0940	75	72	Est. platoon size ambush waiting for sweep to come through Red Eye 901931. 53 spotted the ambush before it was tripped. Mortar attack 30–35 rounds of 82mm and a few B-40 rockets.
0950	75	72	Need 4 cases of M-16 ammo, 1 case of M-79 and 2 cases M-79 HE.
1000	75	72	Dust off complete taking incoming at this time.
1130	75	72	Additional incoming when bird came in with ammo. 5 rounds.
1140	47	bde	Just finished 2nd air strike, when resupply bird landed 5 more incoming rounds all on company CP no damage. Still trying to locate tubes believe to be SE of LZ.
1200	72	21 (A)	Rout of travel for 2183 (platoon) 894972, 904924, 909919, 915914. They will continue on present route towards recons position then when they get to 1st point given they will follow given route to your location.
1300	75	72	(Summary) We SP'd on sweep this morning to check out area of movement and spottings this morning. We got no further than just down the hill from Roberts, and made contact with what appeared to be an awaiting ambush by an approx. enemy platoon. Our point man saw some movement and opened up, then it all broke loose. The enemy advanced towards the patrol, then red leg was coming in and forced the enemy back SE the way they came. At the time contact was made LZ Roberts

started to take incoming, 82mm mortars
and B-40 rockets approx. 35 rounds.
Our people pulled back took cover
while artillery and air strikes pounded
our hilltop. We had 2 WIA's and 1
person suffering from shell shock.
When dust off came in we received 5
more rounds. Later when supply bird
came in we took 3 more rounds of
incoming. We think enemy fled SW
down ridgeline. After air strikes we
heard 3 secondary explosions.

While all of this was going on, we stayed on our hilltop and
no sweeps went out. We were having a quiet day, which was
unusual. We all had the feeling something was going to happen, but nothing did.

Radio Log cont.

Time	From	To	Message
1337	75	72	Sp'd reinforced SRP to sweep contact area.
1350	75	72	Just made contact again
1410	72	DO	Dust off called 3 WIA
1420	75	72	Have 6 WIA
1720	72	DO	Dust off called for 6 WIA at 75 location.
1755	75	72	Received 5 more rounds incoming.
1805	72	bde	Dust off complete for 3 EM at 75 location 3 EM did not need dust off.

2200	0	72	Report of enemy action at Ben Het. The use of P-76 Russian tanks against special forces camp followed by 200+ rds. 85mm. and 140mm rockets. Attack on Cam Rahn Bay Air Force Base and limited probes believe to be the start of Phase 2 in current enemy offensive in 2 core area. 4th Div. intel. from captured documents, POW's indicate enemy forces are in position to hit Hwy 14 and 17 An Khe, fire support bases, air force bases, Pleiku, Kontum and hamlets at minimum, probably will use Battalion size ground attacks, mortars, rockets and sappers. Plan to occur next 72 hours.

ORLL Ending April 30, 1969, RCS CSFOR-65 (R1) (Operations)

Large enemy forces continue to operate in the Tri-Border area, threatening BEN HET. There, on the night of 3–4 March, the enemy launched the first armor attack in the Central Highlands. Recon intelligence indicates the presence of a new NVA regiment, the 28th, in the Tri-Border area.

Elements of the 40th NVA Artillery Regiment employed 85mm guns and possibly 105mm howitzers as well as 122mm rockets, mortars, and recoilless rifles. An estimated eight to ten Soviet PT-76 light amphibious tanks participated in the attack on the night of 3–4 March. For unknown reasons, the attack, which included a battalion of infantry, dissipated before enemy and friendly forces could become decisively engaged. Of the two enemy tanks knocked out, one was evacuated by US forces for extraction of technical intelligence.

One US tank was damaged and two crew members were killed. The remainder of the 1st Battalion, 69th Armor[2], operating with the 1st Squadron, 10th Cavalry in an economy of force role in western and southern PLEIKU Province, was alerted for immediate deployment to KONTUM Province. Moving by night, one tank platoon reinforced the armor already at BEN HET. Company A and the Battalion command post reinforced ground elements at POLEI KLENG. There the tanks were centrally located to react to enemy attacks on population centers.

[2]The Battalion was operating minus Company C, which remained on the Central Coast under operational control of the 173d Airborne Brigade.

During the night, while we were on 50 percent alert, things got worse for Recon. We all wondered what the gooks were up to and how many were around us. We didn't receive any incoming that day at all, which was surprising after our getting hit almost every day for over a week. The letup made things more intense. And we still wondered which platoon was going to sweep north?

Radio Log (Daily) S-3 1/12th March 5, 1969

Time	From	To	Message
0150	75	72	Had a dink on the south side of the perimeter, fired at him we think we got him.
0205	75	72	Getting incoming and ground attack we're being overrun. Request firecracker now.
0210	23	72	81A heard tube popping AZ 30 at 700 Meters.
0210	72	0	Requested spooky on the way, ETA 20 min.
0310	spooky	72	Up on station
0405	spooky	72	Leaving station to another target Spooky 22 will replace
0415	23	72	Had movement on NE side of perimeter employed frags.

0420	23	72	Had more movement, trip flares popped employing small organics
0415	75	72	Dinks had on steel pots and employed very few small arms, they made ground attack using grenades.
0450	23	72	Same LP on NE side of perimeter has movement employed frags.
0615		72	Spooky 22 checked shadow has an ETA 15 min. to LZ Roberts.
0645	31	75	Employ red leg and sweep area as soon as possible.
0746	75	72	We found many drag marks, guts and blood laying around. At this time est. at least 20 enemy casualties. Enemy force was estimated to be platoon size element. Have found bushels of chi com grenades, and B-40 rockets, some were zeroed in on a log but weren't fired. They were found 20 meters away from bunkers. Enemy believed to escape down valley to the west.
0820	75	72	We found some objects laying around undetermined what they are. Could be some kind of enemy land mine. They stand 1 inch off the ground and are 3 inches in diameter silver in color.
0915	75	72	Receiving incoming at this time on LZ Roberts.
0925	72	0	We are taking incoming at this time.
0940	72	0	Still taking incoming on LZ Mile High, have 2 men WIA, 1 is pretty bad calling dust off at this time.
1000	72	0	Dust off completed.

1015   75   72   We found 1 enemy KIA so far, wearing green hat and green socks also found 2 AK-47's, gook hats and sandles.

1020   22   72   2281A has sp'd patrol base.

"2281A" was a short-range patrol from my old squad.

Dean Johnson, who was the squad leader of 1/3, had just returned to the company about an hour earlier after being gone for about two months on R & R and having had a hernia operation in base camp. Like the rest of our squad leaders, he was short, under two months. He could have stayed in base camp with a medical profile, but he was worried about his squad. Just seeing him seemed to up 1st Platoon's morale. He was very well liked and was one of the best squad leaders in the company.

He didn't have to go out on patrol right away, but he wanted to get back into shape and into the swing of things. He took with him Ed Medors, Ken Thomas, and Ray Bethea (who went because Little George was getting short).

They headed northwest out of the perimeter. I said a prayer as we watched them disappear into the wood line; going where they were, they would need a little help from the Big Guy. I went up by the CP so I could hear from the company RTOs how the patrol was doing as they headed to their night location.

A card game was going on in a hootch about twenty feet from the radios. Sergeant Page, Sergeant Revels, Sergeant Treadway, Little George, and a few others were playing. About seven others were watching, most from the 1st Platoon, but they were also there to monitor Dean's patrol. I wasn't going to play, but I saw all of those MPCs. Then Little George said to me, "Hey, blond-headed kid, jump on in; the water's fine."

I had about a hundred MPC, which really wasn't much; each of the other players had hundreds, and Little George had about a thousand. I told him to move over, and I sat down. I lasted ten minutes, and I was flat broke. I stood up and said, "Thanks for the swimming lesson." Everyone laughed. Then I said, "I must be lucky at love."

Little George replied, "Yea, your hand must be sore as hell."

Everyone was laughing, including me.

Radio Log cont.

1330	75	72	Receiving incoming have 5 WIA and 1 KIA dust off called.
1350	72	bde	Dust off completed, dust off on fire, dust off was completed with re-supply ship. Will require a hook to get dust off ship out.
1405	72	bde	Request spooky from 1930 to daylight to cover my 75 tonight.
1430	72	bde	More incoming at LZ Mile High, 4 rounds. 2 WIA
1645	72	0	Incoming rounds at LZ Roberts today, 16-82mm and 3 B-40's. At Mile High 4 CS 82mm, 3-120m, and 13-82mm HE. Also had 48 secondary explosions from air strikes around Roberts.

Dean's patrol made it to their night location without any problems, and we all felt pretty good about that as darkness fell once again in the Plei Trap.

After our nightly routine of bunker guard, radio watch, and nervous sleeplessness, the sun rose in a cloudless sky. For a month or so, each day had been the same—brilliant sun, hot breezeless days. I was thankful we had the shade of the trees.

Radio Log (Daily) S-3 1/12 March 6, 1969

0755	72	bde	Received 4 more rounds of incoming.
0831	75	72	Taking small arms fire in perimeter.
0833	72	bde	Received 9-82mm, 1 B-40 and 1 gas 82mm.

0950	0	72	Secret no Foreigners: Following arc light targets have been requested. Request clearance ASAP. All friendly elements must be at least 3 klicks away from target boxes.

Map 6537-IV Kontum 7146-P YA979938, 986942, 992911, ZA001915
        Kontum 7147-P YA972906, 980912, 983880, 992885
        Kontum 7148-P YA970933, 979938, 992991, 984906
        Kontum 7149-P YA974967, 972957, ZA003962, 001915
        Kontum 7153-P YB856025, 865021, YA845997, 855994
        Kontum 7154-P YA866951, 874948, 853925, 862920
        Kontum 7155-P YA890939, 900941, 893909, 903911
        Kontum 7155-P Time on target requested for 7 March
        thru 9 March.
        Recon has been moved to LZ Mary Lou for stand down.

1120	75	72	Have 2 WIA from sniper fire one was head medic called dust off.
1330	72	0	Our losses at LZ Base from incoming. 462 rounds 81mm HE, 76 rounds 81mm illumination, 200 rounds 4.2 mortar HE, 15 E-8 gas dispensers, 8 sets of sling gear, 7 night devices, 3 M-16's and 1 81mm mortar.
1507	72	0	2 more rounds incoming 82mm at Mile High
1515	72	0	Took 3 B-40's at Mile High.
1545	72	0	We need 400 rounds 4.2 HE, 75 4.2 WP and 400 81mm HE
1555	72	0	Took 4 rounds CS at Mile High

We were sitting around, and some guys had started cooking their C rations. Suddenly we heard *shhhh-booom*. That sent everybody scrambling to the fighting bunkers. Sir Charles was up to his old tricks again. I hated incoming because you never knew where the rounds would hit. You could do nothing but play gopher and keep your eye on the outside of the perimeter for a ground assault.

1625	22	72	Receiving rockets and mortars from the west about 2 klicks.

1635	22	72	Mortars located 883975

The gooks moved into the area we swept a few days ago, those sneaky little shits.

1650	22	72	Incoming stopped, first round sounded like rocket, the rest 60mm 15 rounds total.

We stayed in the bunkers for about twenty minutes, then we got out. The sun was setting, and it was too late to make fires to cook. Besides, nobody felt like eating. I had some cheese and crackers, and they were enough. As night fell, we were put on 75 percent alert. About eight we were hit by incoming again. Besides having our sleep ruined, we were getting pissed off and scared. We wanted to get back at the gooks, but we couldn't. They knew how to screw up our minds.

2002	22	72	Got 3 rounds of incoming 82mm 1 inside perimeter 2 outside neg. casualties.

2003	72	0	Received 2 rounds of incoming 82mm neg. casualties.

2150	21	72	Receiving incoming and SKS small arms fire from the North 10 rounds of 82mm.

At midnight all radio call signs were changed: A Company became 61; B Company, 62; C Company, 63; D Company, 64; Battalion, 95.

Radio Log (Daily) S-3 1/12th March 7, 1969

Time	From	To	Message
0210	61	95	Receiving incoming 4-82mm, 1B-40 in perimeter neg. casualties.
0300	61	95	Our sub 82a has movement about 100m's out employing mortars.

Before we knew it the sun was coming up. Another sleepless night had passed. Even so, the sun always looked good.

Time	From	To	Message
0930	61	95	6182B closed patrol base, on his way in he found 4 propellent tubes, 3 other tubes, tube cover for 82mm and 34" carrying strap.
0935	61	95	6182A closed patrol base he found 3 B-40 rockets ready to be fired. Found 100 meters from 6182B's find at 941910.

At about ten o'clock, the gooks sent us diving back into our bunkers and eating more dust.

Time	From	To	Message
0957	62	95	Receiving incoming 3 rounds of recoilless.
1006	62	95	3 more rounds incoming, 1 man hit in foot.
1113	62	95	Receiving incoming again 82mm 6 rounds.

About half an hour after the last incoming round, the 2d Platoon packed up and moved out on a sweep. They went west, which faked us out; we were receiving all the incoming from the north and northwest. Dean's patrol heard the tubes popping a few hundred meters to their north. They were told to take cover while an air strike hit the area to their north.

Time	From	To	Message
1350	61	95	Just took 3 rounds incoming outside perimeter 60mm.

1400	63	95	Took 2 rounds of 82mm gas.
1537	63	95	Took 1 more round 82mm 1 WIA need dust off.
1603	95	bde	Dust off complete
1725	62	95	6282 just closed patrol base, they found 1 gook canteen, also found 1 hootch 4' by 6' covered by leaves open sides not used within last week. Found trail heading northwest used recently, they destroyed in place.

The 2d Platoon wasn't back a half hour when we were hit by incoming again. The routine was getting old.

1750	62	95	Receiving incoming again 8 rounds of recoilless from NW.
2310	62	95	Receiving incoming, 4 rounds neg. casualties.
2311	95	0	Taking incoming on Mile High 2 rounds neg. cas.

Nobody in the battalion received any more incoming the rest of the night, the gooks probably got tired and went to sleep, after they ruined another night of my sleep. We were put on fifty percent alert for the rest of the night. The light of day came again too soon. My head was heavy from lack of sleep, everyone carried bags under their eyes. We looked like shit.

We were sitting next to the bunkers, cooking up some nasty Cs. Not too much was said; we were too tired to talk. Then someone yelled, "Saddle up" from 3d Platoon's side of the perimeter. We stopped what we were doing and looked at each other. Which way? After a few minutes, Steve came down to the bunker line to give us the word. He pointed, north.

For two weeks, we had wondered who was going that way. Now we knew, but we were a little surprised at the 3d Platoon's selection. It was no secret throughout the company that, overall, the 3d Platoon was the weakest.

Lieutenant Nathan lacked experience. He came to us about

the same time as Lieutenant Scurr of the 1st Platoon, although he was a couple of years older. The platoon did have a couple of good E-6s in Workman and Kellough. About half the platoon were pretty good guys, and I knew a few (Jerry MacDonald, Prentiss Harris, Serros, Lemmens, Heath), but the other half were FNGs and guys untested.

Nobody said a word about the sweep, probably because we didn't know what to say and didn't want to jinx them. I wondered what was going through their minds as they were packing up.

About twenty minutes after we finished chowing down, we heard the clanking of equipment coming from the other side of the perimeter. A few minutes later they filed by where we were sitting. They all had feathers sticking in their helmets (symbol of our battalion, Red Warriors). We didn't know what to say. What do you say to guys who are going to be in contact? A few of us said, "Take care," or "Hurry back." They just nodded. A few managed to crack a smile.

Radio Log (Daily) S-3 1/12th March 8, 1969

0815   62   95   6283 just Sp'd patrol base.

When they were gone about twenty minutes, Steve came down from the CP and told us that the 3d Platoon found nine bunkers about two hundred meters outside of our perimeter.

Little George yelled out, "*Ssshhit*, that's too fuckin close, man!"

Then Happy Jack asked, "What about Dean and them?"

Steve replied, "Dean's going to hook up with the 3d Platoon and come back with them."

That took us by surprise because Dean's patrol was supposed to come back in.

Then Bill said, "I agree with Dean, it's better to be with thirty guys than four."

We all agreed. Nobody questioned his decision.

I thought our shit was weak; all of our squad leaders weren't with us—Jack Shoppe and Jim Leonard were both in for R & R or something, Joe Fegan was at LZ Mary Lou trying to get trip flares because we were low, and Bill Butler was already in for malaria, which he caught after his R & R.

0836	62	95	6283 found bunkers recently used within a week each capable of holding 2 or 3 men, no overhead, one not complete, will destroy in place.
0915	64	95	6482 just SP'd on sweep.

D company also sent out a platoon sweep south of their position. Between us and them was a hilltop 994.

1025	63	95	81e on sweep ran into ambush, pulling back at this time, grid of contact 930930. Spotted 7 dinks neg. casualties. We are setting up ambush at this time.
1058	95	bde	Received 2 82mm and 51 cal. fire into Mile High 2 casualties
1110	63	95	6381e rec. fire again they pulled back to about 100 meters outside of perimeter they are adjusting 81mm mortars.
1125	95	DO	Called dust off.
1130	95	bde	Dust off complete 3 individuals from 63 element.

A few hours had passed; everybody's mind was on the 3d Platoon's sweep and Dean's patrol. We were scared for us and for them. We would be the only reaction force for them. After us, D company was two klicks to our north.

1215	62	95	6283 is at 81a location, 81a will push on with 83.

Dean's patrol hooked up with the 3d Platoon, and they continued on the sweep towards hill 994. Two hours later, Steve came down from the CP again, the look on his face told us here comes some bad news.

"What's up, Ginzo?" I said.

His eyes looked north, and he said, "The 3d Platoon just found a bunker complex, over 150 bunkers a couple days old, three- or four-man bunkers." It didn't take a mathematical genius to figure out how many gooks that is.

| 1425 | 62 | 95 | 6283 at 898988 found 140 bunkers 2 or 3 days old capable of holding 3 to 4 men with no overhead, bunkers are running NE on ridge, still looking around. |

| 1459 | 62 | 95 | Further read out on bunkers found by 83 element 170 total. |

We wondered why 3d Platoon was still out there looking around, why they weren't pulled back and the place blown to hell! Twenty minutes later our suspicions ended. Small-arms fire shattered the silence, coming from the north and echoing through the trees. We grabbed our rifles and ammo. As quickly as the small-arms fire started it stopped; we waited.

| 1520 | 62 | 95 | 6283 element in contact 1 AK-47 firing at them at 904994 on top of hill 994. |

| 1525 | 62 | 95 | Firing has stopped at this time 83 will sweep area of contact. |

We were sitting around dumbfounded, not knowing what to do. That soon changed. *Ssshh boom! Ssshh boom!* Two rounds of recoilless landed outside the perimeter. We dove into the bunkers.

| 1535 | 62 | 95 | Receiving incoming 2 rounds of recoilless rifle, landed outside of perimeter. |

About ten minutes went by. We were still in the bunkers when small-arms fire again erupted from the north, this time with more intensity. M-16s, AKs, grenades, machine guns, and M-79 rounds exploded periodically. All of us expected to hump out to reinforce the 3d Platoon, but the word never came.

| 1543 | 62 | 95 | 6283 has 3 WIA don't know severity yet. |

The small-arms fire stopped, and two more rounds of incoming landed outside the perimeter. Either the gooks were trying to keep us pinned down or they were trying to piss us off enough to send out another platoon. It was hard to figure out, as usual. If they were trying to scare us, it was a wasted effort; we were already scared.

| 1615 | 62 | 95 | 6283 has 4 WIA's 2 are in good shape, 1 bad the other they don't know. |

| 1620 | 95 | bde | Moving a plt. size element to contact area of 6283 will be 6483. |

Word came down from the CP to stay ready. We also were told about D company's platoon going to help. This sort of relieved us, but that didn't change the shit we already were in. The bunkers were an indication that it was us and D company against a possible regiment. But what about the other side of the Hill 994? We would soon find out, so would the 3d Platoon of D company.

Another mortar round landed outside the perimeter, it was a good thing they were lousy shots. But the round did serve its purpose; we went back into the bunkers.

| 1710 | 62 | 95 | Just received another round of incoming. |

| 1726 | 62 | 95 | We took 6 more rounds of incoming |

The daylight was fading fast. No matter what happened now, it was too late to go out.

| 1720 | 95 | 0 | Called dustoff for 4 WIA's from last incoming round at Mile High. |

| 1743 | 95 | 0 | Dustoff complete. |

There was about ten minutes of light left in a day that was draining for everyone—physically because of the adrenaline rushes caused by the incoming and hearing the small-arms fire of the 3d Platoon's contact; mentally draining because of not knowing what was going to happen next, and worrying about who had been hit in the contact. Our thoughts were derailed again when another firefight broke out to the north.

1825	64	95	64 element is 300 meters away from 62 element he said there are dinks in front and in back of them dug in, 6483 in contact.
1835	64	95	6483 element tried to pull back but dinks are in front and in back of them in fox holes, going to stay and fight way out 6483 at 907994.
1840	64	95	Just killed 2 dinks, walked up on our patrol base perimeter.
1841	62	95	We need gun ships for 6283 they are completely surrounded.

Lieutenant Scurr came down to the bunker line. He informed us that the 3d Platoon was surrounded and that our platoon would move out in the morning to get them. D Company could not reach them; it was also in a buzz saw. The small-arms fire died down, then stopped. It was completely dark. I got together with the guys from my old squad, 1/3—Dean's squad. We had not eaten all day, and we knew what the morning would bring. It was like the Last Supper in a way. We decided to cook up the best food we had saved from our care packages. We'd been saving the food for special occasions. This wasn't what we'd had in mind, but it could be our last meal. I cooked up some Spaghetti Os, and for dessert, I had peaches and pound cake.

We did all our cooking in a fighting bunker and sat outside, talking about home. We talked about anything to take our minds off of the situation at hand. We ate what we could, but nobody ate too much because our stomachs were churning.

Word came down to the bunker line, fifty percent alert. Bunker guard was split up. I was paired with Monkey, my hootch mate. We had guard from ten to midnight.

We went back to our hootch to try to get some sleep, which was impossible. As I lay on my air mattress thinking about what morning light would bring, I prayed to St. Jude again to watch over all of us.

After about ten minutes, I whispered to Monkey, "Monk, are you awake?"

He answered, "Are you kidding? How the fuck could anyone sleep, when tomorrow ... ?" He stopped, but I knew where he was coming from.

We got up and sat outside our hootch until our watch. Gunships worked out to the north.

1930	64	95	6483 has 1 WIA, 1 KIA, KIA name Spec. 4 Zufelt
2010	62	95	6283 has movement all around them.
2047	64	95	6483 has freed point element.

Sporadic gunfire and explosions echoed in the darkness. We didn't even hear three rounds of incoming until they exploded on the west side of the perimeter. We crawled back into the bunker.

2100	62	95	3 more rounds of incoming
2135	62	95	Received 3 more rounds of incoming, azimuth 275 2 klicks
2150	64	95	6483 is missing 6 people, he believes they are in the rear, radio is out will find them in the morning. The bunkers they found are being destroyed by concrete piercing rounds.

Things calmed down about one o'clock in the morning. Monkey and I returned to our hootch to try to get some shuteye. I just lay on my air mattress. I had a headache, I was overtired, and my eyes burned. I couldn't sleep, so I just prayed. I said three rosaries before I finally fell out about four o'clock. Morning came, my head was still groggy from lack of sleep, and my eyelids felt like they had grenades tied to them. Strangely, things were quiet, which was unexpected. Maybe the gooks had left. That hope vanished when artillery barrages exploded to the north.

Radio Log (Daily) S-3 1/12 March 9, 1969

0540	62	95	6283 has movement to the south about 200 meters they are employing redleg they said it is heavy movement they will work it in towards them.
0615	64	95	6483 has movement to the NW employing redleg he didn't get a distance but said it was close.
0645	62	95	6283 reported that movement has stopped.
0800	64	95	Made commo with 6 missing people, one is KIA.
0845	62	95	6283 has 5 WIA and 1 KIA, KIA name Dean Johnson E-5
0907	bde	95	Jaguar 25 wants to insure that B co. has enough equipment to get WIA's and KIA's out.

We were told to saddle up; we were leaving to get the 3d platoon. They were still surrounded. I was assigned to carry the radio for Lieutenant Scurr. Happy Jack Regan, Jim Claiborne, Lieutenant Scurr, and myself were cutting point. Behind us was the machine-gun squad with Luke Whitaker, Joe Flynn, and the rest of the 1st Platoon, and then the CP. The 2d Platoon was rear security. We moved out following the foot path that the 3d Platoon used.

0925	62	95	6281 Sp'd perimeter.

My mind flashed back. I was watching the 3d Platoon hump out the day before. Now we were being watched by the 2d Platoon. The only difference was that we didn't have feathers in our helmets. My heart pounded as we moved farther away from the perimeter. The sun pierced through the trees, casting shadows that danced, making it look like everything was in constant motion—trees, termite mounds, small shrubs, and logs. I prayed as we cautiously moved down the ridgeline.

About fifteen minutes into our hump, we ran into the bunkers found by the 3d Platoon the day before. There were nine bunkers in various positions along the path in a U. The bunkers were a few days old, just the way Lieutenant Nathan reported. The brownish orange dirt was still moist. The gooks were set up to ambush anybody who came down the footpath. Nobody did until yesterday—the 3d Platoon. Most of our squad leaders avoided footpaths, but we were stuck on the footpath because we were trying to get to the 3d Platoon.

Things were quiet, no birds chirping, no jungle noise, just the wind ruffling the leaves. We continued on.

1040   62   95   Present location of 6281 (907985) they
                          found bunkers, fresh no overhead
                          reported yesterday by 6283.

We picked up the pace to get to the 3d Platoon quickly because at any time things could change. We force-marched about an hour and had started up one of the ridgelines of Hill 994 when I received a radio transmission on the handset. I took the handset from beneath the green towel I had wrapped around it. I didn't have to pull the whip antenna up; I had it stuck through the ring on the shoulder strap.

"One-Six, One-Six, this is Six. Over."

"Six, this is One-Six. Go," I answered.

"One-Six, we have a slight problem back here. Spread out and hold."

I told LT. He was pissed and said, "What the hell is going on?"

He spread everyone out and motioned to me to follow him back up the ridgeline to see what was going on. As I passed, everyone was in the prone position. Some guys looked back at me, question marks on their faces.

We made it back to the CP and Captain Patrick. There were two guys from the 2d Platoon laying on their backs. Piggy Dumpy (medic Lloyd Pelky) was wiping their foreheads with a water-soaked towel. Captain Patrick was just shaking his head.

"What's up?" LT asked him.

The captain replied, "These two sorry-ass FNG's got heat exhaustion."

I looked at Piggy Dumpy. He nodded, and said, "They passed out; we can't move them."

"I should leave them here," Captain Patrick replied. "We have to move. I'll leave a squad behind to secure them here with Doc until they get their shit together."

LT agreed and said, "We're moving out."

We headed back down the ridgeline, LT motioning to our platoon to get up. We reached the point and moved out. The 3d Platoon called the captain and told him they had movement. The CO relayed the message to me and said, "Hurry, they're in trouble."

We had lost twenty precious minutes. We headed up a ridgeline about fifty meters, then it leveled off. We cut east up the ridgeline until we ran into another footpath, then we stopped, spread out, and waited until everyone caught up. After about five minutes, we moved out.

With each cautious step, my heart beat faster. It was quiet, too fucking quiet. Our eyes darted back and forth, heads turning from side to side. Looking to trees and termite mounds. I was also looking for logs, trees, and natural indentations to dive behind or into when the shit hit the fan. We pressed on, down the worn footpath which followed the contour of the ridgeline. We were three or four meters apart. Claiborne motioned halt with his right arm. He got down on one knee and whispered to Regan, who in turn whispered to Lieutenant Scurr, which I heard. "Bunkers!" LT motioned for the rest of the platoon to spread out and get down. I got behind a tree with LT as Claiborne and Regan moved, like tigers stalking prey, up toward the bunkers. They made it to the bunker line, then split and were lost from sight by the trees. A couple of minutes passed before they reappeared and motioned us forward. I followed LT to the bunker about ten meters to our front while Luke Whitaker and Roger (I didn't know his last name) came up on our left flank with the M-60 machine gun; the rest of the platoon came up and spread out behind trees, waiting. LT and I made it to one of the bunkers that dotted the ridgeline. The bunkers were staggered ten to fifteen meters apart, as far as we could see in both directions. All of the bunkers were identical, fighting positions, with three or four logs for overhead and a sleeping area about eight feet by eight feet, cut three feet deep. The shovel marks could still be seen in the brownish orange dirt; the ground was littered with various objects left behind by the gooks. Empty AK-47 magazines, a few rice pouches, a pith helmet, and some empty envelopes postmarked Hanoi.

"Get Six on the horn," LT whispered to me.

"Six, this is One-Six. Over," I whispered into the handset. The reply came quickly. It was Captain Patrick. I handed the handset to LT. LT told him we were in the bunker complex, and asked what we should do. He listened, then handed the handset back to me and said, "We have to move out, but quick. The 3d Platoon has movement again."

"What about all these fuckin' bunkers?"

"We don't have the time to check, there's too many of them," he said.

He was right about that. The point had checked out about ten bunkers in the immediate area, which took about ten minutes. There were about 170, which the 3d Platoon had estimated the day before. LT motioned to the rest of the platoon, and we moved out.

The order of march remained the same. As we moved from tree to tree, bunker to bunker, I thought of playing hide-and-seek or peekaboo when I was a kid. I was praying to St. Jude as my mind was racing.

Small-arms fire, muffled, was coming from the north. It had to be D Company's platoon on the other side of Hill 994. The small-arms fire was replaced by the *whop, whop, whop* of exploding artillery. The 3d Platoon couldn't be that far away.

1215	68	95	Putting in a battery of 105's every 3 minutes, 62 is about 30 min. away from his 83 plt. and 6483.
1218	64	95	6483 is still receiving sporadic sniper fire, working area with red leg, at this time we have heavy movement on our right flank.
1220	95	bde	Receiving RR fire from the west, 57 type heard about 10 fired rounds are hitting on the terrain feature to the north of Mile High.
1225	95	bde	Received 1 round of 82mm incoming, 1 casualty, dust off called.

We checked out about ten more bunkers within thirty meters up the gradual incline of the ridgeline, then cut to the right to pick up the footpath about twenty meters away. The footpath ran parallel to the bunker line up the ridgeline. We were in double and triple canopy, and our visibility was limited to about thirty meters. We cautiously moved along the footpath, which gradually took us farther from the bunker line that we constantly watched.

After about one hundred meters, I glanced back, everybody was moving in slow motion, five meters apart. Little George was behind me, then came Bill, and then Luke, Roger, and Pat with the M-60. I was thinking that the 3d Platoon had to be very close. I could sense it. Suddenly the pop of AK-47s mixed with machine-gun fire coming from up the ridgeline. I dove behind a tree, then fired my M-16 up the ridgeline. We returned fire; bullets were hitting the trees, thudding into the ground, kicking up dirt and splinters of wood. I couldn't see where the enemy fire was coming from—no smoke or muzzle flashes. I looked over at Claiborne and Regan. They were behind a log, firing wildly up the ridgeline.

"Where are they?" I yelled over to them.

"We can't see them!" they yelled back.

At the same instant, Lieutenant Scurr low-crawled over to me, firing as he came. He crawled up behind me because the tree I was behind was only about three feet wide. He rested his M-16 on my pack with the barrel about six inches from my right ear. He continued to fire away. I thought my eardrum was going to explode.

While I was reloading a magazine, I yelled to LT, *"Get that fuckin' rifle away from me, you asshole!"*

He moved it. There was utter chaos, but time seemed to be frozen. If there was a twilight zone, we were in it.

1440	62	95	In contact at this time, I am trying to maneuver 1-6 element around to where contact was initiated by point element.
1445	62	95	Approximately 200 meters from my 83 element.

After using about ten magazines up, shooting on semiauto, we heard somebody yell from up the ridgeline, "We're up here. Hurry! Here they come. Help us!"

To our shock and amazement, the 3d Platoon was up the ridgeline about fifty meters at about two o'clock, between us and the gooks. We didn't know what to do; we were dumb-founded; we kept on returning fire. Then I heard in my left ear, my right was still ringing, "One-Six, One-Six, this is Six. Over."

I grabbed the handset off my chest and put it to my left ear and answered, "Six, This is One-Six. Go."

It was Captain Patrick. "Get up that fuckin' ridgeline now," he yelled, "Do you copy? Now!"

I yelled to LT, who was behind me, "The CO wants us up the hill. Now!" He nodded to me. I got back on the handset, "Six, I copy. We're moving out."

I took off my pack to use it as a shield. LT crawled up next to me and said, "When we start shooting, you come up behind us." He yelled over to Regan and Claiborne, "Let's go."

They started crawling up the ridgeline, I thought, well, this is it—St. Jude help us. I stuck the handset into a pouch on my pack, got to my knees, popped off another magazine, and re-loaded, trying to cover them.

LT yelled, "Now!" They laid down their volley of fire. I hurriedly put down my M-16, picked up my pack, and threw it as far as I could—about ten feet—then I crawled to it. LT, Regan, and Claiborne were about ten feet in front of me. When I reached my pack, they started to crawl again. I used my pack as a rifle rest, still firing at the invisible enemy. LT yelled again, "Now!" I rose to my knees as they laid out another vol-ley, again threw my pack and crawled to it. A bullet hit the dirt about a foot in front of my head, kicking dirt into my mouth. I tried to spit, but my mouth was too dry. I don't know how much time had gone by, but time didn't matter; we seemed to move in slow motion, but bullets were split seconds.

Again LT yelled, "Now!"

They laid out more heavy fire; I flung my pack, fired, and crawled with a jet in my ass. We did this routine four times and moved about forty feet toward the 3d Platoon's position. We still couldn't see them. I looked ahead and saw three dark figures moving from tree to tree and glimpsed a few others through the smoke and haze. In all my time with the company, I'd never seen the enemy and their muzzle flashes shooting back towards us. I guess I thought it never would happen. Something told me to glance back to see where everybody else was; my heart skipped a few beats; I didn't see anybody over my left or right shoulder.

I yelled to LT, "Stop! Stop! Hold it!" He turned his head. "There's nobody behind us!" I yelled.

He quickly turned his head to look over his left shoulder, then yelled, "Get on the horn."

I fired off a few more rounds toward the trees I had seen the enemy run behind, then pulled the handset from my pack and screamed into it, "Six, This is One-Six. Get these fuckin' guys up here! There's nobody behind us. Do you copy? Do you copy?" I never heard the reply because a rocket exploded about ten feet away on my right, jarring my senses.

We stayed in that same spot, firing away at dodging figures for what seemed like an eternity but was only a couple minutes. I glanced back again and saw our guys slowly crawling, rifles spitting lead. I was overwhelmed with instant confidence.

I yelled up to LT, "They're coming. They're coming."

He looked back, then we heard yelling from up to our right front, somebody must have heard me.

"We're up here! Come on!" It sounded about twenty meters away.

LT yelled back, "We're coming," then, "Let's go, now!"

He rose to his feet in a crouch, along with Regan and Claiborne. I rose into a crouch and grabbed the radio with my left hand; I noticed the enemy small-arms fire had died down. Now I heard only an occasional pop from an AK. We seemed to be putting out more fire; they seemed to be pulling back up the hill.

| 1512 | 62 | 95 | Still receiving sniper fire, working up red leg at this time, we have 1 casualty at this time don't know how bad. |

We moved about five meters. Firing had stopped. I was dragging the radio along the ground. So far so good, I thought, they're gone; or maybe they're all dead. My hopes were dashed by AK-47 fire from the front. We hit the dirt again, firing madly at the trees and termite mounds about thirty meters away. Bullets whizzed through the air.

| 1526 | 62 | 95 | Have 2 enemy KIA laying in front of me. |

Artillery finally started to pound the hill two hundred or three hundred meters away. There were only five or six snipers keeping us from getting to the 3d Platoon, but they kept us pinned down with sporadic bursts of fire. Then without warning two gooks popped out from behind a tree about ten meters to our front. We all saw them and fired. They slumped to the ground almost immediately, another tried to dart back up the hill and got the shit shot out of him.

1540   62   95   My 83 element only has 4 individuals
                       that are able to fire at this time the rest
                       are casualty

"Let's move," LT yelled again.

They laid out another volley of fire for me. I grabbed the radio and dragged it along the ground. We moved about five more meters, stopped for a few seconds, then we moved again.

While moving, I spotted two of our guys laying behind a tree to my right front, ten meters away. They were firing up the ridgeline.

I yelled to LT, "They're over here," and made a beeline for a log. I was sure they were just on the other side. The point and LT kept moving as I cut to my right and up the ridgeline. When I reached the log, I threw my pack and dove at the same time over it. I landed with a thud; my helmet flew off my head and rolled along the ground. I looked around slowly; the sporadic sounds of gunfire disappeared from my ears and was replaced by muffled groans. I tried not to believe what my eyes were seeing. Our guys were laying all over, some moving, others lying motionless. The smell of blood and death hung in the air over the makeshift perimeter. My eyes moved from figure to figure, trying to recognize somebody. I couldn't. Two guys, laying not ten feet from me, were dead, shot through the head. Tears welled in my eyes. I quickly looked away to my right. Lieutenant Nathan was propped up by a small tree; his face was white. He was in shock, shot through the shoulder, staring into space. My mind then panicked, where's Dean, Eddie, Ken, and Ray? Oh my God, no! I looked up to my left. I saw Eddie and Ken; our eyes met. I saw the strain of combat written on their faces. They looked drained of all strength, their eyes with dark circles around them, tears running down their cheeks. We could hold back the tears no longer, I knew right then something had happened to Dean and Ray. They were nowhere in sight. I felt so helpless, I didn't know what to do. I took the handset of the radio and called back to the captain. "Six, this is One-Six. Over."

"One-Six, this is Six. What is your location? Over."

I choked the answer, "I'm in Three-Six's perimeter. Please get up here. These guys need medics bad. Hurry!"

"One-Six, this is Six. We'll be there in about ten. Where is your Six?"

I looked to my left front and saw LT and the point maneuvering towards Eddie and Ken, about fifteen meters away, then I looked over the log and saw the others coming up. I answered, "He's on his way. He's still with the point. ETA five minutes." After the area was secured, LT and the others filtered into what was left of the 3d Platoon's perimeter.

1600	62	95	My 81 element has linked up with 83 and they are maneuvering around to wipe out what dinks are left, the dinks are behind large trees.

Tears were rolling down our cheeks as we tried to help with the wounded while Doc Pelky (Piggy Dumpy) and another medic worked frantically with bandages and tape. Minutes went by. The firing had stopped.

The captain arrived at the scene. He looked around and yelled out, "Pick everyone up and move back down the ridge-line."

We slung our weapons to free both hands to pick up the wounded or carry the dead. I put my pack on, slung my M-16 over my right shoulder, and shuffled over to where Little George and Bill were trying to roll the KIA closest to me into a poncho. I knelt down to help them. They looked at me and shook their heads. We rolled the body onto the poncho. I moved to pick up the ends of the poncho where his boots were. We couldn't pick him up, so we slid him along the ground. We slowly moved down the ridgeline, not even thinking about the enemy. We were devastated.

1659	62	95	At present time I have linked up with all elements, my point element is 200 meters away from top of 994, at present time I have 20 unconfirmed WIA's, we are pulling the wounded back and employing gunships.

We moved about fifty meters and set up a perimeter. We dragged the body over to where four others were lined up, boots sticking out grotesquely from the dark green poncho's they were wrapped in. I stared at the boots and wondered who the men were and how many hearts would break at the news. Little George grabbed my arm and said, "Len, let's go. We can't help them now."

We headed over to the rest of our platoon. LT was putting everyone in two-man positions around the area. Light was fading fast and we would have to spend the night on 100 percent alert in case the gooks attacked. LT pointed to a half-rotten log and told me to set up there. He would be my partner. I went to the log and sat down, took off my pack. Eddie and Ken were together in the position next to me, about ten feet away. I asked if they were okay; they nodded.

Then Eddie said, "Dean and Ray are still up there; they're . . ." He choked up, and I knew what he was trying to say. They were dead. He took a deep breath, then said, "They're about fifty meters up the hill from where you found us." He looked up the hill.

Tears in his eyes, Ken looked at me, and said, "I thought we were going to die."

"Try to get some sleep tonight. I'll keep watch for you." I didn't know what else to say.

"We'll be okay," Ken said.

The gunships that had pounded the hill left as darkness fell. LT told me we had to go back up the hill to get Dean and Ray in the morning. I already knew we had to.

A few of the wounded who were in the center of our small perimeter were moaning; they needed a medevac bad, but we had no LZ. Trees had to be cut out of the way just to get a basket in. We didn't have any axes, only three machetes.

1820   62   95   Starting to cut LZ will call when we can get the dustoff in.

LT told me he was going to help with the cutting, and left our position. I didn't like the idea of being alone, but I really wasn't. Ten feet on my right were Eddie and Ken, and ten feet on my left was the M-60 machine gun with Luke, Pat and Roger. I felt secure.

I felt like somebody had kicked the shit out of me. Fatigue was setting in, and my whole body seemed to be sleeping, although I was awake. Adrenaline works in a weird way. In combat it gets you up, but afterwards it knocks you out—and that's what it was doing to me.

My mind raced through the day's activities. My stomach churned, but I wasn't hungry; I was very thirsty. I took out a canteen and drank it down. It was my second since we'd set up in our tight perimeter, and I was still thirsty. The water seemed to evaporate going down. I could have drunk another, but I wanted to save the two-quart bladders I had left because, next to ammunition, water was the most important element of survival.

I counted my magazines—thirty-three left. I'd shot up twenty-one during the day. Ammo goes fast. I was glad I'd humped it; you could never hump enough ammo or water.

Artillery started to pound the top of 994 again. We could hear the whistle of shrapnel as it ripped through the air.

1830	95 bde	A co. will continue to secure LZ Incoming and will continue to maintain SRP screen 6183 will set up ambush at 948903. B co. will attack to secure Hill 994 and try to link up with 6483. C co. will maintain position on LZ Mile High and maintain present SRP screen, will send 6381 on sweep to west of Mile High, will check on mortar position at 921931. D co. will maintain patrol base and present SRP screen. Has one platoon in contact at 907994 will attempt to link up with 62 element by noon. Recon will secure B co. patrol base at 912978.
1839	S93 M25	Wrap up on today's activity, 62 element made contact and linked up with his platoon, during hook up had sporadic sniper fire. At this time they have 13 WIA 7 KIA at present time they are trying to cut LZ to get basket in. 6483 tried to link up with 62 but also got into contact never made link up, since then he has broken contact. At present D co.

SRP's are picking up movement. On today's contact artillery fired 140 rounds of HE red leg. At present time we are trying to get class 5 into B co. Have planed an extensive red leg program tonight.

| 1900 | 95 | DO | Called dust off for B co. WIA's |

| 1906 | J93 | 95 | Will get a repelling team into 62 element to help cut LZ. |

| 2010 | 62 | 95 | Yesterday afternoon 83 was moving up a ridgeline of 994 saw a dink killed him and was taken under fire by larger unit. They tried to flank the unit but was outflanked by the NVA. The 83 element then fought their way back to the rear about 200 meters down the hill and set up hasty perimeter. He then called in artillery. Today the dinks found him and started sniping 100 meters from him, 62 was taken under fire trying to reach 83, in the last 2 days 6283 has killed 31 unconfirmed NVA, 6281 confirmed killing 5 NVA while 6483 has killed 5 NVA. |

LT came back from trying to cut an LZ. Not too much success. He shook my shoulder and told me to keep my ass awake. I was groggy, my head felt like lead. I asked LT what was going on, and he said that they'd called for engineers to come in to cut an LZ. He told me to keep watch while he caught some shut-eye.

| 2232 | 0 | 95 | Black Jack 25 on the way with engineers, chain saws, medical supplies ETA 10 minutes. |

| 2350 | 0 | 95 | Dust off 32 ETA 20 minutes. |

About midnight, I could stay awake no longer. I woke up LT and told him it was his turn for watch. He asked me if the medevac had come yet. I told him no. We were amazed at how much time it took to get help. We had a few seriously wounded who might die if they didn't get help fast. I prayed for them and thanked God I wasn't wounded. I went back to sleep. I was only asleep about a half hour before LT shook my shoulder. I woke up. I was pissed off. He told me he was going to go see the CO.

I said, "Why is it when it's your watch, you split to the CO?"

"I don't have to answer to you. You pull watch and keep your mouth shut!" he replied.

Once an asshole, always an asshole, I thought.

A prop plane, I think it was a Skyraider, dropped bombs, shaking the ground. We could hear the shrapnel. Smoke reeking of gunpowder and splintered wood choked every breath, drying the nose and mouth and tickling the throat. There was about six hours to daylight, but what would daylight bring? We still had to go up the hill to get Dean and Ray. That was the longest most miserable night in my entire life. Finally, at almost 3:00 AM, the first medevac arrived, with another chopper, probably a gunship escort. The medevac had its spotlights on, and they lit up the area like it was a stage. We hugged the ground, watching our front. I looked back and saw a basket litter come down though the trees. One guy was loaded on at a time and taken up, slowly spinning. Only four were taken out. LT crawled back to my position. He told me Captain Patrick was pissed off and let battalion know it; one guy had died already because of the wait. That gave us eight KIAs.

Radio Log (Daily) S-3 1/12 March 10, 1969

0315   62   95   First dust off complete, it's about time I have 1 more KIA.

A half hour went by before another chopper came in and lowered chain saws and some medical supplies. LT left my position again to go help.

0345   62   95   We got the chain saws and medical supplies in.

Almost immediately the chain saws were put to work cutting down trees to make the LZ larger. At first I felt that the sound of the chainsaws would help the gooks zero in on our position, but then I remembered that our wounded needed help. If it were me, I would have been praying to get the medevac in. Why in God's name was it taking so long?

My mind jumped from fear to hope for the wounded. I prayed again to St. Jude to help us in our time of need. I always prayed when scared or in need of something more powerful than fate. Almost an hour passed before another chopper came in.

0435   62   95   6 more people dusted off.

After the medevac left, I fell asleep. When I woke up it was just getting light. LT was still sleeping so I woke him up. I saw we still had four wounded. Fortunately, their wounds were not serious.

The lighter it got, the more activity there was around the perimeter. Those who could eat cooked C rations; others moved around to stretch their legs. Everyone looked worn out from lack of sleep and despair.

A four-man recon patrol was sent out toward the top of 994. Things were quiet except for the sound of chain saws and the chopping of trees. I couldn't stop myself from glancing at the row of KIAs wrapped in ponchos at the far end of our perimeter. I thought about their families.

0705   95   DO   Called dust off for D co. 83 element 2
                     men.

0850   95   0   Dust off complete.

We sat around, waiting, wondering when we would go to get Dean and Ray. Hours went by. The only thing we heard was that the situation around Mile High had not changed.

0945   61   95   6181B has heavy movement, working
                     up 4.2 on it at this time.

1015   61   95   82A spotted 2 dinks about 20 meters in
                     front of them, fired on them and
                     brought in 4.2 sent 6181 to assist them.

At about 10:30 AM, a chopper came in, dropped off four engineers, and took out the four remaining wounded.

1040	95	0	Pick and shovel team on the ground at 62's location last wounded taken out.
1050	61	95	My 6181 has linked up with 82A they are sweeping the area, so far have found 2 AK-47s, 1 pistol belt and 1 pack.

The patrol that was sent out at daybreak returned. They didn't see anything, but found one AK-47.

It wasn't until 3:00 PM that LT came over to tell me the 3d Squad (Dean's squad), he, and I would be going out to retrieve the bodies. Jim Claiborne found out who was going and volunteered. We moved out an hour later. There were eight of us: Claiborne, Regan on point again, followed by Lieutenant Scurr, myself, Thompson, Medors, Thomas, and Warner. We moved out. Fifty meters away we ran into the 3d Platoon's makeshift perimeter of the day before. It was littered with empty M-16 magazines, a few steel pots and rucksacks, and bloodied bandages. We would pick up those things later; they weren't our main concern. Just seeing that equipment flashed my thoughts back to the scene I saw the day before. I quickly blotted that out in order to concentrate on what we were doing.

We moved about forty meters. We found them laying face down. The point and LT secured the area, ten meters up the hill. LT motioned to me to move up; I turned to Little George and said, "Let's go." We moved up to one body; Ken, Eddie, and Bill to the other. The stench of death forced me to hold my breath as I knelt down next to the mound of decaying flesh. Holding his nose, George was kneeling across from me. I didn't know whom we were kneeling next to.

I said, "Little George, who is this?"

His eyes filled with tears; his voice cracked, "I can't tell; we have to roll him over."

The exposed skin, hands, and the back of the neck were dark purple. The smell got so bad, I rose to my feet, coughing. I backed up to get some air; I felt light-headed. I moved five meters away to the other body, where the others stood. I bent down, holding my nose. The corpse's exposed skin was the same dark purple. This body looked the same, bloated to almost twice its normal size and with dark purple skin. It was difficult to identify. That shocked and frustrated us because Dean was white and Ray was black.

We stood there, not knowing what to do, then Bill said, "Dean wore a class ring on his right hand."

Little George bent over and picked up the sleeve of the right arm. The hand had no ring. He and I quickly moved to the other body, lumps in our throats. Little George picked up the sleeve, the right ring finger was chopped off—it must have been Dean.

We broke out crying. Little George could hardly get out his choked-up words, "Those motherfuckers, Those rotten fuckers."

The others came over; I choked the words out. "Look at what they did, those cocksuckers."

At that time, Claiborne came back from the point and saw us crying. Little George held up the sleeve to show him the swollen grape-colored hand. "The gooks cut off his finger."

Claiborne bolted away, over to the bodies of three dead NVA soldiers about ten meters away, put his M-16 six inches away from one of the gooks' heads, and opened up, firing on semiauto, yelling, "Take this you fucker. Take this." He emptied the magazine into the lifeless head, nobody stopped him; he only did what we all felt like doing.

I counted eight dead NVA soldiers around the area.

George and I took off Dean's pack so we could roll him over onto the poncho we had laid next to him. It finally took four of us to roll him over. When we did, we saw his face was already infested with maggots, flies, and ants. That made us gasp. Little George quickly put Dean's towel over his face and wrapped the poncho over him. The others went to tend to Ray's body. Little George and I stayed with Dean.

The point and LT moved back to us. "Let's go," LT said.

Dragging the bodies of our comrades back toward our perimeter, we slowly moved down the ridgeline. As we passed through, we policed up all of the equipment that was left in the area of contact. I called the CO on the radio and told him we had the KIAs and were heading back. About a half an hour later, we reached our perimeter. While we were gone, the other KIAs had been taken out. As everyone watched solemnly, we took the bodies of Dean and Ray to the edge of the perimeter by the LZ. It was a devastating day for our squad. Now the rest of the platoon who had known Dean and Ray felt the sorrow. Our platoon didn't know most of those killed because they were in the 3d Platoon, but here were two of ours.

Dean had touched everyone; he was respected and liked by all, a true leader and a friend. Ray, on the other hand, had his prejudiced ways, and he hadn't been liked by many. It was ironic that they would suffer the same fate at the same time.

But the tears that fell, fell the same for both. As different as they were, they were part of our family, part of the bond. We stood over them, saying our silent farewells and prayers for a few minutes, then we walked away, remembering them each in our own way.

| 1730 | 62 | 95 | We have the last KIA's on the pad ready at this time. 6281 has closed my location. Within a 20 meter radius of last friendly KIA's they found 8 dead NVA and 12 spots where other dinks have bled profusely with drag marks. They didn't sweep ahead. Still estimate at least 40 body count. |

As we returned to our two-man positions, each in our own solitude, we could hear a chopper in the distance. We knew why it was coming. I didn't want to see Dean and Ray in the state they were in.

As the sound of the chopper faded away, along with the light, I looked up the ridgeline, telling myself I will never forget Hill 994.

| 1745 | 61 | 95 | At 948907 found an enemy mortar site with 1 82mm round and a place where a base plate had settled in the dirt. My 81 element left it intact and will put red leg on it tonight. |

| 1845 | 95 | bde | LZ Mile High taking incoming at this time 5 to 10 rounds. |

| 1905 | 95 | bde | Have taken 35 rounds of incoming all 82mm with misc. recoilless. |

| 1910 | 95 | bde | Dust off completed for one element of 63. |

1920	bde	95	Make max. use of artillery on all suspected enemy positions, react rapidly and with heavy volume to all enemy attacks direct and indirect.
1921	63	95	82B getting sniper fire, rocket and mortars, on his position he is retreating back to our base.
1924	64	95	6483 has closed his patrol base.

We sat in our small perimeter, in the darkness, on 50 percent alert. We heard artillery exploding a few klicks to the north, in the direction of D Company. Around us, it was deathly quiet. I couldn't wait for first light when we would finally leave that place of sorrow, the memory of it etched permanently in our minds.

(Operational Report Lessons Learned 4th Inf. Div. Ending April 30, 1969)

On 10 March, Company D, 1st Battalion, 8th Infantry located two 105mm howitzers which had been heavily damaged by artillery and air strikes. Both howitzers, of US manufacture (1942 and 1945), were evacuated. In its Spring Campaign in KONTUM Province, the 40th Artillery Regiment lost nine artillery pieces to allied artillery and air fires.

2100	64	95	83A has dinks to the south putting in red leg trying to run them into the surprise.

Radio Log (Daily) S-3 1/12 March 11, 1969

0017	0	95	The 1st bde. found out the hard way how to attack NVA bunkers. The bunkers had 5 ft. of overhead and front ports 3-5 inches wide 3-4 inches high, and 6-12 inches above the ground. Fields of fire were cut to shoot ankle to

knee high. U.S. troops drop when fired
upon and then were in a tremendously
dangerous kill zone. On March 10, U.S.
soldiers attacked 3 times and were
repelled, the 4th time they took the
bunkers standing up.

Before I knew it, the night had passed without incident.
Daylight. Thank God. We saddled up and headed back to our
patrol base; the battle for Hill 994 was a memory.

0725   62   95   62 sp'd for patrol base.

0745   95   bde   Just received 8 rounds of recoilless at
                     LZ Mile High.

We moved slowly toward the patrol base, sweeping the area
at the same time. We took a different route to prevent the enemy's ambushing us. We didn't see any sign of him. I was
glad.

1445   bde   95   Contact of A co. and C co. 1/14 at
                     9992. Enemy appears to be to north and
                     west about 2 klicks east of Mile High,
                     they are moving up blue line running
                     NW. Alert your people.

Late in the afternoon, we finally reached our patrol base on
Hill 1018, now known as LZ Blackfoot. I was never so happy
to see our bunkers before. We were home. Recon occupied our
bunkers in the perimeter. As we filed in, nobody said a word.
They just watched us.

1500   62   95   62 has closed the patrol base

1518   95   62   Be on the alert for enemy moving east
                    to west, be cautious putting your SRP
                    screen out tonight, they are expected to
                    be in vicinity of LZ Dot in 2 hours.

A few SRPs were put out, the rest of us cooked Cs. It was
back to the daily routine.

Nothing happened that night, no incoming, no sightings from the SRPs.

The following morning, choppers came in and took Recon out. The choppers left us some hot chow—chicken, green beans, mashed potatoes, quarts of chocolate and of regular milk. At first I thought battalion was trying to give us something to appease us. I only took a few bites of the chicken—who could eat greasy chicken in the morning? I ate the green beans and mashed potatoes and drank a quart of white milk.

About two hours later, men were puking all around, some moaning, doubled over from stomach cramps. Doc Pelky said it was food poisoning. I couldn't believe it. My stomach churned, but I didn't throw up, so the culprit must have been the chicken. My stomach felt terrible and I had taken only two bites. An hour went by and the count of the sick rose. The food poisoning spread like wildfire.

1155   62   95   We have 37 people that are sick with stomach cramps, vomiting, etc.

As it turned out, about half of our already low-strength company was sick. Those who weren't sick sat around watching those who were. The smell of vomit hung in the air, and there wasn't anywhere in the perimeter to go to get away from it. It was hot; there was no breeze. In a way I wished I was on SRP.

1245   62   95   At present time we have 40 EM sick.

Late in the afternoon, we heard a short burst of rifle fire from the southeast. A SRP from the 2d Platoon was shot at, so they called in artillery and moved their location.

Night came, another day had passed. Those who'd been sick all day started feeling better. They were bitching, but I didn't blame them. Our morale was low enough. There was no way anyone of us would ever eat hot chow flown out to us again. We would stick to care packages from home and C rations.

For the next few weeks, we stayed on Hill 1018 (LZ Blackfoot). Every day was spent in the same fashion—the company sent out SRPs; we went on a few platoon sweeps; and we sat around the perimeter, writing letters home. The daily routine was boredom—nothing happened, and there was no sign of the enemy.

One day I asked Eddie what had happened when he went

Boarding trucks at Ban Me Thuot in November 1968 for "the move north" to Pleiku.

Members of the platoon, relaxing for a change, on one of many no-name hilltops we climbed in the Central Highlands. November or December 1968.

Ken Comeaux filling canteens at Ya Krong Bolah.

That's me on the left and "Little" George Thompson crossing the Ya Krong Bolah in January 1969.

Me (left) and Ed Medors digging fighting positions at L Z Punch Bowl, January 1969. Note hills towering over our positions.

This picture was taken from a ridgeline above our perimeter at L Z Punch Bowl as we were going out to set up an ambush. Two weeks later the army made this site a fire base!

"Happy" Jack Regan (left) and I getting ready to move out of L Z Punch Bowl, January 1969.

Steve Turzilli with his arm over my shoulder, in early May 1969.

On R and R at Cam Ranh Bay in June 1969. It was hard to believe there was a war going on.

A few members of 1st Platoon clearing a hilltop. At rear is Warner (WIA, May 31, 1969). Sehman is in the middle. At bottom are (from left) Lieutenant Scurr (KIA, May 31), Taylor (WIA, April 1969), Medors, Click, Mong, Gilbert, Claiborne, and Leonard (KIA, May 31).

(Standing, from left) Sgt. Cribb, Luke Whitaker, Fegan, Kutchman, Treadway, Bill Warner, Ken Thomas, ?, Elmore, Lieutenant Scurr. (Kneeling) Me, Pelky, Johnson, Claiborne, Moran, Rainey.

"Body count" as a result of the Battle of Suoi Tre, March 1967. Photo courtesy of Gary Silva.

out on that SRP March 5 with Dean. I told him that if it was too hard to talk about, he didn't have to answer. He said he didn't mind telling me.

EYEWITNESS ACCOUNT

EDDIE MEDORS—1st Platoon, 3d Squad

Remember when Dean Johnson came back from R & R on March 5? I still don't know why he went on that patrol with us. He told me that he wanted to get back into the swing of things. Ray went because Little George was getting short.

Anyway, we headed out on March 5, and we set up at the base of the hill. I call it Forget-Me-Not Ridge.

After we set up on the fifth, the next morning, on the sixth, they started to fire mortars at you guys. Remember when they sent in the smoke rounds? We couldn't see them, so they sent in a spotter plane and told us to sit tight. And that the 3d Platoon would swing by us the next day.

The 3d Platoon swung by about noon on the eighth, and Lieutenant Nathan told Dean that we could go back to the company or stay with them. Dean called us over to the side and told us. Ken, Ray, and I told him that we had already been out going on three days. And we'd take our chances on going back to the company. But Dean said that he'd feel safer with a platoon, so we said okay.

So we started up. The LT went by the book. Sent out flankers and the works. We got about halfway up, and the flankers on our left spotted movement. The LT stopped us and sent out more men to check. No sighting. Dean looked at me and said, "This is not good, Ed. They're working their way in behind us." He also told the LT; Dean checked the rear, too. No movement there yet. I'd say we were approximately two hundred meters from the top when the point made contact. That's when all hell broke loose. I still say if the point hadn't made contact until a few minutes later, Charlie would have got us all in the first whack because I could see a big clearing up ahead.

The first round wasn't really too bad, I guess. No wounded or dead. But that didn't last long. After about five minutes into the first round they hit us from three sides. Front, left, and rear. Dean was on my left, and I don't remember who was on my right. All of a sudden, my ears felt like they were blown off. Smoke all around and a fire over my head. The LT and sergeant yelled that they were firing RPG rockets at us. I looked over at Dean, and he had his head laying on his left arm. And the man on my right was hit, too. I yelled for a medic and shook Dean. No response. The medic checked Dean and said it was too late for him. Then he patched up the guy on my right. Then there was a yell for a medic at the rear. He started down, and he got hit. About that time, the sergeant told the LT that we needed to pull back because they were getting at us too easy. We started to pull back, and I grabbed Dean. The sergeant told me to leave him because we couldn't do him any good. So I picked up one of the other wounded, and the sergeant told me not to worry, we'll come back after him.

We pulled back to a flat spot with a big tree laying down the middle of the ridge, longways. We put the wounded under it, and the LT split the platoon up on each side of the tree. Then things calmed down, except for a few sniper shots, which were hitting their marks.

On the morning of the ninth, it was about the same way. Snipers picking our men off, one at a time. The LT yelled over to our side to watch for friendlies coming down from the top. D Company was trying to get to us from the other side. And our company was coming up from the rear.

We heard a firefight break out on the other side of the hill. Ray was on my left, he asked me for a cig. I gave him one. Then he said "No sweat, Ed. Help is on the way." At that time, we looked up the hill. It seemed to me that it was crawling with people. Ray and I yelled out, here they come. Lieutenant Nathan told us not to fire because they might be friendly. So we watched. I don't remember who yelled it out first, but me, Ray, and two others opened up on them. I think all four of us got hit at once. I was lucky my bullet was stopped by an M-16 magazine. This was about a half hour before the platoon got to us. They were trying to finish us off before you guys got to us. And they were doing a good job of it. They had to know you guys were coming because, about five minutes before the platoon got to us, they (Charlie) started yelling. The sergeant yelled over and said they were going to charge us again. I looked around on my side of the tree, and I knew my side of the tree couldn't take another charge from Charlie. So I took a new clip and put it in my rifle, put one in my left hand and one in my mouth. I looked up to the sky and told Him to get it over with. Then Claiborne and Happy Jack from our platoon popped their heads up in front of me. Our platoon saved our asses, and all I could do was cry.

(Operational Reports Lessons Learned 4th Inf. Div. Period Ending April 30, 1969)

When intelligence reports indicated that the 66th NVA Regiment was moving south toward the CHU PA, the 4th Infantry Division continued its efforts to envelop the enemy. On 14 March the 3d Battalion, 12th Infantry combat assaulted from the vicinity of LZ SWINGER to establish a new fire base, LZ CIDER (YA828798), 27 kilometers southwest of POLEI KLENG. The 1st battalion, 35th Infantry, which had been deployed to BEN HET in anticipation of further attacks in that area, helilifted to blocking positions west of the PLEI MRONG CSF Camp.

The enemy conducted harassing attacks to cover his withdrawal. While his already decimated artillery shelled BEN HET, SWINGER, and CIDER, his infantry and sappers attacked US patrol bases. On the night of 28–29 March, two companies of the 3d Battalion, 12th Infantry repulsed a sapper attack on their ridge-top patrol base (YA8285), killing at least 33 of the attackers. The enemy continued harassing attacks into early April. The Division responded by requesting Arc Light strikes on suspected enemy headquarters and assembly areas. By mid-April, the 66th NVA Regiment was no longer a threat to KONTUM Province. Similarly, the 24th NVA Regiment ceased to be a threat to Highway 14 and northern PLEIKU Province.

The most successful enemy operation of the reporting period was a sapper attack on the 584th Light Engineer Company at TAN PHU (AR764813). Early on the morning of 21 March, under cover of mortar and rocket fire and a diversionary infantry attack against the adjacent Special Forces Camp, 35 to 40 sappers breached the Engineer perimeter. Employing satchel charges and B-40 rockets, the sappers destroyed or damaged practically all of the engineers' heavy equipment, including a 80 to 120 ton-per-hour asphalt plant, four 20 ton Euclid dump trucks, three 5 ton dump trucks, a D7 dozer tractor, and two 2C ten truck-mounted cranes. After 15 minutes of destruction the sappers withdrew, apparently with minimal casualties. Only two enemy killed could be confirmed.

March ended; I marked another month off my monthly calendar on the side of my helmet cover—seven down, five to go. March had taken its toll. Every company in our battalion suffered casualties. It was the worst month since I'd been in country. About a week into April, we received mail—the division paper, the *Ivy Leaf*, dated March 30, 1969, and a few of us got care packages from home.

We were sitting around reading our mail when Lieutenant Scurr came down to the bunker line with a big grin on his face. I continued to read my letters from home.

He broke the silence with, "Well, we made the front page. Did you guys see it?"

I answered, "No, where?"

"Under '289 NVA fall,' " he replied.

Ivy Leaf
March 30, 1969

"The northern sector of the Plei-Trap Valley erupted again on March 9 as two platoons of Bravo company 1st Batt. 12th Inf., while reconning in force 13 klicks northwest of Polei Kleng, exchanged a withering volume of small arms and automatic weapons fire with an estimated NVA company. When contact was broken by the enemy the two platoons swept, finding 36 enemy dead. U.S. casualties were light during the day long battle."

I picked up the paper, so did a few others. I read it and said out loud, "Thirty-six enemy killed," we found eight, "what's this thirty-six shit, and we suffered light casualties? Shit almost our whole 3d Platoon was wiped out. What a bunch of shit!"

LT yelled over to Claiborne, who was sitting on the bunker next to ours, "Hey, Claiborne, I have good news for you. You and I are getting Bronze Stars for that contact a few weeks ago. It's in the paper."

I was shocked. I looked up at him standing there, gloating, and said, "What are you talking about? You mean to tell me just you and Claiborne are getting Bronze Stars? For what? What about me and Regan? We were with you—we were part of the point also!"

The smile left his face. Then he said, "I think I forgot to put you two in my report."

That statement made me furious. I started yelling, "What about Eddie and Ken? Hell, if it wasn't for those two, the 3d Platoon might have been wiped out! This whole thing sucks, the army sucks, and you, LT, can take your medal and jam it up your ass sideways!"

"You can't talk to me like that!" the LT snapped back. "I'll court-martial your ass!"

"Go ahead, see if I give a fuck," I yelled back. I turned and stormed away, kicking a roll of empty sandbags into the air, wishing it was the LT's head. As I walked, I thought to myself, no wonder our squad leader Joe Fegan kicked LT's ass a few weeks ago. If I'd stayed by the bunker, I would have too. But I was worried about the repercussions, LBJ (Long Binh Jail), that always loomed on everyone's mind.

For a few days, I didn't talk to the LT; he didn't talk to me either. I asked Monkey if he wouldn't mind being the LT's RTO. I would be Sergeant Cribb's. He agreed, told the LT, and that was that.

About April 14, we were finally told to saddle up; the choppers came in, and we piled on. As the chopper took off, I looked down, knowing we would never see that hilltop again. Our stay there had cost us dearly. God rest their souls.

Dean H Johnson	SGTE5	KIA March 8 1969	Grid YA903992
Raymond Bethea	SP4E4	KIA March 9 1969	Grid YA903992
Clarence Burleson	SGTE5	KIA March 9 1969	Grid YA903992
Jerry MacDonald	SP4E4	KIA March 9 1969	Grid YA903992
Edward Millison	SP4E4	KIA March 9 1969	Grid YA903992
Clarence Nofford	SP4E4	KIA March 9 1969	Grid YA903992
Robert Pretto	SGTE5	KIA March 9 1969	Grid YA903992
Thomas Turner	SP4E4	KIA March 9 1969	Grid YA903992

W.I.A.-Thirteen

Chapter VII

THE VALLEY

Yea though I walk through the valley of the shadow of death, I will fear no evil, for I'm the evilest son of a bitch in the valley.

When the choppers landed, we found ourselves back on LZ Mile High fire base. We were brought in for a short rest and to get replacements for our depleted company. Our strength was down to about seventy-five. We stayed in fire base for a week or so, getting about fifteen replacements. The only thing good about fire base was breakfast, eggs (I don't know if they were real or not, but they tasted pretty good), biscuits, fried potatoes, milk, and coffee. I even ate a few dinners that weren't bad at all. I figured the food was probably freshly cooked and hadn't lain in a chopper for who knows how long.

About April 21, we were choppered out of fire base to Hill 1274 (Ngok To lum), called LZ Ouachita. It was located two klicks northwest of where D Company had a platoon on Hill 1483 (LZ Delaware), the same hilltop they were on when the battle for 994 took place a month earlier. The rest of the company was west about three klicks, on a Hill 816. We didn't know where we were until one of the squad leaders informed us.

Captain Patrick went on R & R, and the company was commanded by Lieutenant Scurr. We found this out when we landed. When you're a grunt, in the mountains, every hilltop starts to look the same. I couldn't believe we were put back into the same AO, only north about two and a half klicks from Hill 994. Knowing this spooked me, but I didn't know if everyone else knew. Things got so screwed up when we moved locations, setting up a new perimeter.

The hilltop was surrounded by thick forest of mahogany and teak trees. The LZ was large enough for a helicopter to land. A mortar platoon arrived the next day. It was the first time that we secured a platoon of four-deuce mortars.

Our platoons were spread out around the hilltop, under the trees. It felt weird not being able to see any other hilltop through the trees. It was like being under an umbrella with a hole cut in the top. Nights were like being on SRP or LP. It was dark as hell on watch as we stared at the sky and what stars we could see. But it beat staring into pitch-black darkness. All of us hated the hill; it was unlike any we had ever been on.

We all became star gazers, and you could always find something to talk about, back home, the World. Little George had about two weeks left. He was the shortest out of anyone I was close to from the 3d Squad. He would be with us maybe two more days, max. We all thought he should have gone in at two weeks. He was scared, nervous, and wide-eyed. We all felt what he felt and what he was thinking.

We thought a guy should go in when he had three weeks to go. We all had the heebie-jeebies, and short-timers' nervousness wasn't good for them or for us.

The morning of the twenty-third, we were sitting around with nothing to do. Happy Jack was carving something out of a piece of wood. I walked over, sat down, and asked, "Aye, Happy Jack, what ya making?"

"Ayyyee, I don't know, maybe a peace symbol or something," he answered.

"A peace symbol? Ayyyee, I do believe you have something there," I answered. I thought for a minute and said, "Let's make some peace symbols out of melted lead, can we do that?"

He looked at me and said with a smile, "I'm ssshhurre!"

I had to laugh, Happy Jack always spoke Bostonian. He had a way about him that lifted my spirit as well as everyone that knew him. "We can use a few M-60 rounds; we got a shitload; go get a few from my pack," he exclaimed.

He was right about that, we had a shit-load of 60 ammo. Everyone except the RTOs carried about fifty rounds. The gun squad carried four or five hundred rounds, so total, we had a few thousand rounds in our platoon.

I went over to Happy Jack's pack and retrieved ten rounds.

By then Eddie, Ken, and Little George wondered what we were up to. They came by.

"Somebody get some C-4 and an empty can," Happy Jack said as he kept whittling away. I started bending the bullet head between two rocks back and forth, loosening it enough to pull it off. I'd never seen a bullet out of the brass casing before. I stared at it and said, "I didn't know the lead was in the middle."

"That's why you're a grunt," Ken answered.

We all laughed. Little George came back with C-4 and an empty cracker-and-cheese can. Every one of us pitched in; all the cartridges were taken apart, and the lead put into the can. Happy Jack was finishing off his wood masterpiece. We sat around in anticipation.

"Do you think we could have used those ten rounds?" Ken asked.

"Buddy if we needed those ten rounds, we are in deep shit," I answered.

As soon as I finished talking, small-arms fire exploded to life about two klicks away. We looked at each other, and Little George said, *"Ohhh sshhit!"*

I looked at Happy Jack. He was finished carving and held the peace symbol in his hand.

"Let me have a look-see." I passed it around. I was glad we were doing something to keep our minds away from the firefight raging to the southwest.

Happy Jack said, "Get some water; we have to cast our mold."

We were determined to finish what we started. I poured a little water onto the ground; HJ took the peace symbol, pressing it into the mud. We lit a piece of C-4 and placed the can on a can stove. After a few minutes, the lead from the bullets oozed out, filling the bottom of the can. With a couple of small sticks, we picked the bullets out. Word came down that C Company had made contact two klicks to the southwest. No word that we were moving out. Good news for now.

HJ took the wooden peace symbol carefully out of the now dried mud, it looked almost perfect. I took the can of melted lead and slowly poured it into the dirt mold. Presto chango—we had a fucking peace symbol made out of machine gun bullets. We took the gunpowder, poured it around some ants and termites and watched like kids as they crawled over themselves before they were burnt to a crisp.

After a couple of minutes, the lead cooled. I picked it up and said, "I got dibs on this baby!" It was almost perfect. We had only enough lead left to make another, thin symbol, which didn't turn out as well as mine. After hearing a fire fight break out, there was no way we could use any more ammo for peace symbols.

All day, jets and gunships raced over our hill to pound the valley. But we couldn't see what was happening. That night was one of those nights that we had to try to block out our hearing to sleep. The next day somebody was going on sweep to C Company's aid.

The morning daylight always brought the news. The 3d Platoon was going on sweep, which amazed them and the 1st Platoon. Green troops going into a contact area? For what? Lieutenant Scurr was CO, *Why send a green platoon?* Nobody knew why, but that's what happened. The 2d Platoon sent out a SRP right before the 3d Platoon left.

Radio Log S-3 1/12 Inf. April 24, 1969 (Radio Call Signs) 41(A Co.), 42(B Co.), 43(C Co.), 44(D Co.), 75(Battalion)

0743	42	75	4252 element just sp'd the patrol base. srp #3
0753	42	75	4253 element just sp'd the patrol base
0919	42	75	At present time my 4253 element is in contact area of C co. yesterday, neg. findings yet.

Late in the morning small-arms fire broke out, it had to be our 3d Platoon.

0955	42	75	4253 in contact at this time has some dinks spotted, putting M-79, 81 and 4.2 on contact at 888028 have 2 WIA's.
1003	42	75	Ran into 9 or 10 enemy have 2 WIA's in fire fight at this time.

We thought for sure that the call would come down to saddle up. But it never did because C Company was closer to them than we were.

| 1020 | 43 | 75 | I am prepared to move out with 2 light platoons in 15 min. it will leave my hill light. |

| 1100 | 42 | 75 | 4253 element was walking up ridgeline at 888018 and at bunker complex that we found previously, we received much automatic weapons fire. |

| 1145 | 42 | 75 | At present time the 4253 element is receiving fire again, request Tac Air at this time. |

| 1147 | 42 | 75 | Threw a grenade and got a hell of a secondary out of it. |

Sitting around, hearing the small-arms fire, an occasional explosion, and knowing it was our guys in contact really worked on everyone's mind. We felt helpless. We also wondered how Lieutenant Scurr was handling the situation. The same situation had happened the month before, being scared not only for the guys in contact, but for us. What was going to happen? How many gooks? We thought they had to be part of the same regiment we had fought on Hill 994, two klicks away. We figured they had never left the area, just moved over a tad.

| 1157 | 42 | 75 | Have spotted dinks and have a large cache? |

| 1215 | 42 | 75 | Have most of my element in the contact area pinned down, trying to work the flanks around to free them. |

| 1219 | 42 | 75 | The dinks are in bunkers, there is a big cache in there and that's what they are trying to protect. |

| 1245 | 75 | bde | Dust off called for 42 element at 1243 hrs. |

| 1310 | 75 | bde | 4351 and 52 have sp'd to assist the 42 element, 4353 element is staying behind to secure LZ. |

1315	75	bde	Dust off complete at this time for 42, 2 individuals.
1316	42	75	My element has backed away from being pinned down. Although they are still getting occasional sniper fire. Request some immediate air support.
1317	75	bde	Dust off 39 ETA 15 to 20 min. For 1 man from B co. wounded in crotch, he will be transported to LZ Mile High by LOH and dust off will pick him up at LZ Mile High.
1440	75	bde	Dust off complete for 42 individual.
1445	75	bde	At present time 42 element is out of contact and we are employing an air strike.

Jets were streaking by overhead to drop their payloads. The ground shook. Explosions ripped through the air.

1500	75	bde	So far 42 has 3 WIA's and 2 KIA's all the wounded have been dusted off.
1510	BC	64	Reference medevac, 1 shot in leg 4th med. 71st evac. cond. O.K. 1 shot in groin cond. unknown.
1545	75	bde	The 4351 and 52 elements have just sp'd for contact area, also have been getting secondary explosions approx. 3
1610	43	75	In contact at this time, have 2 WIA's.
1633	42	75	Need dust off for 3 individuals, 2 from 43 element, 1 gunshot wound in hand, 1 shot in back, and 1 from 42 element with some shrapnel in left arm.

| 1719 | bde | 75 | To S-3 from S-3 air. Reference air strike 24 Apr 1969 4 dud bombs 500 to 750 lb. 883014 Be extremely careful and report exact location should you find any. |

| 1719 | 42 | 75 | I can get to ridgeline in 10 min. and 43's location in 30. |

| 1719 | bde | btn | Want either 19 or 64 at Mile High tonight, and make every effort to get 43 out ASAP. |

| 1730 | bde | 75 | From Bde Co. to Bn. Co. want you to pull back and saturate area with red leg and air strikes, do not proceed any further into contact area. |

It was already too late to send us out, so we spent all day listening to the battle rage southwest of us. A day of nervous waiting. Although nobody talked about it, we all knew we had to be going out when morning came. Unless the 3d Platoon was coming in, and that possibility dimmed with the fading light.

| 1733 | 75 | bde | Requested spooky |

| 1740 | 43 | 75 | My CO is KIA |

| 1745 | bde | 75 | You have only shot 280 rounds of arty, that is peanuts want you to saturate area. Also want you to move your Z44 up. |

| 1800 | 75 | bde | From F64 to bde S-3 reason being for not employing as much red leg as desired is because of troop disposition. Also don't want to move Z44 element because they have a good position and if they move and make contact we don't have anything to support them. |

1810   68   75   43 element KIA's 0-3 Blair and 0-2
                    Bosquet.

Darkness came, and the word spread around the perimeter
that C Company had lost its commander. The small-arms fire
had stopped. We set up our watch and tried to sleep. For the
rest of the night, artillery and the 4.2 platoon fired support into
the valley.

Morning came quickly, as it always did. I had forgotten the
last good night's sleep I'd had. When we were told to saddle
up, it was no surprise to anyone. We heard choppers over the
valley.

Radio Log S-3 1/12 Inf. April 25, 1969

0725   75   bde   Dust off complete for 43 element took
                     4 WIA's and 3 KIA's.

About a half hour after we heard the choppers, small-arms
fire shattered the morning silence. It was too early for that shit,
I thought. I said my daily prayer to St. Jude as we moved out
southwest down the ridgeline.

0815   44   75   Have some dinks spotted and drawing
                    fire.

0820   44   75   Have some dinks pinned down in
                    bunker complex employing red leg.

We cautiously moved toward the small-arms fire and explosions made by artillery, about a klick away. We had only gone
about three hundred meters when somebody yelled, "I'm hit!"

Confused, I hit the dirt. I didn't hear any shooting nearby,
just small arms and artillery five hundred or six hundred meters away. The 2d Squad was on point, I was with the 3d
Squad right behind them. Monkey, who was with Sergeant
Cribb and the 1st Squad, called me on the radio, wanting to
know why we had stopped. I told him to wait one until I found
out what was going on.

I looked in front of me. The squad was spread out, the men
on their stomachs, I looked behind me, and guys were still
standing. I yelled over to Claiborne, "Jim, what's going on?"

"I think Taylor is hit," he yelled back.

Just then two guys got up, picked up someone, and moved toward my position. As they got closer, I recognized Taylor. He was hit in the leg.

I got on the radio, "Two-Six, Two-Six, this is One-Three. Over."

Monkey answered, "One-Three, this is Two-Six. Go."

"Get Piggy Dumpy up here. We got a guy hit in the leg. Over."

"Will do. Out."

"What happened?" I asked Taylor.

He was in pain but answered, "Sniper."

"Where?"

His reply, "Don't know, didn't see shit."

Doc Pelky was there in a jiffy and quickly patched Taylor up, giving him a shot of morphine. It looked like the bullet had gone clean through his lower leg, shattering the bone. We joked with him, telling him he had a million-dollar wound; he was going home. In a way I envied him.

Sergeant Cribb told everyone to spread out and take cover. Monkey called in what had happened.

| 0822 | 42 | 75 | 4251 element has received some fire, 1 man hit. |

We stayed in our position. But we received no fire whatsoever. Then we moved back up the ridgeline so Taylor could be dusted off. In the valley, the contact was still going on.

| 0903 | 44 | 75 | Have a good position, all my people are spread out in good blocking positions, there is no way the dinks can get out. There are several dinks in bunkers, will be working up red leg. |

| 0907 | 44 | 75 | On first contact this morning, we found light machine gun and a base plate to some kind of mortar. |

| 0945 | 75 | DO | Called dust off for 1 man from the 4251 element that was wounded in leg. ETA 45 min. |

| 1030 | 75 | bde | Run down on casualties. C company has 3 KIA's that have been evac'd and 4 WIA's which have also been evac'd. B company has 2 KIA's still out there, had 5 WIA's 3 of which were evac'd 2 were field treated and will remain in field. Also have 1 WIA waiting to be evac'd. |

We sat around our hilltop, waiting for the medevac, all dressed up and nowhere to go, wondering what would we do next. The battle in the valley raged on.

| 1105 | 44 | 75 | Receiving 60mm mortar fire and small arms sniper fire requesting gunships. |

| 1115 | 44 | 75 | Have policed up tripod for the base plate I found, all I need is the tube which we are looking for now and I'll fire back at them. |

The medevac came in, and Taylor was put on it. The lucky shit was going home. He'd only been with us about three months. His boots were still black!

| 1120 | 75 | bde | Dust off complete for 4251 element. |

| 1130 | bde | 75 | From Bde CO to 19 need to know how many 105 rounds you have fired since 0900 this morning. (55 HE, 35 WP) battery is firing 6 rounds every 5 min. |

Because it took so long for the medevac, the 2d Platoon was already gone, out on sweep. Thanks, Taylor. You kept us from going back out, at least until the next day. I hope you had a good trip home.

For the rest of the afternoon, we sat around listening to a variety of ordnance punish the valley and surrounding ridgelines. The ground shook, and we could feel and hear the power unleashed.

One of our OPs picked up some movement, so, weapons pointed, we got ready behind our fighting bunkers. Come on you assholes, it's payback time I thought as we peered through the trees.

1145	cid	75	Cider 20 on station gave him D co. contact grid and requested some tac air.

1150	42	75	4251 element has movement to his front, is working up small organic mov't on a 225 AZ about 400 meters.

1211	bde	75	Buckeneer 6 on station with flight of 3 gunships to support 44 element.

After the gunships expended their ordnance, the four-deuce started pumping out rounds. I liked having the mortar platoon right there; it was a morale booster. When the sky was clear or there were just a few clouds, we could see the shell once it left the tube, but on its descent, our eyes would lose it in the trees.

Nothing happened. We waited as the minutes and hours passed.

1450	cid	75	Cider 20 left station and cider 24 will replace him and be up shortly, so far 4 air strikes have gone in.

Phantom jets, helicopter gunships, four-deuce, 105s pounded the valley. It was goddamn exciting. Hit them!

1546			For information purposes only, we employed 1 flight of 3 gunships and 4 air strikes in vicinity of D co. contact (87203).

1550	19	cid	We diverted the air strike on above grid for the people on LZ Sioux due to the fighters only have 05 on station and can't wait for the 43 element to pull his people in, we diverted it to grid 885014.

| 1620 | 44 | 75 | Still have 1 sniper giving us harassment fire, plan to move to location previously talked about, also have found 4 ruck sacks SFRF. |

1630 cid24 75 Leaving station at time he got from his higher severe weather warnings.

1635 59 75 Tonight we will try to get 7 CSS so get in NL and make sure they are all correct.

1640 43 75 Banjo 89 EMs 3 Offs EMs att 2.

1700 75 bde PLANS SUMMARY: A co. will continue to maintain defensive positions on LZ Mile High and will continue to maintain a Squad from his 51 element securing bde relay station on superstition mountain. Will maintain 1 SRP vic LZ Virgin and 1 SRP LZ Cacti. Also will maintain his 4152 element securing LZ Delaware.

B co. will continue to maintain defensive positions on LZ Sioux. 4251 will maintain LZ Ouachita.

C co. will prepare positions on LZ Sioux and prepare to attack on order to clear the valley from grid 888011 to 084016.

D co. will construct and maintain blocking position at grid 872023. Continue to maintain SRP 46 LZ Alamo.

Recon will continue to maintain defensive positions on LZ Roberts and will maintain present SRP screen.

D co. 1/22: will move from present location to LZ Ouachita, and construct defensive positions at that location. Will not have a company or plt size element on stand by reactionary force due to the tactical situation as we are fully committed. Air Strike requests for 26 April 69 on following grids: 3 strikes on grid YB883012 and 3 on grid YB886014.

Combat sky spot requests on following grids for 26 and 27 884013, 883015, 881016, 879018, 877019, 877023, Requesting: LOH tomorrow at 0800 hrs to check in on Cmd B push for approx 2 hours and 2 re-supply birds all day to check in on my AL push.

Requested that at grid 864005 to be called LZ Navajo.

Darkness fell, we were told again that it would be fifty percent alert for the remainder of the night.

Radio Log (Daily) S-3 1/12th Inf. 25 April

1720	44	75	They have 1 dink, 2 AK-47, 10 ruck sacks, 1 light MG.
1710	75		Called Dust off for EM for 44 man has stick in the leg.
1900	DO	75	Dust off complete at this time.
1940	44	75	Has dinks on the ridgeline jumping up and down and screaming is employing HE large organics.
2010	44	75	In the 10 ruck sacks that they found, they found clothing, bed gear, and 1 shirt with the number 11 on the upper left shirt pocket.

2350	44	75	Says that the CSS are coming too close to them, they have gotten shrapnel from them, Neg. casualties.

(Operational Reports Lessons Learned 4th Inf. Div. Ending 30 April 1969)

On 25 April, the 1st of the 12th captured additional documents identifying a regiment-sized unit. The participation of a battalion of infantry in the tank attack on BEN HET indicates the presence of additional units in the area.

After five months of relatively light activity in DARLAC Province, Camp Strike Force (CSF) and 4th Infantry Division elements operating southeast of TIEU ATAR (ZV021622) captured prisoners and documents identifying battalion-sized infiltration groups moving through northern DARLAC toward PHU YEN and KHANH HOA Provinces. In spite of extensive reconnaissance, allied elements have not yet located the enemy's main body.

Throughout the night, artillery fired an occasional volley, along with our four-deuce platoon. After pulling watch, I fell in and out of sleep until the morning light started the new day. The day dawned cloudy, and a light mist was in the air. We ran out of malaria pills, which didn't bother me because I had started throwing them away after the March contact, I wanted to get malaria; it was a way out of this madness. Mosquitoes never bothered me. I was lucky, I guess.

Radio Log (Daily) S-3 1/12 Inf. April 26, 1969

0714	42	75	Need some malaria pills want you to try to get them.
0730	44	75	Have 2 dinks in the open to the east working up 4.2 on them.
0740	44	75	Found a shirt in pack, over left pocket had K-3 also name.

0744	cid	75	Cider 20 on station says the weather is too bad to get air in put all my fighters on 1 hour stand by.

All of us just sat around, sipping on coffee or cooking C rations. Every once in a while, I got up and walked around, stopping at each bunker to talk. At times, boredom really·sucked.

The 3d Platoon was still out there somewhere along with D and C companies. The 4.2 mortar platoon was still pumping out a few rounds every five minutes. We were baffled at what was going on.

0818	44	75	Have a dink behind a tree about 50 meters away, dropping 4.2 on him.
0833	44	75	Will have the packs back to a LZ in about 30 to 45 you will be able to get a LOH in at that time also need M79 HE. Also employed 4.2 on that dink if it didn't kill him it shook him up.
0835	cid	75	Cider 20 said the weather is not improving any have diverted him to CSS done by radar on grid 8896.
0840	42	75	Do you still want that squad in a blocking position? Neg. just get out your local security.
0845	44	75	The dink that was just behind the tree is KIA they shook him up with large organic and killed him with M-60. Also the earlier spotting of dinks in the open they were 50-75 meters in front of the moving SE to NW they had full packs and green fatigues, no head gear weapons UKN. Also starting to get ruck sacks back to LZ to evac them.
0855	bde	75	The combat Sky Spots #3 and #5 are not clear we called back to Div but couldn't clear them. (878030, 872033)

0925	43	75	4351A just SP on a small sweep down the finger south about 20 meters.
1000	44	75	Policed up 1 Russian carbine with grenade launcher bolt action at grid 873022.

The hours passed; we sat around, wondering what was going on. Waiting for a call to saddle up—anything, nothing. The day dragged on.

1035	42	75	Pass on to 68 that we would like the body bags and stretchers as soon as possible.
1050	44	75	Just picked up an AK-47 believed to be one of the weapons that the individuals were carrying this morning when we shot at them they probably dropped it. Approx same grid as other weapon.
1600	44	75	Just had a Chu Hoy come up to my perimeter with a white flag in one hand and a grenade in the other. Had 2 people of the 44 element to try to retrieve him and he reached for the pin he was then KIA'd by us.
1610	cid	75	Cider 23 on station.
1620	44	75	The Chu Hoy green uniform had blue undershirt on no hat looked like he had a long stick or weapon they are not going to check it out.
1640	cid	75	My higher has restricted the tac air to troops in contact only we still may be able to get some but it would be around 1730 and the weather is closing in so it doesn't look too good.

1800   75   bde   PLANS SUMMARY: A co. will
continue to maintain defensive positions
on LZ Mile High, and will continue to
maintain 1 squad from his 51 element
securing bde relay station on LZ
Superstition Mountain. Will also
maintain 1 SRP vic LZ Virgin and 1
SRP LZ Cacti. Also will continue to
maintain his 52 element securing LZ
Delaware.

B co. will maintain LZ Sioux and SP
one 5 man patrol at 0600 to secure the
MIA's. 4251 element will secure LZ
Ouachita.

C co. will continue to maintain
defensive positions on LZ Sioux and SP
one 5 man patrol at 0730 will check out
contact area.

D co. will continue to maintain
blocking position at grid YB 872023
and will continue to maintain SRP 46
on LZ alamo.

D co. 1/22 will maintain positions on
LZ Ouachita.

Recon will continue to maintain
defensive positions on LZ Roberts and
will maintain present SRP screen. Will
not have a company or plt size element
on reactionary stand by due to tactical
situation as we are fully committed.

We were put on 50 percent alert again for the night. A day
had passed, and we didn't move. Something big was going on
in the valley, but we weren't a part of it. Why? Maybe tomorrow we'll move out was on everybody's mind.

Things were fairly quiet during the night, but sleep evaded
me. Something had to happen in the morning. How long could
we sit on our asses when around us all of this fighting was go-

ing on. We only caught bits and pieces of what was happening. The wait was frustrating because it gave us too much time to think of what was going to happen. The anticipation of getting killed or wounded was working on our minds. After a restless night, morning light finally came, along with supply Hueys.

Radio Log (Daily) S-3 1/12 Inf. 27 April

0700	19	71	Have small organics and large org. ready to move at 0800. Move them in this order, small org. to Ouachita, put them on top of hill, large org, on the nose, and then the security.
0705	44	75	Found another light machine gun, with a 200 rd. drum on the gun, and another drum in the ruck sack.
0720	42	75	My 53R is about 200 meters outside of the perimeter and negative sitrep not at the bodies yet.
0730	43	75	Have reached the contact area have 2 dink bodies one laying across a machine gun both are untouched. Also policed the machine gun and 2 AK-47 magazines. Later I want to send a plt down there and check it out further.
0810	bde	75	Want to know if you have recovered your MIA's yet, (neg.)
0825	43	75	Have secured one of the MIA's and moving on to the other one. Also ran across the cache found previously it contains RR rounds 82 rounds and 60mm rounds.
0826	43	75	Sitrep on the movement my element had so far they have had neg further.

0828   cid   75   Cider 26 on station putting air strike at 0900 hrs for 874022 will divert it to 884020.

0835   F19   G19   Want to send a plt down into the B co. contact area and secure that area and the cache in that area.

0900   42   75   My SRP 23 has loc my MIA's they will be moving back to the patrol base with them.

0905   bde   75   From S-2 to S-3: Once both bodies are out and back on a LZ you may move one plt into the cache area. Only one plt may be moved. Keep this HHP informed. "Don't screw it up."

All kinds of fighting were going on—there were air strikes in the valley. Choppers came in with more mortar rounds, along with a few 81mm mortars and their crews. We also heard through the grapevine that the 3d Platoon recovered the two KIAs killed on the twenty-fourth and twenty-fifth.

0907   19   42   When the bodies are on the LZ you can move a plt into the cache area. Keep me informed on when the bodies are back in the LZ.

0953   bde   19   IFFV would like BDA of air strikes at YB 884016, YB 885015, YB 883015, request VR when you receive LOH submit BDA for air strikes to BDE. Commanders conference 28 April 1030 hr. in the DIV war room lunch will follow and conference will resume again we will pick up commanders in the RON bird 3/8, 1/12, and 1/22. Pick up will be at 0830.

1000	42	75	He has the 2 bodies on the LZ at this time.
1002	42	75	So far in this one cache we have 100 60mm rounds—75 RR 4 ea and 5 ea 82mm rounds they are all beat up pretty bad some of them are still in the canisters but have holes in them from the grenades we threw in there previously.
1010	44	75	Current location for 4453B is 876023, east of his location are some small hooches and a blue line where he will be getting some water. He will be moving his element to the northeast to where the complex is.
1014	cid	75	Have put in 879025 put 2 flights and at 872012 put in 1 flight.
1055	bde	75	Expect that weather not flyable for the 1215 and 1300 AS TOTs targets are too close for CSS. Request clearance for these 2 CSS for 1215 and 1300 874030 and 873042.
1055	42	75	Total cache found 27 each 75RR, 102 each 60mm, 1000 each AK-47 rounds 100 each 7.62 rounds and 5 each 82mm.
1124	75	bde	The bodies from the 42 element are enroute at this time to Mary Lou on bird. Inform your 64 of this.
1125	75	bde	All the above cache has been blown in place and the elements have returned to the patrol base.

| 1126 | 75 | bde | Status on my move from LZ Delaware to Ouachita follows 7 sorties complete to present 2 of which were 4.2 sorties and the rest of the small organics are expected to be moved by 1200 hours. Have approx 22 slick sorties remaining to complete entire move. |

Before I knew it, it was already noon; time went by quickly because of all the commotion that was going on. We didn't budge.

| 1207 | 19 | bde | BDA of area requested earlier. Est 35 bunkers uncovered 3 of which were huge with the tops blown off probably were the secondaries that took place. Est size 6×10×8. Also observed 4 hooches 3 of which were still standing and 1 partially knocked down, could have been moved in the area but weren't observed. They were the size of a connex container. Also there were 6 large cave type bunkers with camouflage burned off by nape but untouched by destruction of air strikes also found a Vietnamese bed looked like blond wood it was intact without a mattress looked like someone might have dragged it out of one of the hooches that were burned down to save it. Also observed in some of the bunkers that had the tops blown off, shiny objects looked like lids to cans? The air strikes were very effective but didn't destroy the area completely there is still a lot of things to be uncovered. Requesting hornett 44 back so we can mark some targets in that area for the tac air. Est approx ⅓ of the complex destroyed by the air strikes. |

| 1225 | 43 | 75 | 4351 element just SP there last location. |

1226   75   bde   Correct location for the cache that 42
                     found 875010.

1230   42   75   Reference the cache bunker, its mouth
                     was 31×41 and dug back into the hill
                     approx 4 feet was camouflage of palm
                     leaves and bushes to camouflage it
                     from the air. There were fuses in the
                     cache all the 60 mortars were complete
                     but we destroyed it all. (Save them if
                     you find any more.) Also found 3
                     different kinds of propaganda leaflets.
                     Will look ??

1235   43   75   This morning found 2 NVA bodies
                     wearing green fatigues with no
                     markings. Also 1 MG with 1 clip of
                     ammo in round canister. 2 AK mag 1
                     empty and 1 full. Also one was wearing
                     a GI pistol belt with canteen cover.

1241   01   75   The small organics for B co. are 100%
                     complete. The 4.2 is approx ½ of the
                     equipment moved with 6 to 7 sorties of
                     class 5 plus my packs. Then the 4251
                     element is left to go.

The choppers stopped coming in; the move was completed.
The afternoon slipped by.

1615   bde   75   From S-3 bde to 1/12th Co. reference
                     the restriction on your C co. going into
                     that contact area it has been lifted by
                     General Pepke. You may maneuver into
                     that area. Come up with a plan this
                     afternoon so I can present it to Col.
                     Dukeman.

1630   75   bde   PLANS SUMMARY: A co. will
                     continue to maintain defensive positions
                     on LZ Mile High and will continue to
                     maintain 1 squad from his 51 element

securing the bde relay station on Superstition Mountain will maintain 1 SRP vic LZ Virgin and 1 SRP vic LZ Cacti 4(1)51 provide security for 4.2 and plt 81's on LZ Quachita.

B co. (-) will occupy blocking position vic 881012 and will provide supporting fires for Co. C and will prepare in assist of sweep of area if necessary. Will block enemy movement to the southwest. 4251 will occupy blocking vic 829015, and will block enemy movement to the northeast. Will maintain support of Co. C if necessary.

C co. will sweep from LZ Sioux northwest towards D co. searching and destroying the contact area.

D co. will maintain present blocking positions and will be prepared to assist C co. on order. Will maintain in SRP 46 on LZ Alamo.

Recon will continue to maintain defensive position on LZ Roberts and will maintain present SRP screen.

D co. 1/22 will move to blocking positions 887020 and block enemy movement to the north and northeast and will be prepared to assist Co. C if necessary and will be prepared to sweep from blocking position to the southwest.

Will not have a company or plt size element or reactionary stand by due to the tactical situation as we are fully committed.

Requesting 2 re-supply ships all day to check in on our AL push and a LOH at 0830 to check in on our Cmdd B push.

Darkness fell; another day shot in the ass.

2150   0   75   Wanted to know what unit, location, and day that the M-60 was lost (April 24, B co. 882014)

During the night, the artillery and mortars continued to fire, but we had no idea at what. As usual. When morning came, we were told to saddle up. We got our gear together, then waited. As usual. The valley was alive with activity.

Radio Log (Daily) S-3 1/12 Inf. 28 April 1969
71-DCO 1/22

Time From   To   Message

0745   71   75   Have completed the sweep of the movement area of last night. Found Ho Chi Minh foot prints very fresh it rained last night and they showed up well. There were some sumps in that area they might have gotten down in the sumps when the red leg was being employed. Also there is a strong odor of "dead" out there. This was to the north of the perimeter. Neg other findings. Have some birds that just checked in will be continuing our move.

0815   Z44   75   The Z4435 element has movement waiting for large organic.

0830   Z44   75   The movement for the Z4453 element is in grid 883024 west.

| 0850 | 43 | 75 | So far we haven't seen anything except for those two NVA KIA's they are about 50 meters back between us and Sioux. |

| 0900 | Z44 | 75 | Z4453 element employed 12 rounds of large organic called intermission will wait for 10 min and kick out a small sub to check it out. |

About 9:30 a chopper landed on the pad. A few minutes later, we heard a weird noise, like a large squeaky door. A few of us went to see what happened. We found the chopper sitting half on the pad, half off, its nose in the air. Nobody had been hurt except a few egos, pilot and copilot. It broke up the monotony.

Radio Log April 28 con't.
19- Batt. LOH (Major Owens) CiD-spotter

| 0956 | 19 | bde | Have spotted 2 dink trucks at grid 852978 both are military type trucks both about 1½ tons. They were camouflaged with brush but it was old and dry they were parked in a dig out area dug out by a dozer. There is a narrow road running parts of it had been scraped by a dozer. There is a bridge at 845994 looks to be made of bamboo but it will hold a truck. These locations are very vague as I was unable to get a good plot due to the bird that went down on Ouachita. Reference the bird down, we have been landing birds on this pad for the last 6 days. What happened? The bird landed too far back and slid over backward. Won't be able to get a hook in there it will blow it down the hill. |

| 1025 | 43 | 75 | Have come across a bunker complex at 884015 will give further read out. |

| 1030 | 19 | bde | Will be sending a crew in to sling out the trucks will consist of a QIC, 2 engineers W/500 lbs of C-4, and 2 pad men along with 12 men from A co. Will require 3 slicks and 2 gun ships to perform this will be expecting a 1300 PZ time. Will call for the hook once the people have a LZ and security. |
| 1130 | 19 | bde | In the pack we policed up from out D co. yesterday we have intell reference the following units B-3 front, C-23, K-3RN, C-18 co. K-E Bn. to C-18, C1, D1 Trang. C-13 co. C-14 co. X-3 co. E-28 co. and K-3 Bn. Also the C-9 co. C-10 co. C-11 co. C-12 co. |

At noon, we put on our packs and headed out of the perimeter. This was what we had waited for.

| 1202 | 71 | 75 | 4251 element just SP the patrol base. |
| 1210 | 43 | 75 | At location 884015 found 3 bolt action rifles 1 B-40 rocket launcher 6 packs, medical supplies, pioneer tools. |

I was assigned to the rear element, carrying the radio for Sergeant Henkel. Up near the point, Mong carried the radio for Sergeant Cribb. We headed northwest from our hilltop down the steepest part of the hill. Henkel told me he would bring up the rear, in front of him Williams, then Bill Stout, a guy from the 3d Platoon who had just come back from R & R in Hawaii, then me. I was fourth from the rear. It was slow going, steep as hell, and we had to hold on to small trees as we descended. After about forty-five minutes, the column stopped moving. We sat in place for about fifteen minutes. While we waited, I talked with Bill, who told me how great Hawaii was. He'd met his fiancée there, and he had a tough time leaving her to come back to Vietnam. I understood that. He asked me if I'd been on R & R yet, I told him no, that in two weeks I'd be starting my eighth month in country.

Bill laughed and asked me when I'd be going. I told him I hadn't made up my mind where I wanted to go yet. I'd heard good things about all the places—Taipei, Bangkok, Singapore, Sydney, Hong Kong, Tokyo, and Hawaii. I was more confused than ten FNGs.

Then Sergeant Henkel got my attention. He was about ten meters from me at about two o'clock. He said, "Find out what's going on. This isn't a good place to be stuck."

He was right. The slope was so steep that if something happened, we'd have trouble. I got on the horn. "One-Five, One-Five, This is Two-Five. Over."

Mong (Monkey) answered, "Two-Five, This is One-Five. Go."

"Yeah, Monk. What's going on? We're stuck on that steep son of a bitch you just went through, or is it still that way by you? Over."

"We have a bomb up here," he said. "We're trying not to upset it. Over."

I turned and told Henkel, but in a few minutes, we started to move again. For fifteen or twenty minutes, we climbed down while air strikes pounded the valley about a klick away. The ground shook; the explosions rocked the surrounding ridgelines.

1300   cid   75   Cider 25 on station with 3 air strikes
                      going we diverted the first one.

The ground finally leveled off, and we slowly followed the level ground for twenty or thirty meters to our left. I was trying to close the gap in front of me, which had opened to a twenty-meter interval instead of the three we normally kept. I closed the gap as fast as I could, then I had to stop. The accordion was now closed.

Guys ahead of me were gawking at something. We went about twenty meters, and then I saw it, an ugly, black, bullet-shaped thing about the size of a coffee table. It was a dud 750- or 1000-pound bomb. The ground still shook from the air strikes dropping in the valley. The bomb on the ground took my breath away.

About three meters from the bomb, a half-uprooted tree, about twelve feet in diameter, was leaning grotesquely over the edge of another steep drop. Panic grabbed me. With the ground shaking from the air strikes, I was afraid the dud would explode and wipe us all out. Dear God, don't let it go off, please, I thought. We quickstepped out of there. The farther we got the more my heart calmed down, but I could not forget what it looked like. Deadly.

About twenty more meters and the easy humping ended. The ridge dropped off again about thirty degrees. The column cut back to our right. Again, the way was so steep we had to hold on to small trees to go down. About thirty minutes had gone by since we passed the bomb. We slowly descended; the air strikes continued; the ground shook. About ten meters in front of me, the ground leveled off again, I couldn't wait until I reached it.

I glanced back and saw the others carefully climbing down. About five meters separated each of them. I turned back; my feet finally touched the level ground. At the same instant, a roar like thunder came from up the hill. I quickly looked back up the hill. I was shocked to see a large tree flying down the ridgeline like a torpedo. Debris was flying; it was coming right for us. I yelled, "Look out!" but my voice was drowned out by noise. Fear took over. I took off, running to my left about ten meters, and hid behind a huge teak tree. I watched helplessly as the tree thundered down like a runaway locomotive, ripping ground like a giant plow and slamming into the ground I had just left. The noise was deafening; the ground shook like an earthquake. The wooden torpedo came to rest, then sudden silence.

Then screaming sounded from up the hill. I ran over to the tree in panic, laying next to the tree was the guy behind me, Bill. I couldn't believe my eyes; he lay there motionless; dead. I started crying.

Bill didn't have any arms, and blood oozed out of him onto the ground into a puddle. I looked for his arms and his M-16, but I couldn't find them. I got on the radio, crying, "Get back up here, hurry, Monk! You hear me? Help, hurry, oh God help us."

Henkel and Williams were screaming up the ridgeline. I couldn't see them. I lost control, and I didn't know what to do. Mong came on the radio, "Two-Five, Two-Five, What's happened? Over."

"Monk, Get back here. Hurry." I answered. "We need a medic. Hurry. A fucking tree, a tree!"

I couldn't talk anymore. I guess I was in shock. Everything happened so fast. The tree was the one we passed earlier, the half-uprooted one with the bomb next to it. The bomb. Did it come down with it? My mind was so fucked up. How could this happen? Why? It could have been me. Seconds earlier, it would have been.

I thought of Bill. He hadn't known what hit him. I thought of his fiancée, his mother. They don't know; I do. Minutes went by before the others came back. Nobody said anything; a few went up the ridgeline to see what they could do for Henkel and Williams. A few more minutes went by before Mong and Sergeant Cribb returned with Doc Pelky. Doc hurried up the ridgeline to see what he could do. Sergeant Cribb called battalion.

| 1345 | 42 | 75 | Have 3 individuals hurt by a fallen tree and 1 killed. 1 broken arm, 1 broken leg and 1 with internal injuries at loc. 889019. |

Sergeant Cribb requested a medevac immediately, and Bill was wrapped up in a poncho by a few guys. We waited. Mong asked me what happened. I told him what I thought. A fucking tree! I asked about the bomb over and over. They looked for it, but nobody saw that ugly thing anywhere, thank God. Doc Pelky came back and said, "Henkel is in bad shape; I don't want to move them from the steep slope." A few guys tried to clear an area so a basket could be dropped in; that was the only way they were going to get out.

| 1530 | 75 | DO | Called dust off for the 4251 element will be DO 30 in 30 min. |

| 1540 | 43 | 75 | Will have an LZ cut in 30 min. Want to extract the Intel. out and have a EM with a 101 temp. |

| 1540 | 42 | 75 | The individuals that are hurt: one has broken back and rib cage, one a broken hip, one a broken thumb, and one killed. |

| 1600 | 75 | bde | Requested a hook for 1615 and the slicks and guns to pick up our people at 1645. |

1702	Bde	75	From 19. The hook is working for you now use him for extracting the truck.

It took almost two hours before a medevac came in to extract Henkel and Williams. A medic I didn't know broke his thumb somehow. For some reason, the medevac didn't take Bill's body. I stayed with the 1/3 squad that carried him back up the hill. We left a trail of blood behind us. We never did hook up with the 3d Platoon. We took a different route back up to our hilltop. I couldn't help but wonder whether the hill would ever let us leave its unlucky grasp. How could we fight the unexpected?

1800	75	bde	PLANS SUMMARY: A co. will continue to maintain defensive position on LZ Mile High. and will maintain the 1 squad from his 51 element securing Bde relay station on Superstition Mountain. Also 4152 securing LZ Ouachita. Will maintain SRP vic LZ Virgin and SRP vic LZ Cacti.
			B co. will move from present location and search and destroy to set up a blocking position at grid 877016. His 4251 element will move from LZ Ouachita and set up blocking positions at grid 887020.
			C co. will continue to search and destroy in bunker complex moving towards D co. location.
			D co. will maintain present location as a blocking position and will maintain his SRP 46 on LZ Alamo. Also maint his 4451 pres loc. Roco will continue to maintain defensive positions on LZ Roberts. Will also maintain current SRP screen.

D co. 1/22 will move from present location sweeping and searching set block position at grid 882026. Will also SP his Z4453 element to move from present location to 878027.

Will not have a company or plt. size element on reactionary stand by due to tactical situation as we are fully committed.

1830   71   75   People injured today were D-026 back injury, D-100 leg and hip, medic code name Hudson had a broken thumb, man killed was D-091 and also sent in D-128 for az. Rundown of what happened. They were moving down the side of the hill when they stopped for a break. Noticed a tree with a 750 bomb dud near the roots of the tree. Air strike was going in nearby and probably jarred the tree loose. When it hit the ground it started rolling and that is when people got hurt.

There was only about an hour of light left by the time we made it back to LZ Ouachita (1274). My ass was kicked from the hump back up, and I was mentally drained. A platoon from A Company was watching us as we came in. No words were exchanged. The body wrapped in the poncho said all that had to be said.

As night fell over the hilltop, all was silent. The chopper that had fallen off the pad was gone by then, but nobody cared enough to ask how they got it out. That night on my radio watch, I thought that the time to go on R & R had arrived; I had waited long enough. My reaction to the situation that day was the indicator to me. I was near to some kind of emotional breakdown. I thanked God that I hadn't gone on R & R yet. That was my way out without showing any kind of weakness to my buddies.

I tried to block what had happened out of my mind. I focused my thoughts on R & R. Where would I go? It didn't really matter; whatever sounded good, I would take. In the morning, I would tell Sergeant Cribb that I was ready. I prayed myself to sleep. He was there again when I needed him—St. Jude, thanks again. I believe in you always.

The following morning, I went to see Sergeant Cribb.

In a Carolina drawl he said, "Blond-headed kid, I was wondering if you ever was going on R & R. How long you been here?"

"Going on eight months."

"It's about time, son; where?" he said.

I said, "Let me know what allocations come down; I'll decide later."

He shook his head. He treated us all like we were his own sons. He understood and cared about us all. First Sergeant (Top) Page was like that, too. We had the utmost respect for them; they held us together. They also had to take orders from the captain and our lieutenants, who were twenty something years younger. That had to be tough, but they were army all the way. Cribb and Page were career soldiers in their forties. With families back home, it must have been very hard for them.

I went back to the guys and told them I was going on R & R soon. Everyone was happy for me, and, of course, *everyone* tried to tell me where to go. About an hour later, we were told to saddle up; we were going to try to meet Lieutenant Scurr and the 3d Platoon, again.

Radio Log (Daily) S-3 1/12 Inf. 29 April

TIME FM TO

0840   42   75   current location for B co. 878016.

0855 4251   75   4251 sp'd NL at this time.

We headed out of the perimeter in the same direction as when Taylor was hit in the leg by a sniper four days earlier. Things were quiet as we passed through the area where Taylor was hit. Nothing happened. We continued. The gooks must have left the area, I thought. I hoped. About a klick out from our perimeter, we reached a small hilltop, 900. There we waited for the 3d Platoon.

About noon they came straggling into our makeshift perimeter. They were worn out, unshaven. They had bags under the eyes from lack of sleep. Stress written across their faces. It was good to see them. Lieutenant Scurr was the only one who cracked a smile.

| 1215 | 43 | 75 | 4353A found Cache 20 rounds mortar, pack, and MG ammo |

| 1350 | 43 | 75 | 43 element found a bunker complex to SE of his NL. Also found the M-60 that was lost by the 42 element. Found some mortar rds. and other ammo. Will give a count on it later. Across the blue line to the NW found 11 bunkers, they were 3 man sleepers. One was a kitchen with 4 stoves in it. They burned all hooches and are destroying the bunkers as much as possible by hand. To the west there is another complex which could be a possible hospital. Checking all of them out now, will give a read out later. |

We headed back to our hilltop. It seemed that we had found new strength from each other. It had taken us four days to hook up, and each of us experienced those four days in his own way. It made us feel strong, although you could not detect anything on our faces.

After a couple of hours, we were back at our patrol base, LZ Ouachita, weary and thankful nothing else had happened. C Company was still sweeping the valley, looking for whatever it could find. Lieutenant Scurr called in to battalion with his find before he hooked up with us.

The day came to a close. It was silent.

| 1833 | 43 | 75 | 886015 found 1 pr. bino's, 1 crescent wrench, 5 pr. fat, 1 screw driver, 52 ChiCom grenades, 39 B-40 boosters, 36 rifle grenades, 1 SKS rifle, 1 ea B-41, 6 ruck sacks, 4 canteens, 11 sweat shirts, 1400 rds. MG ammo, 14 bars TNT, 8 gas masks, 7 ea 82mm, 25 mortar fuses, 7-75RR, 10 ea concussion grenades, 83 |

> B-40 rockets (30 still in container—2 per container), 93 60mm, 13 mag AK-47, 4,000 rds. 7.62, lea wire cutter, 5 hats gook type, 1 aiming stake, 1 82 111, 1 VC flag, and small bottle of UNK pills, 2 wallets—nothing in them and miss documents.

1900	75	bde	42 element found at 876017. 15 bunkers look to be storage bunkers with OHC—Approx 2′ OHC. Also a 4′ × 3′ tunnel 6′ long. Also 2 small shacks with square hole in bottom—looked to be rice storage cache but had been evacuated. Also 1 dink body wearing khaki uniform, NVA type, killed by small arms fire from our 43 element when they had their contact.
1901	75	bde	The 43 element had neg findings.
1902	75	bde	42 also found 2 empty boxes, 1 was wooden 75RR box 18″ × 36″ × 8″, and 1 was metal UKN what it contained 16″ × 12″ × 4″. Also a kitchen bunker with OHC approx 2′ with stove pipe sticking out.

The following day we sat around; no patrols were sent out. We figured we would leave the hilltop soon—why stay when the gooks were gone? We wanted to leave, and I hated this dreaded hilltop. Word came down to saddle up and wait in place; we did. Choppers were supposed to be on the way, but they never showed. We sat around, cleaning weapons, bullshitting about the World, and listening to music on AFVN.

Hours passed, and music filled the air, songs that fit the times, "Good Times, Bad Times" by Led Zeppelin, "What Becomes of the Broken Hearted" by Jimmy Ruffin, "Who's Making Love to Your Old Lady" by Johnny Taylor, "Get Back" by the Beatles, "It's Your Thing" by the Isley Brothers, and "We Gotta Get Out of This Place" by the Animals—we *all* sang that one. "Magical Mystery Tour" by the Beatles, which we were on. Songs that got our minds off of what was happening and songs that reminded us of the Nam. It was a never-ending cycle.

I wrote home to my parents without mentioning the tree, just as I never mentioned the contact of March eighth and ninth, I didn't want to worry my folks. I'm sure nobody else wrote home about bad times.

The following morning, the choppers did come to take us away. Only a few knew where we were going. I was glad we were leaving. As the chopper lifted away from the pad, I looked down at the valley, so green, so peaceful. It was hard to comprehend that we lost three KIAs and eight WIAs. I didn't know how two died; one KIA and two WIAs, I knew how. The question in my head was why? For ammo, weapons, supplies, and trucks? What a waste. Before long, feet dangling in the wind, we were gone. The chopper blades deafened our hearing; our asses numb with vibration, grasping each other's packs with one hand, clutching our weapons with the other, wondering where we were headed.

Hill 1274 was now a memory, along with Hill 994.

Lawrence Budzinski SP4E4 KIA April 24, 1969 Grid YA884014
Randle Ruggs   PFCE3 KIA April 24, 1969 Grid YA884014
William Stout   SP4E4 KIA April 28, 1969 Grid YA893017
WIA-Eight

Chapter VIII

THE AMBUSH

After a forty-minute flight, the chopper banked to the left and descended. The terrain had changed somewhat; there weren't as many mountains. We landed on a hilltop called LZ Carmen, Hill 727, somewhere southwest of Kontum. How far, only a few knew. The hilltop had no trees, just large rocks on one side and a large boulder in the center. Bunkers were already in place.

As the choppers left, we knew one thing already—we were going to fry on that hilltop. Shirts immediately came off; it was time to work on tans. Most of the brothers stayed in the bunkers that afternoon. We sat around, wrote letters for a few hours as the sun beat down. To avoid getting sunstroke, occasionally, we went into the bunkers. Tans returned quickly.

The sun finally faded to the west, along with the last day in April. I scratched off another month on my helmet. Eight down, four to go. By rights, I still had ten more days before I was really *there*, eight months, but a lot of us just scratched months; it looked better on the helmet. It don't mean nothin' until you're in double digits (days) anyway.

(Operational Report of the 4th Infantry Division for Period Ending 30 April 1969, RCS CSFOR-65 (R1))

(10) With the offensive of first-line enemy forces defeated, the 4th Infantry Division returned to large scale support of the Republic of VIETNAM pacification program. The 1st Brigade airlifted out of the PLEI TRAP Valley and then travelled by convoy and C-130 aircraft to a new area of operations far to the east of the Division's usual sphere. Establishing its base at AN KHE, the former home of the 1st

Cavalry Division (Airmobile), the 1st Brigade began operations in support of pacification in BINH DINH Province.

(11) At the close of the reporting period the Division was
deployed over an unprecedentally wide area of the Central
Highlands.

(a) The 1st Brigade with the 1st Battalion, 8th Infantry;
3d Battalion, 12th Infantry; 1st Battalion, 69th Armor; and
2d Squadron, 1st Cavalry (−) continued pacification operations in coordination with province and district authorities in
BINH DINH.

(b) The 2d Brigade continued its Operation PUTNAM
PANTHER west and northwest of POLEI KLENG, with the
1st Battalion, 12th Infantry on LZ MILEHIGH (YA936930),
and the 1st Battalion, 22nd Infantry occupying patrol bases
halfway between POLEI KLENG and DAK TO. South of
KONTUM City, the 2d Battalion (Mechanized), 8th Infantry
and 3d Battalion, 8th Infantry conducted pacification operations. The 1st Battalion, 14th Infantry departed the 2d Brigade's area for operations with the 3d Brigade against rice
caches and infiltration routes of the 95B NVA Regiment in
southern PLEIKU Province.

(c) Under 3d Brigade control, Operation GREENE
QUEEN, with the 2d Battalion, 35th Infantry, two air cavalry and two ground cavalry troops, conducted reconnaissance of suspected infiltration routes between TIEU ATAR
and BAN BLECH Special Forces Camps. The 1st Battalion,
35th Infantry, conducting search and clear operations west of
the OASES, prepared to join the 1st of the 14th for operations against the 95B Regiment's infiltration routes.

For the present, the Division will remain dispersed over a
vast area, assisting the local VIETNAMESE authorities and
self-defense forces. The ARVN 24th STZ confronts the only
substantial threat in the Highlands—the concentration of the
28th NVA Regiment and other enemy units in the vicinity of
BEN HET. Should first-line NVA units attack in force, the
Division will reinforce the 24th STZ as required to defeat
the invaders.

AVDDH-GC-MH 21 May 1969
SUBJECT: Operational Report of the 4th Infantry Division for Period Ending 30 April 1969, RCS CSFOR-65

In April, CSF from TIEU ATAR made contact with infiltrating NVA forces. A task force of the 4th Infantry Division, inserted to block the infiltration routes, made moderate contact with infiltration groups which attempted to avoid decisive combat. Captured documents and prisoners mentioned Infiltration Groups 1062, 1063, and 1064; and the 12th and 19th Regiments, apparently the infiltration groups' training regiment designations.

b. Estimated Enemy Composition, Strength, and Disposition as of 30 April 1969:

UNIT	EST STRENGTH	PROB. LOCATIONS
B-3 Front HQs	1000	Unlocated in Cambodia
Elsm 316th Trans Gp	500	Kontum and Pleiku Prov
40th Arty Regt HQs	300	Tri-Border Area
30th Bn	300	Tri-Border Area
32d Bn	300	Unloc west of Polei Kleng
33d Bn	300	Tri-Border Area
41st Bn	300	Tri-Border, Plei Trap Area
42d Bn	300	Unlocated
303d Sapper Bn	300	Tri-Border Area
K-31 Arty Bn	300	North and NW of Pleiku
28th NVA Regt	1600	Tri-Border Area
66th NVA Regt	1200	Northern Plei Trap
24th NVA Regt	1200	SW of Kontum
95B NVA Regt	800	Base Area 202 (VC Valley)
966th NVA Inf Bn	300	NW of Pleiku
K-16 Armor Bn	200	Unloc in Tri-Border Area
K-20 Sapper Bn	250	North of Tanh Canh
K-37 Sapper Bn	250	SW of Kontum
408th Sapper Bn	250	NE of Pleiku
K-28 Recon/Sapper Bn	250	West of Polei Kleng
K-25A Engr Bn	250	Tri-Border Area
K-25B Engr Bn	250	West of Polei Kleng
304th LF Bn	250	East of Tanh Canh
306th LF Bn	250	SW of Mang Buk

H-15 LF Bn	250	NE of Pleiku
X-45 LF Bn	250	West of Pleiku
Hqs & Spt Units 18th NVA Regt	500	Vicinity BR 7363
7th Bn, 18th NVA Regt	450	Vicinity BR 6672
8th Bn, 18th NVA Regt	450	Vicinity BR 5950
9th Bn, 18th NVA Regt	300	Vicinity BR 6936
Local Guerrillas	2500	
Infrastructure	6000	
Total Enemy Forces	21900	

K-16 Tank Bn	200	Tri-Border Area
U/I (37mm AA)	300	Tri-Border Area
E-301 LF Bn	300	Base Area 237
K-394 NVA Bn	800	Base Area 740
631 NVA Bn	500	NW of Pleiku

PLEI TRAP TOTAL	7500	Est. Strength
	4500	Local Guerrillas and Infra
	12000	Pleiku & Kontum

*Left out from 31 Jan 1969 (OR-LL) *=Author's Tabulation

320th NVA Inf. Regt	1400
1st NVA Inf. Regt.	1415
95C NVA Inf. Regt.	1200
407th Sapper Bn	300
	4315

*Left out Since 31 Oct 1968 (OR-LL)

101D NVA Inf. Regt.	1800
40th NVA Arty Regt	1200
K-39 NVA Inf Bn	300
966th NVA Inf Bn	250
	3550

3550 (Left out since 10-31-68)
4315 (Left out from 1-31-69)
21900
29765 Total
2100 (Added from General Pepkes Report)
31865 Total

AVDDH-GC-MH

SUBJECT: Operational Report of the 4th Infantry Division
for Period Ending 30 April 1969, RCS
CSFOR-65 (R1)

c. Enemy Battle Losses (1 Feb–30 Apr)

(1) Personnel:

	KIA (BC)	1434
	NVA CIA	13
	VC/VMC CIA	25
	TOTAL	1472

(2) Weapons:

	S/A	234
	C/S	65
	TOTAL	299

(3) Ammunition:

	S/A rds	368881
	C/S rds	1712
	Grenades	690
	Mines	261

(4) Miscellaneous Captured Items:

	Explosives	762 lbs
	Documents	1158 inches
	Rice	303.6 tons
	Salt	1103 lbs

(5) Enemy Facilities Destroyed:

	Structures	614
	Fortifications	2391

d. Enemy Capabilities, Vulnerabilities, and Probable
Courses of Action:

(1) Enemy Capabilities:

(a) Elements of the 40th Artillery Regiment can still conduct attacks by fire in the DAK TO-BEN HET and DAK

SEANG areas utilizing 85mm and 105mm howitzers, 122mm rockets, mortars, and recoilless rifles.

(b) The 66th and 28th NVA Regiments can conduct attacks in up to multi-battalion size against BEN HET, DAK TO, POLEI KLENG, and KONTUM City.

(c) The K-25A and K-25B Engineer Battalions are capable of extending the road systems in the PLEI TRAP area. They are also capable of building fortifications and artillery positions, while at the same time committing company-sized elements to attack lines of communication.

(d) The enemy can mount battalion-sized armor attacks against BEN HET Special Forces Camp and possibly conduct convoy security in the PLEI TRAP road system, once the K-25A and K-25B Engineer Battalions complete the roads in the PLEI TRAP.

(e) The K-28 Sapper Recon Battalion can make company to platoon-sized reconnaissance of allied installations and conduct sapper attacks against these installations.

(f) The 20th Sapper Battalion has the capability to attack allied installations and conduct in-depth reconnaissance of the same installations.

(g) The 304th Local Force Battalion can conduct mining and small scale ambushes along Highway 14 North of KONTUM City. This unit can also conduct company to battalion-sized attacks against villages and hamlets along Highway 14. The 306th Local Force Battalion is capable of conducting company to battalion-sized attacks against the villages and hamlets in the MANG BUK Special Forces area (AS9842).

(h) The 24th NVA Regiment is capable of conducting multi-battalion attacks against allied installations in western PLEIKU Province.

(i) The K-31 Artillery Battalion, employing 122mm rockets and 82mm mortars, can conduct attacks by fire against allied installations in the PLEIKU-Camp Enari area. All or part of the 966th NVA Infantry Battalion, elements of the 24th NVA Regiment, and the K-37 Sapper Battalion can follow up attacks by fire with ground attacks.

(j) The 408th Sapper Battalion can conduct sapper operations in up to company strength against allied installations in the KONTUM City area.

(k) Local Forces can conduct attacks against lightly defended villages and hamlets anywhere in the 4th Division's area of operations. They can also interdict lines of communication utilizing mines, B-40 rockets, small arms, and automatic weapons.

(l) The K-34 Artillery Battalion can perpetrate standoff attacks against installations at BAN ME THUOT employing 75mm Recoilless Rifles, 60mm and 82mm mortars, and 122mm rockets while the K-39 Battalion provides security.

(m) The 95B Regiment has the capability to conduct attacks in up to battalion strength against fire support bases, isolated camps, and populated areas; interdict LOC's by ambush and mining, attack bridges, interdict the pipeline along Highway 19, and disrupt the pacification program by terrorism and attacks on lightly defended and undefended hamlets.

(2) Enemy Vulnerabilities:

(a) Enemy units are vulnerable to artillery and air strikes when in bivouac or when massing for an attack.

b. Replacements: A total of 224 officers and 4282 enlisted replacements were received. During the same period, Division losses were 148 officers and 3013 enlisted personnel. Emergency leaves processed during the reporting period totalled 235.

c. Promotions: A total of 5067 enlisted personnel were promoted during the reporting period.

d. Casualties:

Unit	Hostile Wounded	Dead	Missing	Non-Hostile Injured	Missing	Dead
1st Bde	453	104	7	44	0	0
2d Bde	263	49	0	35	0	2
3d Bde	327	34	0	27	0	2
DIVARTY	81	11	0	11	0	0
DISCOM	18	0	0	17	0	0
2-1	45	3	0	17	0	3
1-10	61	3	0	16	0	1
1-69	38	4	0	6	0	0
4th Engr	17	6	1	12	0	1
4th Avn	12	1	0	6	0	0
124th Sig	11	1	0	1	0	0
HMC, 4th Inf Div	2	0	0	1	0	0
4th MP	0	0	0	3	0	0
4th Admin	5	0	0	1	0	0
Scout Dog	3	1	0	0	0	0
K/75	5	3	1	3	0	0
4th MI	0	0	0	0	0	0
TOTAL	1341	220	9	200	0	9

e. Morale and Personnel Services:

(1) Decorations Awarded	Feb	Mar	Apr
Distinguished Service Cross	0	0	0
Silver Star	19	15	78
Legion of Merit	2	1	3
Distinguished Flying Cross	5	6	33
Soldier's Medal	16	0	13
Bronze Star (Valor)	75	33	132
Army Commendation (Valor)	44	15	47
Air Medal (Valor)	10	10	12
Bronze Star (Service)	120	113	154
Army Commendation (Service)	518	562	1256
Air Medal (Service)	306	387	291
Purple Heart	152	297	367
TOTAL	1267	1439	2386

(2) Badges	Feb	Mar	Apr
Combat Infantryman Badge	919	843	241
Combat Medical Badge	76	42	54
Aircraft Crewman Badge	2	44	15
Miscellaneous Badge	0	16	63
TOTAL	997	945	373

For the first few days in May, we sat around on LZ Carmen, not doing much of anything but sweating, getting tan, and being bored. One afternoon, a supply chopper came in to drop off water and C rations, along with two boxes of M-79 rounds, which we needed like the clap. We already had more than enough. Lieutenant Scurr came down from the CP with one of the boxes and dropped it by our bunker and said, "The captain wants you guys to fire these rounds off tonight on bunker guard, about one every half an hour. Make sure where the LPs are and shoot them far enough down the hill." He turned and went back up to the CP.

We looked at each other and started laughing—a first, we get to thoop some rounds. It was something to do. As soon as it started to get dark, we began thooping, aiming at tops of trees silhouetted down the hill about two hundred meters. About every five minutes, all you could hear was *thoop*, then a few seconds later *wham*, followed by giggling. We were having fun for the first time in a while. We each took a turn, Bill, Monkey, and myself, but LT got pissed and jumped out of the bunker, yelling, "I told you guys one every half hour! That's an order!"

What a bummer, he ruined our fun. We waited until he was asleep, about a half hour, then we started thooping again. This time we shot farther down the hill, judging how far we could make them go by counting seconds before impact after we pulled the trigger. We couldn't even see the explosions; those suckers were really going far out there. It was midnight before we were bored with it. We did accomplish one thing—no LP slept while we were on watch. They answered every sitrep called by the CP on the radio that night.

About a week went by. A few patrols went out without finding anything of the enemy. Then one day, the early morning silence was shattered by an explosion and small-arms fire, two or three klicks away, which only lasted a couple of minutes. We wondered what it was, but I continued heating Cs with my hootch mate Monkey. RTOs hootched together because we were RTOs for the platoon and weren't assigned to a particular squad. But my heart was still with the 3d Squad, 1st Platoon, the 1/3 elephant.

LT came running down from the CP, yelling, "First Platoon, saddle up!"

"Oh shit, what did the asshole volunteer us for now?" I said to Monkey.

LT told us that a division LRP (long-range patrol) was in contact about three klicks away, and we were the closest company, so they were sending our platoon as a reaction force. The copters were on the way. We packed up and went up to the landing pad. We waited only about five minutes. My heart was pounding within my chest. I'm sure I wasn't the only one whose adrenaline was flowing.

"I'm getting too short for this shit," Bill exclaimed.

We heard the choppers coming before we saw them, four choppers for thirty guys. The choppers came in, one at a time, and we loaded on. Our chopper took off, shaking loudly. It dropped a little before building enough lift to go up. Choppers always scared me because they shook so much, and their noise was deafening. We weren't in the air too long, about ten or fifteen minutes, before the chopper banked and started to descend. As we got closer to the ground, I saw we were landing next to a wooded ridgeline, in what looked like elephant grass. We descended until we were about fifteen feet from the ground then hovered. One of the door gunners yelled out, "You guys gotta jump!"

I thought he was kidding; he wasn't. I looked around— Happy Jack, Ken, and Eddie had already jumped.

LT yelled at me, "Get goin'." I looked at Bill. He didn't want to jump either, but we had no choice. This had never happened before—why jump when the LZ wasn't hot? I looked down and saw the others waving for me to jump. I was going to take my pack off and throw it first, but then I thought of the possibility of my breaking a leg or foot with the increased weight, so I left it on and jumped.

The ground was soft, and I didn't break anything. The jump just rattled my head a little. We spread out and secured the LZ while the others came in after us. Only one guy got hurt in the jump, and that was Jack Shoppe, who fractured his ankle.

We had radio contact with the LRPs, so I called them. "Two-One, this is One-Six. What is your Lima [location]."

"Just walk straight toward the wood line about thirty Mikes [meters]."

I told LT, and we moved out toward the wood line. No small-arms fire. Things were quiet. Thank God, again. We made it into the wood line, and all four of the LRPs were spread out about ten feet apart, facing up the ridgeline.

"Glad you guys are here," one of them said to LT. "You

must have scared the gooks away, but we got three of those fuckin' monkeys."

He explained to LT, "We were right here; we heard some noise up the ridgeline coming down this footpath," he pointed. About ten feet away was a wide path five feet wide. "We saw them about thirty meters away and blasted two claymores. We got the two gooks walking point; the others scattered. Joe cut one down with his Swedish K. Don't worry; the rest are long gone. Come on, I'll show you." I followed the LT and the LRP team leader. The rest of the team remained spread out, just in case.

We walked up the path about ten meters and found two dead NVA lying side by side. One had half his head blown off, brains oozing out onto mother earth. The other had one arm ripped off besides having his chest ripped open. Flies covered their exposed parts. About five meters away on the other side of the path, the third NVA was lying face down, with three bullet holes across his back. It didn't bother me to look at them. I thought of the Vietnamese as lesser humans than I was. Seeing a dead dog would have bothered me more.

My emotions had changed from when Ken Comeaux and I killed the two gooks on my first SRP back in October. Being at the eight-month mark of my tour, I was better seasoned. I was getting used to the jungle. When you live day after day in the jungle, you become a part of it. Your hearing gets sensitive to its sounds. You can distinguish between a four-legged animal and a man walking. You can tell the difference between the sound of wind in the trees and that of leaves being crushed, and you can judge the distance of unusual sounds. You become better at seeing with hardly any light, with or without a moon. You learn to automatically use your peripheral vision to locate movement or whatever.

Living and learning to survive like an animal. Survival of the fittest, kill or be killed, only the strong survive. Trying to stalk the enemy like a tiger stalks its prey. Living on the border between life and death, knowing that at any instant the silence could be broken by bone-shattering metal.

We talked with the LRPs for a while about what they did. They specialized in long-range patrols that lasted, usually, four or five days. They didn't hump too far because helicopters would take them out and pick them up at agreed LZs. They could carry whatever weapons they wanted. In the team we reacted to, one guy had a Swedish K, one had an AK-47, one had a sawed-off pump shotgun, and the other an AR-15. They had to rely on each other, evade the enemy until they could spring an ambush, call in artillery and air strikes on enemy infiltration routes, etc.

No thanks, I thought. I hated short-range patrols. LT called the CO and told him what was going on. The LRP team called brigade or division to send out a chopper to pick them up. We expected the choppers to pick us up also. But I should have known better. Never expect the army to do what was right; it never did. The word from the CO was that we had to hump back to our hilltop. In other words, we were to sweep on the way back, after securing the LRPs while they boarded the chopper. We'd caught the raw end of the deal again. LT was glad we had to hump back, but he was the only one. We stayed in the wood line as the chopper came in to extract the LRP. The team apologized as they headed for the elephant grass. This time the chopper landed. We were stunned. We could have broken our necks jumping out of the choppers. Then I thought that maybe being division LRPs wasn't so bad; they seemed to get a hell of a lot better treatment than we did. The thought didn't last too long before I said out loud, "Fuck that."

"What did you say, Leninger?" LT snapped back at me.

I said, "LT, I was thinking out loud."

He told me to keep my thoughts to myself. We moved out toward the company perimeter through the elephant grass, then we entered one of the many "Twilight Zones" of Vietnam. Places that seemed to have stopped in time, dense jungle that nobody seemed to have entered since the beginning of time. The same kind of jungle that we found around Duc Lap.

We hadn't brought machetes because (1) nobody thought we would need them, (2) nobody said we should bring any, and (3) we left within ten minutes of being told to saddle up. In other words, our shit was weak for this kind of terrain. We had to pull in the flanks and hump in a single line. The guys on point had a hell of a job trying to knock down the foliage. I wasn't worried about finding any gooks in that tangle; they weren't that stupid.

The air was dead, no wind. We made about four hundred meters in two hours. We were not going to make it back to our company perimeter, so we set up in a small clearing in a maze of foliage.

While we were sitting around bitching, we heard movement

to our right. After listening for a few moments, we could tell it was some four-legged creature. Suddenly, a deer appeared about twenty meters away. Lieutenant Scurr shot a quick burst from his M-16. When the deer fell, he ran over and jumped on it and knifed it in the chest four or five times to make sure. The deer never had a chance. LT called the CO, who relayed the info to battalion. Excited, battalion said they were sending a chopper to pick up the dead deer. We just couldn't believe that. A few guys took the deer to a small clearing.

The chopper was there faster than a speeding bullet and lowered a sling to take the deer out. Jack Shoppe also got on the chopper. It was a good thing Scurr had bagged the deer. Otherwise Jack would have had to walk back with us, with a broken ankle.

Everybody was pissed off; we felt like we'd been pissed on. Nobody brought any C rations. I had all of my shit because of the radio, so I had my Cs, water, etc. I gave away two of my meals. Happy Jack got chicken and noodles, and Double G got a can of beefsteak. I had enough crackers and cheese and a couple cans of fruit to hold me over. That night we pulled watch, but everybody fell asleep. If anyone could have got through all the brush without us hearing it, more power to them. I'm sure the gooks were watching us from a ridgeline, laughing at us.

We started humping at first light and broke out of the dense shit about 10:00 AM Once we broke out, it only took us about two hours to the perimeter. Guys bitched all the way, especially Chuck Zeller, who bitched about everything anyway.

Shortly after the LRP reaction and the deer experience, we got word from division that Raymond Johnson, nicknamed Coon Ass by most in the 1st Platoon, was mauled to death by a tiger on his first division LRP. He was a good ole boy from Louisiana, just like Ken Comeaux, and they'd been close until Ken became our company supply guy at LZ Marylou in April. He'd transferred two weeks prior. He didn't want to go, but he'd put in for the transfer a few months earlier when he first came to us. Problem was, he grew right in with us, became part of our family. He was one of our guys. His death upset us all. How and why could that happen.

I thought back to the patrol with Monkey, Jim Leonard, and Claiborne when the tiger we'd heard walked by us and nothing happened. God, what a way to go.

We stayed on LZ Carmen a few more weeks until the familiar call of "Saddle up" rang out around the perimeter. We were humping out. A few R & Rs had come down, one to Singapore and the other to Taipei. I had let both slip by, and now we were on the move. I amazed myself. We humped a couple of days into terrain thick with trees, bamboo, low elephant grass, ridgelines, and small hills. At times it was open for ten to twenty meters, easy humping. We set up every night, but didn't dig in.

We made good time, two or two and a half klicks a day. The weather was hot, and water was going fast because we were sweating so much. What gave me—and everyone else—a case of the ass were little black bugs that flew like they were drunk and got into your eyes, mouth, nose, ears, and down your neck. When we stopped for breaks, the little shits would land on our arms. If you took a finger and touched them, the bugs didn't move, so you would squash them. Even so, they drove us nuts. After a while, because of them we didn't even want to take breaks. But at times they seemed to concentrate in swarms—we could move twenty or thirty meters and they would be gone.

After two days of humping, we were beat. We thought that was because this was the first real hump we had been on since February and we were out of shape. But it was really the heat that got to us. The third day of the hump, May 27, before we humped out, I found out from 1st Sergeant Page that an allocation had come down for an R & R to Hong Kong. I had first dibbs because of my time in country. I told him right away, "I'll take it. When?"

Top said, "As soon as we get through humping." We humped about a half hour before we were held up. Word was passed back to us that the 2d Platoon point had found some bunkers. That started my heart pumping. I knew I was going on R & R soon. I didn't need this now. Oh God, not now! Please. I prayed to St. Jude as we waited. Why didn't I go on R & R when I had the chance? Now I had the chance, and I couldn't get out.

RADIO LOG (DAILY)

S-3 1/12 Inf. May 27, (Radio call signs) 92(A), 39(B), 18(C), 20(D), 96(E-RECON) 60(BATTALION), EMPIRE 81(Lt. Col. Carter), O(DIVISION OR BRIGADE)

TIME	FM	TO	
0725	39	60	He is SP'ing at this time.
0805	39	60	At grid 130775 found fresh diggings on bunkers, also found a steel pot, further readout follows.
0815	39	60	Wants guns over him if possible.
0820	39	60	Also found a GI gas mask and some kind of spoon and an AK bayonet.
0835	39	60	Also found one chi-com grenade and dink shirt, believe to have found the southern end of contact area. Will move on to my objective and send an element back to check it out.

We moved out, slowly, cautiously. The feeling of soreness and aggravation that I had was replaced by the high from the adrenaline flowing through my veins. The column snaked its way through the foliage in such a way that we didn't see any bunkers, but we were sure they were there. I didn't want to see them. I'm sure most of the column didn't.

TIME	FM	TO	
0850	bde	60	General Irsik will visit Marylou at approx 1000 hrs today. Then he will visit 1/12 and 2/35 and possibly Plei Morong. Col. Daniels may be with him.
0852	18	60	At 132767 found 8 fighters, 4 sleepers, 1 latrine, 1 mess with 4 stoves. Appeared to be VC or NVA. Approx 2 weeks old, set up in triangle, not finished.

0900	96	60	Present location for A co. 128798. Setting up an ambush here to make sure no one is following us then we will move into our objective. Also at this location there is a trail running north to south, recently used, will check it out 500 meters in each direction.
0903	35	96	Want you to move into objective 7 by tonight and clover leaf it.
0925	BH	60	Black Hawk 30 on station will stop by and coordinate.

About an hour later, we were held up again. More bunkers had been found. Things were looking mighty fucked up. All I could do was pray. All of us were wide-eyed, scanning the surroundings through the small trees, where shadows danced so peacefully.

TIME	FM	TO
0935	39	60	At grid 124776 found 12 bunkers. 4×4×3 neg. OHC., neg. recent use. Also at this location found 1 gook gas mask, the old type with canvas mask cover and plastic eye piece covers.

Nobody said anything, and I couldn't find out on the radio what was going on. I was told they would get back to me.

TIME	FM	TO
0945	18	60	All the 18 elements have closed and they are SP'ing at this time.
1000	39	60	Same location found some more bunkers 4×4×4 with 2 feet overhang. 1 82mm round, a song book, and 3 old gook ruck sacks. There are 18 bunkers and 2 kitchens.

1025	18	60	Present location for 18 element 125764. At this location will be setting up and clover leafing the area.

1035	18	60	Will be sending the following elements clover leafing. 70(–) 125764, 16(–) 125768, 80(–) 115750.

After a while we moved out again. Everyone looked at me questioningly. I shrugged my shoulders. I didn't know what was going on; that always angered me. I called Monkey, who was with LT. He didn't know anything either.

TIME	FM	TO	
1105	18	60	At 125758 found a trail 1 foot wide running north to south. Recent use 1 week, also a marking of 2 sticks in a V-shape with 3 sticks running across the wide end.

Suddenly small-arms fire exploded about a klick away; someone was in contact. We didn't know who. We held again. This time everyone was pulled in, and we formed a perimeter.

TIME	FM	TO	
1130	18	60	Made contact, 7 dinks moving to the west, think we got one when we initiated contact. Neg friendly casualties.
1135	18	60	Grid of contact 125767, just received some more small arms fire, going out after them at this time. Using Black Hawk 30.

I thought for sure we were going to move out and help whoever was in contact, but we just sat, listening to the firefight. After a few minutes, two squads were sent out to recon the area.

TIME	FM	TO	
1150	39	60	3980 and 70 elements have just SP their perimeter.
1155	18	60	Receiving B-40 and small arms fire, believe to have 2 WIA friendlies. Further read out follows.

Gunships were called in, and we could hear them working out, firing rockets and miniguns. The firefight intensified, but all I could think about was, I'm not going to get out for R & R, boy, I fucked up. Nobody talked for a while. We just listened. Then word was passed around that one of our patrols had spotted gooks and that we should be on the alert. No talking or moving around. Shit—nobody moved or said anything for a while. Why even tell us? We were wrapped in our own thoughts, some praying.

TIME	FM	TO	
1330	39	60	80 element has dinks in the open, will lay dog until they get close then we will eliminate them.
1335	60	bde	2'd set of gun ships making their run.
1340	39	60	Dinks are coming from the south to the north.
1355	39	60	Dinks are 150 meters across an open field in the woodline at approx grid 124774. They were proceeding to cross the open field when the gun ships came on station. They ducked back in the woods. My 80 element still has movement over there believe when the gun ships clear out they will try to cross the field and we will eliminate them.
1408	60	DO	Requested a dust off to be standing by for 18 eta when we call 05 min.

| 1420 | 18 | 60 | One of 18's plt. to the east is still receiving small-arms fire. |

| late | | | |
| 1350 | 60 | bde | No confirmed casualties report yet. Last word 10 WIA and 1 KIA. |

The battle raged on, artillery and then gunships pounded the area to our south. The afternoon wore on, more explosions drowning out the small-arms fire. We found out it was C Company that was in the shit.

TIME	FM	TO	
1430	18	60	One of my plts. is receiving small-arms fire from the east.
1445	35	60	Reports a large secondary from red leg from Nicole.
1445	60	bde	Message from Bde CO to bde. Make sure you get red leg resupply into both Nicole and Penny.
1540	Bde	60	Let us know as soon as you get your 18 element a secure LZ, and we will have the Bikini birds come in and get them.
1540	60	Bde	My 18 element has a secure LZ at this time. Empire 81 is on the way to my location (2 minutes out).
1550	60	Bde	We have 5 people dusted off at this time, and Bde. has the Bikini birds on the way.
1555	60	0	We have 3 KIA's and 29 WIA's (Cobras are on the way at this time).
1556	60	0	Bikini birds are on station at this time.
1600	60	0	Black Hawk is on station.

1610	60	Bde	P-81 has left this location at this time.
1611	075	E60	Have 4 men on board: Dnelson, Bozinski, Killer, Iojem.
1630	Bde	60	18 is 2 minutes out.
1635	Bde	60	Empire 81 took Sgt. Graves to My Loc.
1637	Cid	60	Cider 22 on station.
1645	18	60	Believe to have 3 KIA's and 6 WIA's, 3 of which are litters, left.

After a few hours, one of our patrols killed a gook a few hundred meters from where we were set up, but we continued to sit in place.

TIME	FM	TO	
1650	39	60	Just killed a dink in the open area.
1655	bde	60	From Empire 81. Before you release the birds make sure you have good radio contact with all units on the ground.
1700	BK	60	Bikini 16 reports small-arms fire from the west of 18 LZ.

The suspense was frying my mind. I wanted something to happen just to get the suspense over with. I was convinced that I wasn't going to see my R & R. Two mortar rounds landed about twenty meters outside our perimeter, but we didn't know for sure whose they were. We were told they were incoming. I didn't want to hear that. How in the fuck do they know we're here, I thought.

TIME	FM	TO	
1735	35	60	39 is receiving incoming 82mm rounds. (2 rounds)
1750	35	60	Just received another secondary.

1751	bde	60	Request you call a dust off.
1755	60	bde	Requested dust off to be stand by at Korium with guns.
1825	60	0	Another secondary.
1810	92	60	Empire 81 is KIA.
1815	bde	60	Will have a spooky coming up on your B co. internal at dusk.

Light was fading fast. I was glad because we wouldn't hump in the dark; we'd dig in. Right before dark, we got the word that the battalion commander, Lieutenant Colonel Carter, had been killed. He landed in a LOH (loach) to go to the aid of C Company. Most of C Company's cadre had been hit.

It was dark; we couldn't see each other. I heard LT's voice as he wandered around to each position, telling everyone, "First Platoon, saddle up. We're moving out. Grab on to the pack of the person in front of you. We have to set up a blocking position. Try to be quiet."

About four "What's!" came out of the darkness, then someone asked, "LT, what the hell is going on?"

"Battalion wants our company to block the gooks," he answered. "They think there's a regiment around."

There was a lot of confusion while we tried to form up in a single file while World War II Skyraiders bombed and strafed in the darkness. There was so much fucking noise, we could hardly hear ourselves think, let alone try to hump in the dark. Battalion must have really had a case of the ass because of what happened, and they were trying to close in and block the gooks, hoping to destroy them with firepower. All I prayed for, as we moved out, was to keep the gooks from running into us. We'd never fought at night before, and I thought we might very well shoot each other.

TIME	FM	TO	
1816	60	bde	Requested 1,000 rounds re-supply for 105 HE Nicole.
1825	60	bde	Moving 39 element down to link up with our 18 element.

1830	cid	60	Cider 24 on station with spads.
1832	60	bde	Empire 81 at my location.
1835	bde	60	Sending down another LOH to Nicole so your 35 won't have to come back to Marylou to refuel.
1850	92	60	The 18 element is receiving small-arms fire and B-40 rocket fire.
1855	bde	60	Spooker 21 will be at station at approx 1910 hrs.
1900	bde	60	You can have the spads for 15 more minutes.
1908	92	60	At present time we have checked fire red leg and will be employing the spads. What happened was the 18 element got split up all over creation and the dinks got between them. At present time 35 is trying to get everyone together. When the spads are complete we will start the red leg up again. Still receiving fire and B-40 rockets.

Holding on to each other, stumbling, and swearing, we groped through the jungle like blind men. The air was heavy, and it was hard to catch my breath. The air was filled with gunpowder smoke. The sound of explosions was deafening, and the noise jarred my senses. We slowly moved toward the contact area until we were only a few hundred meters away. Then we held up. Thank God for small favors. We were split up and put into two-man positions about five meters apart. Flares illuminated the sky overhead, making it almost as bright as day, an eerie daylight, but at least we could see somewhat. The flares made shadows dance as they fell to the earth.

We weren't in position more than five minutes when some-one yelled, "Gook," from down to my right. Then someone yelled, "Don't shoot." Nobody did. Shortly thereafter, word was passed down the line that a gook had wandered through our position, running like hell. Nobody shot for fear of stirring up a firefight between us. What a lucky gook.

TIME	FM	TO	
1940	39	60	Just had a dink come up inside our perimeter.
2110	60	bde	Requested 1 LOH first light, cav troops first light, 2 slicks to back up our dust off, also at first light.
2130	18	60	Will have to get 11 WIA's out tonight and 15 out tomorrow. Subtracting everything that will leave our strength at 40. Empire 81 was hit with sniper fire in the neck, shoulder, and knee. He was in the C co. CP at the time.

For the rest of the night we were put on 100 percent alert. There were no more sightings. The area stayed lit; helicopters came and went. They must have been dustoffs. We sat waiting for more gooks to try to slip through our blocking position, but no more came. They had to be somewhere near. I prayed for daylight.

TIME	FM	TO	
2140	60	DO	Requested Dust Off for 11 individuals. DO 62 ETA 20 min.
2145	35	18	You will be the 11th man out of there tonight.
2210	60	bde	Night location for C co. 125766.
2310	0	60	The first contact was inacted at 1130 to 1540, and the second contact was started at 1850 to 2145 when they stopped receiving sniper fire.

Totals	KIA	WIA
C company	8	39
HQ.	1	5

RADIO LOG (DAILY)
(call signs) 92 (A company) 39 (B company) 18 (C company) 20 (D company) 96 (E company Recon) 60 (Battalion) 81 (Batt. commander) S-3 1/12 Inf. May 28.

TIME FM   TO

0001   —   —   Log opened equipment check.

0045 comp 60 92,96,20,39, sitrep n/c.

0130 Dust 60 First ship Dustoff 62 took 6 WIA's.

0145 Dust 60 Second ship took 9 WIA's, Dustoff 63.

0150   18   60 2 of the WIA are now KIA.

0220 Dust 60 Third Dust Off complete, took 7 WIA
                to include 18.

The darkness finally gave way to the welcome light of early dawn. I felt recharged and relieved. Word was passed down that we were moving out to set up another blocking position. It seemed the higher-ups were determined to get the gooks wherever they went. They couldn't be far. A and D companies were also sweeping the area.

TIME FM   TO

0620   39   60 The 39 element has SP'ed to establish a
                blocking position to monitor traffic
                aroused by 20 element sweep.

We moved about a klick, then set up again into blocking positions. After a short time, somebody opened up with a brief burst from a M-16. We didn't know what was going on.

TIME	FM	TO	
0908	39	60	Just reported, another 2 dinks, came up on us from north to south we opened up on them believed to have KIA'd one of them.
0920	39	60	Had 2 dinks wearing green fatigues, no head gear, and 2 AK-47's they were about 25 meters away when we opened up we knocked one down and the other fled to the west.
0950	35	bde	After we finished these last 4 sorties completing our D co. would like to release the birds to you then call them when we want to extract our C co.

We found out later that two gooks had been spotted on our left flank. One was hit, and the other took off. A squad was sent out to the spot but all they found was blood marks.

First Sergeant Page came over from the CP to talk to Sergeant Cribb, who was sitting next to me. Page said, "We need some of your boys to cut an LZ so we can get some resupply in."

I couldn't believe my ears; my mouth dropped open. Top Page looked at me and said, "Leninger if you guys can cut an LZ large enough for a chopper to land, I'm letting you go on R & R," he smiled.

I got so excited, I jumped up, tripping over my pack and falling back to the ground. "Really!" I said in disbelief.

Sergeant Cribb said with a smile "Take it easy blond-headed kid; we don't want to have to call a medevac for you."

I was shaking. "Where do you want us to start?" I motioned to the guys in my old squad—Happy Jack, Eddie, Ken, and Bill. I was so excited, they were all laughing at me.

I motioned to them. "Come on guys, lets go." I took off my shirt, grabbed an ax, and asked Top Page, "Where?" He told us to head up to the CP and we would get the location up there. I led the procession. On the way, I picked up Luke, Roger, Jim, and Good Buddy (Elmore). We had three axes; the rest had machetes. I double-timed up to the CP. Along the way, guys were asking, "What's up, Len?" All I could say was, "I'm going on R & R, man, no time to say hello, good-bye, I'm late, I'm late, I'm late."

By the time I reached the CP, there were about twelve of us, most from the 1st Platoon, a few from the 2d Platoon. When I reached the CP, Steve Turzilli was standing there, his shirt off, holding a machete. I said, "Hey, Ginzo, how ya been, buddy." I hadn't seen him for a few days because of all the movement going on.

He said, "You know the deal—we cut an LZ for a bird to land. I hope we're both going out, I have three weeks left. I hope the fuck we're both going out."

In my excitement I had forgotten how short he really was. I said "Ginzo, that would be fuckin' great man—me and you, buddy!" We slapped hands and gripped.

We had the common goal, to get out. Things didn't look good, and we both knew it. Here was our chance.

Steve led the way, stomping through the brush for about ten meters. Suddenly he looked up and said, "Here!" I looked up and around, he was right. I believed we could do it. "Len, you guys with the axes"—when Steve talked you paid attention or he would kick you in the ass. Everyone respected him because he was an old-timer and everybody's buddy, especially the 1st Platoon. "Cut the trees down so they fall toward the middle; we will work on the outside, then in." We spread out, making sure nobody was in the general direction of where the tree would fall. Chopping like madmen, we hacked at the jungle and trees. The trees here were ten or twelve inches in diameter, soft wood. A few good whacks, and they headed down where you wanted them.

Over the months, we had become experts at clearing perimeters and cutting LZs. We called "Timber!" or "Heads up!" as the trees were falling. When a tree fell, guys with machetes would rush to it, hacking off the branches and foliage. Some of us took our frustration out on the bush, I know I was. I had getting out to drive me on. Between swings of the ax, I heard the faint sounds of small arms, but I didn't care; I was a cutting fool.

TIME	FM	TO	
1057	20	60	Spotted some dinks trying to carry away bodies at 125767, opened up on them don't know if we got any, further read out follows.

1105	20	60	Have the dinks pinned down, are not receiving return fire at this time, they are going to try to capture them. (the dinks are unarmed)
1125	35	60	The dinks are dragging the dead dinks to the south not the north as suspected previously.
1127	35	60	Reports 4 dinks KIA'd by napalm, and 1 KIA by red leg. Also have 3 more KIA's from the 18 element to be extracted at time request bird. (you have Bikini 22 working for you use him)
1135	35	60	20 has 2 more Dink KIA.
1145	bde	60	Reference these last 3 friendly KIA's were they found this morning (affirm). Also do you know if there are any more KIA out there. Also were any of these 3 men stripped of equipment.
1210	35	60	Hornett 44 spotted one more dink KIA'd by napalm just to the west of the contact area.
1215	60	bde	Total count of NVA KIA's found to date 9 for 20 and 1 for 39.
1219	92B	60	Just SP'd an OP.
1222	35	60	20 just policed up another dink killed by 18 element, also found another dink KIA'd by Napalm.

LATE
| 1145 | Pad | 60 | The 3 KIA's have arrived at this location. |

| 1310 | 20 | 60 | Policed up 3 more dink KIA's that were eliminated by the 18 element yesterday. They were found in bunkers bandaged up also another one laying to the west KIA'd by small arms. |

| 1320 | 60 | bde | Total enemy KIA's reported today so far 16. |

| 1330 | 60 | bde | Reference the 82 mortar tube reported earlier, that is a false report there was negative tube found this morning. |

| 1332 | 20 | 60 | Found a dud 105 round, and a couple of bunkers that took direct hits from red leg. Also will be moving west 250 meters then make a left and go back down through the contact area (118772). |

| 1345 | 60 | 20 | Want you to police up as much dink equipment and uniforms as you can for their intelligence value. |

| 1350 | 92A | 60 | Reports a bird taking ground to air fire from a 220 AZ about 2 K away. (It was reported that a bird from the G element was taking small-arms fire from general grid 173725. |

| 1401 | 20 | 60 | Just reported at his turn around point a bunker complex that is still smoldering and there are still a lot of human parts laying around. |

| 1406 | 96 | 60 | The Medic that we were supposed to send back has left my location. |

| 1415 | bde | 60 | Message from Bde S-3 to all CO's. All Batt. commanders are invited to a luncheon for Col. Duquemin at Highlander Heights on 29 1300 hrs May 69. Batt. CO's who are unable to provide their own transportation will contact Bde S-3 NLT 29 1100 hrs May 69. |

Hours passed; we kept cutting, alternating on the ax every hour and breaking for water about every half hour. Ginzo came over to tell me that he was going up to the CP to man the battalion radio and to see if he could get a chopper, any chopper heading back to Kontum. We had until five o'clock to catch one, because at five o'clock, except for medevacs, they stopped flying. That gave us almost three hours to find one. We had cut down most of the trees we needed. It was now a matter of cutting the center of an opening about forty meters in diameter inside the LZ so a bird could land. It was a beat-the-clock situation; we had to complete the LZ within an hour or so to have a shot.

TIME	FM	TO	
1445	20	60	Just ran across another bunker complex will take a little longer to go thru this.
1505	Bde	60	Once you feel that D co. has situation under control have A co. and B co. continue to sweep to the West.
1508	20	60	In the last bunker complex found a 60mm mortar round and all the bunkers in the complex had rice spread around them. Also estimated that there were 5 enemy KIA'd 3 by small arms and 2 by red leg.

We took the fallen trees and made a makeshift pad, trimming branches so they wouldn't interfere with a landing chopper. I looked at my watch. It was 3:30. We were finished. I thanked everyone and headed up to the CP to find out what was happening. Ginzo was sitting by the radios. "Hey Ginzo, put a fork in us; we're done, man," I yelled to him as I walked up.

He looked up and said, "You better start praying then because the only free choppers are taking what's left of C Company out. It doesn't look too fucking good."

I sat down next to him, sweat dripping off me. "Steve, keep trying, man. Where there's a will there's a way," I said.

"I hear that. You might as well go cool out and get some chow. I'll call you if anything happens. Okay, buddy?"

I got up and went back to 1st Platoon and my gear, praying as I walked.

TIME	FM	TO	
1532	60	bde	We are ready to start moving our 18 element LZ call sign 18C LZ call sign 26X to be conducted on our AL push.
1610	39	60	Reference the dink 39 shot this morning he was downed but when we went to police him up neg. findings other than blood spots.
1620	60	bde	Just located 7 more enemy KIA's by red leg in the contact.
1625	60	bde	So far have a total of 28 enemy KIA's to date.
1635	35	60	20 found 1 more dink KIA'd by the element that is sweeping the area to the North.
1639	BH20	60	Black Hawk 10 reported finding at grid 098766 10 bunkers and a trail running NE-SW also 1 Pith helmet laying on the trail all were recently used, possibly today. (35 said to adjust some red leg on it and will work out the gun ships on some packs he found in the open.)

1640	20	60	Reports 2 more dink bodies and 2 drag trails.
1643	60	bde	Total dinks to date 31.

The time passed quickly. The closer it got to five o'clock, the more nervous I became, bitching and moaning. Everybody tried calming me down. At 4:45 I ran up to the CP to see Steve. He had the same look on his face as I had on mine, worried.

He just shook his head. "I can't believe this shit; not one fucking chopper in this whole fucking division."

I turned and walked back, swearing my ass off. Nobody said anything as I passed. They all knew what was going on.

Five o'clock came. I kissed off my R & R. I sat back down next to my pack. Happy Jack came over, sat down and said, "Look at it this way, Jack, you probably would have caught the black clap on R & R, and your thing would have fallen off. And then what?"

Happy Jack always made me laugh. I said, "Yeah, you're right."

Then I heard someone yell, "Blond-headed kid, get up to the CP, ASAP!"

"Hey, Leninger, get your ass up here."

Until I heard the "Get your ass up here," I thought somebody was fucking with me. I jumped to my feet and took off toward the CP.

First Sergeant Page was waiting for me. "Get your gear son. There's a supply chopper on its way back to Kontum. ETA about fifteen minutes. Bring Warner back with you."

I ran back to my area. When I reached my pack, I was so excited, I was shaking. All I could say was, "I'm goin', I'm goin'." I reached into the pouches on my pack for the cans of my favorite C rations and put them on the ground. "Here, you guys, divvy this up. I don't have time." Then I took off my canteens and two-quart bladders, I kept one two-quart bladder and said, "Here you guys take this too I'm sure you'll drink it!" I also gave my air mattress to Ken, and three bandoliers of M-16 ammo to whoever wanted it. I didn't have time to say good-bye to everyone. I just looked around real quick and said, "You guys take care. I'll see you later. Keep your asses down." I grabbed my pack, the radio still in it, and yelled over to Bill,

"They want to see you up at the CP!" I took off running. He followed walking. At the CP, Top Page said, "Take the radio out of your pack. Give it to Warner."

I looked over at Ginzo. He had his head down. He was busy as hell getting coordinates from the map, talking to the chopper. I asked Top Page, "What about Steve? He's going too, right?"

He looked away and said, "Give the radio to Warner." He walked over to the radios and Steve. I bent over my pack and looked at Bill. Our eyes met. We didn't say anything. We both wondered why Steve wasn't getting out.

In the distance, I heard a chopper coming. My heart raced. Captain Patrick gave the order, "Pop smoke!"

I put on my pack as soon as I heard the pop. I looked over at the pad and saw red smoke hugging the ground like a fog. The chopper was closer. I could hear the *wop wop wop* of the blades. I looked over at Steve. He still had his shirt off, and the look on his face told the story. He wasn't going with me. The chopper was over the pad, hovering higher than the trees, sizing up the LZ, judging whether he could fit.

Come on. *I* know you got plenty of room. Dear God, bring him down, I said to myself.

After a few minutes, the chopper started down, and someone yelled, "Leninger, get ready." I already was. The chopper landed and kicked off a few boxes of C rations. I turned to my left. Steve was standing next to me, and he said to me, "Take care, I'll be gone by the time you come back." He reached out with both arms and gave me a hug.

"Ginzo you should be going, too. Why the fuck not!" I said.

"Go on before he leaves without you," he said.

I turned and headed towards the waiting chopper, holding my helmet in one hand and my M-16 in the other. I got on, the chopper lifted up slowly. Tears welled up in my eyes. I was happy and sad at the same time as I looked down at Ginzo, who was giving me the thumbs-up. Then the chopper banked to the left, and we were gone.

TIME FM TO

1800   39   60   Banjo 84-4-7-1. (84 EM—4
                        officers—7 NCO—1 FO)

| 1845 | 60 | bde | Plans Summary: A co. Will SP at 0730 hrs attack to seize 10 at grid 107792. B co. will attack to seize objective 11. 104758 C co. will continue to maintain defensive positions on LZ Nicole. D co. will attack to seize objective 12 at grid 113758 Recon. Will continue to maintain defensive positions on LZ Nicole and will maintain 1 SRP vic LZ Carmen. Will not have a company or platoon size element on reactionary stand by due to the tactical situation as we are fully committed. Also requesting a LOH 0730 and 2 re-supply slicks all day. Would like to request an air strike on grid ZA 098766 in reference to Black Hawks spotting of 10 fresh bunkers and fresh trail. |

As the chopper gained altitude, I pulled my legs in and sat in the middle. I felt drained. Fatigue set in, and the vibration almost numbed me into a sound sleep. I had learned to sleep under the weirdest situations. In the air, I felt safe, out of range of small-arms fire. I was never fired on in all the time I spent in the air, and I didn't expect that to change at all.

After a half-hour flight, we started to descend. That woke me up. We were coming into LZ Marylou, Kontum. I became excited. I was on my way to Hong Kong and women unknown. The sun showed orange and red in the west, and daylight was only going to last another fifteen or twenty minutes. Too late to get nabbed for bunker guard. I would sleep like a baby. I looked forward to that. We landed; I gave thumbs-up to the door gunner and headed over to the battalion area. I went straight to the transients' tent for a cot.

TIME	FM	TO	
1915	20	60	2016 (-) closed, found 50 more of the same type bunkers also parts of bodies laying around believed to be 3 enemy KIA. (red leg)
1935	60	bde	Total dink body count to date 33 KIA.

As I was getting my shit straightened out, one of the guys yelled out, "Hey, who ya with?"

I couldn't see who it was because by now it was pitch-black inside the tent. I answered, "B Company."

Then he asked "Are ya going home, my man?"

"No. R & R, man!"

"I hear that; I remember mine; me and my buddy Sam here are getting out this motherfucker!"

"I could dig that," I answered.

Then he said, "Oh man, I'm sorry—we're in D Company. I'm a little fucked up. Hey, you want a beer?"

"Naaa, I'm fucking beat. Besides that's one less for you guys. Enjoy it, man." I grabbed my dirty towel and my 16 and headed out of the tent to the shower, thinking about the buddies I had left. I looked up at the star-filled night and prayed as I walked, not only to thank Him but for protection for those I left. I arrived at the shower, took off my filthy fatigues, got in, and pulled the chain. Cold water hit my sweaty head. It felt so *good*. I bent over and, with my hand, groped the floor for a bar soap. After a short time, I found one about half-used, I lathered with one hand for a while then I thought, what the *fuck* am I doing? I let go of the chain and used both hands. I had almost forgotten how to wash; I hadn't had a shower since the end of February. I washed my hair three times, then I just stood still and let the water spray on the back of my neck. God, it felt good. I looked at my skin-diver's watch, which glowed in the dark. It was after eight o'clock.

I was in the shower almost an hour and a half. I must have dozed off standing up. I put my pants back on and left my filthy boxer shorts there. My arms, shoulders, and legs were sore as hell. I shuffled back to the tent, carrying my shirt in one hand, my M-16 in the other. I entered the tent, and someone yelled, "Who's there?"

I answered "B Company." I could smell the hootch they were smoking. They were giggling and asked me if I wanted a hit. I put my 16 and towel on the bunk and shuffled down the wooden planks, reaching my hand out towards the red glow in the darkness. I never saw the guy's face. I took two hits, passed it, said thanks, and went back to my bunk. I moved the 16 over a tad, used my pack as a pillow, and zonked out as echos of laughter and talking passed through my head.

TIME	FM	TO	
2015	20	60	Found AK rounds, 4 B-40, 3 60mm Mortar and a small book maybe a diary will be back hauled on first available.
2145	comp	60	96,39,18,20,92 sit-rep no change.
2400	—	—	LOG CLOSED.

LATE
ENTRY

1920	20	60	The 20 element found 7 bodies just before dark by one of the elements sweeping the contact area.

I woke up in the morning with sweat rolling down the back of my neck. I sat up. Nobody was in the tent. I looked at my watch. Eight o'clock. Damn! I missed chow. I hurried to put my shirt on, left it unbuttoned, grabbed my 16, and ran over to the mess tent. But I arrived too late. An E-6 was standing at the entrance. As I tried to pass him, he said, "Hold up, young trooper. Where do you're think you're going?"

"Come on, Sarge. I overslept. I'm hungry as hell."

He gave me one of those lifer looks and said, "That's too fucking bad, boy. Get your ass out of here. And button up that fucking shirt."

I glared at him as he turned and walked away. But one of the cooks said, "Hey, man, come here." He was holding a biscuit with some eggs sticking out of it and said, "It's cold, bro, but it beats nuttin'." He handed it to me.

I said, "Thanks, brother; you don't know how I appreciate this." I chomped it down in no time and headed over to the headquarters tent to check in. I was told there wouldn't be a chopper going to Pleiku until late afternoon. I said, "Great! What do I do until then?"

That was the wrong thing to say. An E-5 standing about fifteen feet away heard me, whipped around, and said with a smile, "I have something for you to do until this afternoon."

I realized my mistake too late. I got stuck again, filling sandbags. The army always had you; there was no way out. You were always the grass and it was the lawn mower.

RADIO LOG (DAILY)
S-3 1/12 Inf. 29 May (call signs) 92(A company) 39(B company) 18(C company) 20(D company) 96(E company Recon) 60(Battalion) 81(Batt. commander)

TIME	FM	TO	
0735	39	60	B co. SP'd.
0830	60	bde	Requested to get the tracker dogs we requested to our trains pad ASAP as we have a bird working now.
0844	96	60	9616 element just SP'd.
0850	bde	60	The dogs will be at your trains area in about 30 min.
0905	20	60	D co. just SP'd.
1015	96	60	Reconing by fire, and will move on to object 10.
1020	96	60	96 SP'd.
0920	39	60	39 at obj. 11.
0930	96	60	A co. 500 meters east of obj. 10.
0940	39	60	Present location for B co. 107778.
0948	bde	60	Request to know if your CO will need transportation to HH for the luncheon at 29 1300 May 69, for Col. Duquemin. (affirm transportation requested.)

| 0950 | bde | 60 | LOH en route, (turned it back and requested it for 1300 hrs. this afternoon). |

| 1007 | bde | 60 | Would like permission to bring 2 slick loads of replacement officers and Sr. NCO8s to LZ Nicole on the Am of 30 May 69. |

| 1012 | 60 | bde | Permission granted reference last message if they are in proper uniform. |

| 1036 | 20 | 60 | On the dinks they found the letter "T" in white over the left breast pocket (4 have it). |

All together there were four of us. We took turns, holding the bags and shoveling, the sun beat us up, we sweat until noon then broke for lunch.

TIME	FM	TO	
1110	96	60	96 is at objective 10.
1130	39	60	At grid 114786 3970 found a well used trail, 3 ft. wide possibly used yesterday by 50–100 people.
1150	20	60	Platoon for 20-@116763 at this location found 2 trails one running on a 210 and the other running on a 220 AZ will set up at this location for a little while and send out elements to check out these trails. Then will move on to the objective and set up a night location there.
1225	96	60	9680 present location 107790 found a trail running due south and used in last 3 to 4 days by a company size element.

The guy I was filling bags with was from Washington state. We talked only about home. He found out about Chi-town, I

found out about Seattle. It passed the time. The four of us
shammed for over an hour and a half in the mess tent before
we were told to leave, then everyone in the detail split in different directions.

TIME FM TO

LATE
1326 bde 60 From S-3 air. There are no pre-planned
               air strikes for 30 May due to the truce
               only troops in contact will receive tac
               air. (What Truce?)

I went back to the tent; it was like an oven. I grabbed my
funky towel and headed to the shower. The detail was over as
far as I was concerned.

TIME FM TO

1415 20 60 Night location for D co. 114764.

1550 39 60 3970 saw 1 dink and fired on him they
              had no return fire. They are bringing
              Black Hawk 20 over his 70 element.

1558 39 60 The dink that 3970 shot at was at grid
              108773, also they have confirmed that
              they killed the dink.

At about 4:00 P.M., a guy yelled out, "All you guys going to
Pleiku get up to the chopper pad on the double!" I ran to the
tent, got my gear, and headed to the pad. Six of us headed for
Pleiku. We got on, and the chopper took off into the clear blue
sky.

TIME FM TO

1615 60 bde Plans summary: A co. will continue to
               occupy obj. 13 at vic 094785.

               B co. will continue to occupy obj. 14 at
               vic. 098774.

C co. will continue to maintain defensive positions on LZ Nicole and have 1 ambush vic. 168773.

D co. will continue to occupy obj. 12 at vic. 114764. Recon will continue to maintain defensive positions on LZ Nicole. Will also continue to maintain a SRP vic. Carmen, and 1 ambush vic. 168794.

Will prepare to maneuver units to the west & south when the truce is over. Will not have a company or plt. size element on reactionary stand by due to the tactical situation as we are fully committed.

Requesting 1 LOH at 0730 for 2 hours to check in on Cmd push, and 2 resupply slicks all day to check on our AL.

1642	60	0	The dink that 39 killed had neg. weapon or pack, looked like he was going after water.
1625	60	bde	Requested transportation for my 81 and 75 for the change of command ceremony tomorrow.
1626	39	60	Have confirmed dink KIA also spotted another running to the South have Black Hawk 20 looking for him.
1632	39	60	3970 grid of contact 107773 no weapon found was wearing a khaki shirt and green pants also was wearing a dink hat. The other dink took off in a southerly direction on a 160 AZ.

A half hour later, we landed in Camp Enari. I took my time walking to the battalion area because I didn't want to check in too early for fear of getting put on bunker guard. All the guys told me to stay away from the transient's barracks until it was dark, so I didn't really find out what to do about my weapon, pack, ammo, grenades, and shit. I couldn't walk around with all that ordnance, so I sat down on the side of the road to have a cigarette and think for a spell.

TIME	FM	TO	
1700	39	60	3970 just closed also have a man slightly wounded by a hand grenade thrown by the dinks it is very minor and won't necessitate any med attention, also said the dinks had a B-40 that they tried to fire and it misfired attracting their attention they eliminated that one and the other got away.

While I sat there, a lot of things passed by me. There were plenty of jeeps, trucks, and base-camp commandos on foot, headed up to the PX. A couple of them asked me, "Are you okay, man?"

I answered "Yeah. What's it to ya!"

They looked away and kept walking. Their fatigues were starched and tailored. Their boots were shined, and they wore OD baseball caps. My fatigues were a faded green, dusty, grimy; my boots looked like tan Hush Puppies; my steel pot was also light tan. I was bush, and stuck out like a sore thumb. Where am I going? I thought to myself. I don't feel like shamming until dark. I'll take my chances. I started walking. Walk tall, sharp, I thought, look good. I represent something. I'm bush. I hated it already; fuck bunker guard. If I got nabbed, fuck it; it might be an experience. I walked tall, weapon slung over my shoulder. Your left, your left, you had a good home but you left, your right, you had a good home, but you left, your right, danced through my head. At times, I thought I'd been brainwashed because I liked the attitude in a way. I was proud that I was a grunt.

In a short time, I arrived at the front gate of the 1/12th area. I looked up at the sign mounted above the road, WELCOME TO THE RESERVATION 1ST BN. 12TH U.S. INFANTRY. Underneath it was a small sign which read FIGHTING FOURTH'S FINEST!

I checked in at headquarters, the first building on my left.

Two clerks were still there; the rest had left for the day. One of them told me to sign in on B Company's roster and handed me a clipboard. I signed in. He then told me that chow was being served in the mess hall across the street and to turn in my weapon to the weapons shack down the street, if Smitty was still there; if not, wait till after chow. How in the hell was I supposed to know who Smitty was. Fuck it. I went to chow. I walked in the mess hall, M-16 slung downward; guys looked up, then continued eating. A sergeant major walked up to me and said, "No weapons in the mess hall, boy. You have to check it into the weapons hootch."

"Now?" I answered.

He said, "If you want to eat."

I thought so, and turned to walk out. An E-5 stood up, blond hair with a short mustache, and said, "Follow me."

He headed out the door in a hurry, I followed. He walked briskly across the street, down a wooden sidewalk to the right, and two buildings over, then he cut left along the building. I watched him and thought, where's the fire, man? I was still walking along the street; he was almost at the end of the building, about thirty meters in front of me. He then took a right. I took my time. I turned right. One building over, the door was open. I went in and said, "You Smitty?"

He answered, "Yeah."

He told me to print my name, sign next to it, and add the serial number which he read off. He took Black Beauty from me, then he told me to write in how many magazines I had, and grenades. He said, "You better hurry up to catch chow, man. They stop serving in ten minutes." I yelled my thanks as I bolted out the door. By the time I reached the mess hall, it was empty. But I managed to enjoy some chicken casserole. Base camp sure has some good-ass cooks, I thought.

As I walked out the mess hall, a deuce-and-a-half was loading a few guys for bunker guard. Half of them were grunts. They must have been going home or been on R & R like me. I would remember that tomorrow. I walked down the street to the transient building as the sun set in all its splendor. I watched the sunset for the first time in a while. It was quite a sight—reds, orange, blue, all in different shades.

Inside the light blue building, I sat on an empty bunk, pulled out my Panasonic radio, and tuned in AFVN, then lay down on the cot. I felt naked without my M-16. I hoped nothing would happen. I was convinced nothing would; this was a huge camp.

I wondered what my company was doing. I clutched the medals and blue plastic cross from the rosary around my neck and prayed the men would be all right. Then I drifted into sleep.

TIME FM TO

1930 bde 81   Constmt. order for temporary cessation of offensive operations in RVN from 30 May 0600 to 31 May 0600. The following instructions will govern action of US forces during this period. US forces will be prepared to react decisively to any enemy attack. Each commander is authorized and directed to take all actions necessary to carry out the inherent right and responsibility of a commander of self defense of his force. These actions will include but are not limited to:

1. ILLUMINATION. 2. DEFENSIVE AMBUSHES OR ROUTES OF APPROACH TO FRIENDLY POSITIONS. 3. AERIAL RECON. 4. GUNSHIP COVER OF CONVOYS. 5. EXISTING SRP SCREENS, LP's, and OP's.

The following will not be conducted: H & I fires, recon by fire offensive RIF (Recon In Force) and sweep operations.

Report immediately all NVA — VC initiated incidents.

Resume all normal operations 31 May. No public conversation will be made regarding cessation and/or these instructions.

2230	39	60	39 has movement West 150 out on their perimeter, employing red leg.
2315	39	60	Employed 11 HE on the movement neg movement at this time.
2345	comp	60	96,39,18,20,92 sitrep n/c.
2400	—	—	LOG CLOSED.

I woke up. Sweat was rolling down my neck. The radio was hissing. My watch was glowing in the darkness. It was after twelve. I took off my boots. I'd never slept with them off before, and I was sure those puppies needed air, lots of it. I rolled over to sleep on my stomach. I hadn't done *that* since in-country R & R back in October. I thought about Hong Kong and Oriental foxes. I fell asleep.

My deep sleep was broken by voices and laughing. I opened my eyes. It was morning, and guys were going to breakfast. Others were still asleep on their cots. I looked at my watch: 6:30. My head felt like lead, and I needed more sleep. I could get chow later. I woke up at 8:00. I missed chow, but I felt like having a cheeseburger anyway. I grabbed my pack to head over to HHQ to see the company clerk and start things rolling for R & R.

I walked through the door, looked around, and saw about ten clerks sitting at their desks. The tapping of typewriter keys filled the air.

One of the clerks sitting in the front asked me, "Who ya looking for?"

I answered, "B Company clerk."

He pointed to a guy with short blond hair. I walked over to him and stood. He was typing; he looked up and said, "Hi, I'm Mitch Wilson. You must be Leninger."

The tone of his voice startled me; it was very feminine.

"So you're going to Hong Kong? How much time do you have left? How's everybody in B Company? Did you know Jerry Sehman? He just went home last week. He was a mail clerk here for B Company."

I answered his questions. Jerry was in my squad, so I knew him very well. I wanted to know about Jerry.

"Jerry used to talk about all you guys all the time," he said. I hadn't seen Jerry since February when he got out of the

bush and took his sham mail-clerk job. He was very close to
Dean, our squad leader, and all of us in 1/3. I pulled bunker
guard with him; he was from Iowa somewhere, a good dude.
I wish I would have seen him before he left, but that's the way
it was in Nam. I was glad he made it home. Mitch told me
what to do—turn in my pack, get my duffel bag out of storage,
etc. He then advised me to stay away from the transient tent
during the day, or I would be nabbed for some detail. He told
me to report to him the next day for orders and tickets. He was
a good clerk, and he knew his base camp.

RADIO LOG (DAILY)
S-3 1/12 Inf. "RED WARRIORS" 30 May, 1969.

TIME   FM   TO

0925   39   60   3970 element on their sweep thru the
                   contact area. Policed up the second dink
                   that they KIA'd yesterday. He was
                   wearing green fatigues and web belt
                   carried 2 chi com grenades 1 M-16 rifle
                   with an empty mag. Also 2 AK-47
                   magazines and a note book.

I sat and talked to Mitch for two hours, then left to do my
chores. I turned in my pack, then went to the storage area to
check on my duffel bag. I hadn't seen it since I arrived in
country. It took the clerk a while to find my duffel bag, and I
started to panic. What prevents these guys from ripping off the
contents of everyone's bag? I thought. What about the guys
who are killed? Did they mail their belongings home?

After about ten minutes, the clerk came out with my bag. It
looked full. He handed it through the wooden window. I took
it off to the side, took the key from my wallet. On top was my
shaving kit with tooth brush, shaving cream, a bottle of Canoe,
Gillette razor. I laughed. Then I took out my folded khakis,
spit-shined low-quarters, and civvies. Things were in order. I
emptied my bag, then put the goodies back, and handed it to
him. He asked me when I was going on R & R, then told me
to come back the morning I was leaving with my orders. I
headed up to the PX, thinking about cheeseburgers and what I
had to get for R & R, if anything. The PX was like a department store, selling a vast variety of stuff. I looked at the 35mm

cameras. I needed one, but I might need the dough on R & R. They had some neat stereos, top of the line. My buddy Joe had given me three hundred bucks to buy an Akai 1800 SD, a reel-to-reel recorder with an eight-track player. Joe, an Italian from Melrose Park, was one of the only guys I grew up with who wrote me. At home we called him Tilt or Tilt a Whirl because his head tilted to one side. We double-dated a lot when I was in high school.

I had about five hundred MPC in my pocket. I would get more on payday, the first of the month, two days away. I got a cheeseburger; it wasn't the greatest, but it did the job. I spent most of the afternoon up at the PX. Then it was time to head back to chow at battalion. I was beat from shopping, seeing things I wanted to buy. I did buy film for the guys—instamatic and 35mm, and film for my Kodak Brownie. After chow, I walked out the door into an E-5 nabbing guys for bunker guard as they came out of the mess hall. I had forgotten about that shit.

TIME   FM   TO

1600   60   bde   Plans summary: A co. will move from present location attack to seize obj. 16 vic in zone 080757.

B co. will attack to seize obj. 17 in zone 095753.

C co. will continue to maintain defensive positions on LZ Nicole. Will maintain ambush vic 170767.

D co. will attack to seize obj. 18 and constitute SRP screen from 105758 to 107738. Recon will continue to maintain defensive positions on LZ Nicole. Will also maintain 1 war party 168793 and will maintain 1 SRP vic LZ Carmen, and will stand by as a reaction force for operation to the west.

Will not have a company or plt. size
element on reactionary stand by due to
the tactical situation as we are fully
committed.

Also requesting 1 LOH at 0730
tomorrow for 2 hours to check in our
A, and 2 re-supply slicks all day to
check in our AL push.

Requesting a troop of Yellow Scarf
(Armor) at 0900 to screen the north and
south flanks of our moving elements.

1630	30	60	Night location for 3970 plt size ambush 106779.
1637	60	bde	From S1 to Empire S1 we only have 5 tubes in our 105 battery.

Others were standing to the side already. I joined the group.
Two of the guys must have been drinking and smoking all day;
their eyes were red and blue, no white at all. Two more guys
joined the group as the deuce-and-a-half drove up. We climbed
on. The truck took us around the block to the weapons building. We could have walked, but that was the army. We got our
weapons, then back on the truck. It took us to the bunker line.
While we were bouncing along, the E-5 took our names. No
way out of it, they were slick. We arrived at the bunker line on
the far southwest corner of Camp Enari. A twenty foot tower
with a bunker next to it.

The E-5 yelled out, "Okay, four guys jump out!"

I was in the back so I jumped out; three others followed.
The two guys who were high were still on the truck, babbling
away. I was glad; for sure, they were prime candidates to fall
asleep on bunker guard.

The truck took off to the next bunker, about one hundred
meters away. We walked into our bunker. There were four
dusty cots and a fighting position with about ten detonators for
claymores. By the luck of a draw, I won first watch, eight to
ten. Standing in a twenty foot tower, with an M-60 machine
gun, gave me a sense of power.

The bunker line seemed well defended. There were tanks

down toward the helicopter pad to my right, roll upon roll of barbed wire, numerous trip flares, there were fougasse (fifty-five-gallon drums) buried out there. The wire stretched more than a hundred meters; it was different; it was kind of neat. I wanted Charlie to attack so I could tear him up. Nothing happened during my watch except for a few flares being fired occasionally to light the area. After my watch, which went quickly because I was amused, I woke the next guy and went to sleep, thinking about the next day. I was to get paid and set up my R & R.

I said my prayers, as I did every night, to protect me and my company in the bush.

Before I knew it, I heard the sound of a truck. Daylight, time to go! I thought. No. It was the middle of the night, and an E-5 was checking us out. At about 7:00 AM, a truck picked us up. Bunker guard was over. After we turned in our ammo and weapons, we went to chow.

Radio Log: S-3 1/12 Inf. 31 May 1969. Radio Call Signs: (96 A Co., 39-B Co., 18-C Co., 20-D Co., 92-E (Recon), 60-Batt., 35-Maj. Owens, O-Division

TIME	FM	TO	
0905	39	60	Have 10 dinks in the open at grid 097761 working up red leg and maneuvering at this time.
0930	20	60	2070A saw 8 dinks in the open fired on them.
0950	96	60	70 and 16 have closed neg findings and we are SP'ing at this time.
0955	20	60	Location for contact 112753 the dinks are moving to the west.

After chow, I went for some new clothes and to take a shower.

It was ten o'clock as I entered HHQ to find out about my R & R. Mitch had my orders and my pay for the month. He

told me I would be leaving in the morning for Cam Ranh
Bay.

TIME	FM	TO	
0957	bde	60	Have a set of guns coming out.
1009	60	bde	Gambler guns on station will be working for our D Co.
1025	35	60	When I came for ammo the dinks had drug the 8 wounded or killed back into a bunker complex to the south just in the wood line off the contact area. I can see some of them laying in the bunker complex at this time. Employ some concrete piercing in the complex and then have B Co. sweep it.
1030	Gam	60	Reports that he saw 3 dinks running from where they are working out going after them at this time.
1055	39	60	Maneuvering 1-6 element to the east at this time.
1058	60	bde	Requested set of guns (Buckneer en route 15 min ETA).
1100	35	60	35 Hit. dinks are trying to get out employ red leg. Hit below left collar bone.
late 1100	35A	60	Told 39 to back off.
1110	20	60	Getting hit around perimeter also my 2080A element getting hit.
1113	60	bde	Requested FAC on station.

1130	bde	60	To e81 from 075 - 35 will be O.K. shot through left shoulder - have 10 dinks in the open - 3 in west woodline - weapons all over the place. Dinks attempting to leave. Suggest send LOH to stop them.
1140	39	60	39 hit need more people. Have quite a few casualties.
1145	Buck	60	Have spotted the tube firing at 39.

After I'd shot the shit with Mitch for almost two hours, it was time for lunch. He told me to come back after lunch and everything would be set. I went to the mess hall.

TIME	FM	TO	
1200	20	60	Contact broken at this time.
1215	39	60	Contact broken but every time we open up we get incoming B-40's.

I returned to headquarters for my last instructions. It was just after 1:00 PM when suddenly a guy stormed thru the side door yelling, "B Company walked into a battalion ambush!" My heart stopped; I jumped to my feet and yelled, "No! Can't be!" I ran to the door and followed a few clerks to the commo building next door. All I could think of was that he had made a mistake. It couldn't be true. Oh God, don't let it be true.

RADIO LOG

TIME	FM	TO	
1300	bde	60	Shamrock guns en-route
1315	39	60	We have 20 WIA's, 4 KIA's

About eight guys were standing around the battalion radio operator, trying to get details. I pushed my way through them to get closer. One clerk said, "Hey, who do you think you are?" I yelled into his face, "Get out of my way, you asshole.

That's my company!" He stepped back, and I got behind the RTO, who was writing a transmission on a piece of paper. "LZ Nicole—D and B Company in contact. B Company in ambush, est. battalion, many casualties. D Company contact unk. enemy size, few casualties. Line numbers to follow." Time stopped. I don't know how long I stood there.

I felt a few taps on my shoulder; one hand stayed, resting. I turned. It was Mitch, the clerk. I looked at him and said, "My God, no! What am I doing here? I should be with them. I could help. I know I can." I had never felt so alone in a room filled with people. I started to cry. I couldn't handle it, not again. And I wasn't with them to help. I walked outside. I didn't know what to do. Mitch, and a couple of other clerks I didn't even know, tried to comfort me, but I told them to leave me alone. I had to be alone.

RADIO LOG

TIME	FM	TO	
1350	20	60	Reports 10 enemy KIA'd by small arms.
1400	bde	60	ETA on gun ships for your 20 re-supply 30 min.
1440	60	bde	Second air strike complete requested shamrock to come back up.
1445	20	60	All my personnel back in perimeter had 3 WIA's one was evac'd the other 2 aren't serious they can wait although they won't be able to hump. Est. 10 dink killed. Not a confirmed count as there are dinks laying all around the perimeter. Don't want to SP any sweeps until I can work some red leg in.
1447	35A	60	Spotted 2 individuals believed to be friendly on east side of road.

| 1450 | 35 | 60 | Requested to have the dust off and other ships to come up on station at this time. Have them come up on B Co. internal. (Our dust off is up at Dak To will get one from Pleiku.) |

| 1500 | 39 | 60 | B co. receiving B-40 and small-arms fire again. From the west. |

I sat for a while, praying for St. Jude to help them. I tried not to paint a mental picture of what was happening. I knew what kind of terrain they were in. I had a constant battle in my head, trying not to think about it. Thinking about it. Time slid away.

RADIO LOG

TIME	FM	TO	
1525	39	60	The guns are running the dinks out of the wood line and B Company is cutting them down as they come.
1600	60	96	SP for B Company at this time. Loc. 099760.
1615	60	bde	Sending in 2 re-supply slicks with class 5 they will pull out the wounded 4 sorties 5 men each.
1628	96	60	A co. SP'd
1630	cid	60	Cider 24 on station with spads.
1635	DO	60	Total wounded taken out 11 so far.
1645	bk	60	Bikini 15 just took out another 5 WIA from 39 total 16.

1700	075	60	Your 39 has 4 KIA that need to be evac'd he has more KIA's doesn't know how many yet. He needs another slick to get the 4 KIA's out. He doesn't want to move and leave the MIA's.
1701	39	60	Load of WIA's 5 aboard total 21 WIA.
1710	75	60	Load of KIA out of 39 6 aboard. Total to date 6 KIA - 21 WIA

"Line numbers coming," somebody yelled from the commo room. I was at the door in no time. The speaker box was on, the voice rattled off line numbers "D-011, D-013, D-031, WIA." I looked over the RTO's shoulder at B Company's roster—Baker, Boone, Heinicke. I didn't know them. "D-069, D-073, D-021." My eyes darted to the names next to the numbers.

Page, Warner, Price, I knew two of them. Top Page. Bill Warner, he carried my radio. He was in my squad. Numbers echoed through my head; I was dazed; more and more WIAs. My eyes searched the roster. Then came the numbers that were KIA, "D-045, D-082, D-089." Jim Leonard, a good friend from my first patrol. He'd been the patrol leader when we killed two gooks back in October. Lieutenant Scurr my platoon leader. I looked at the last number. Steven Turzilli.

I yelled out, "No, oh God, no!" It was Ginzo. My heart was torn in half. All I could think of was to run; I darted out the door screaming, "No, no!" I ran as fast as I could down the street. I was pursued by two clerks, yelling for me to stop. I ran faster and faster, not knowing where I was running to. I tried to get as far away from everyone as I could. I ran until I could breathe no longer; my nose and throat were filled with mucus. I was sobbing and out of breath.

I sat down on the side of the road coughing, crying, and spitting. I was completely overcome by emotion. The two clerks finally caught up. One was Mitch, our company clerk. They sat down, one on each side of me, and put their arms around my shoulder. They tried to comfort me. Mitch said, "Jack, there's nothing you can do. It happened; it's not your fault."

"I should be there," I replied through my gasps. "I want to be with them."

"It could have been your number that they're calling down. You're lucky to be here," he answered. I didn't look at it that way; I didn't care about my survival at that point. All I knew was that maybe I could have helped in some way. I told Mitch, "I don't want to go on R & R, I want to see them, fuck R & R! Steve, oh God, why Steve." I was broken; it finally happened; I wanted to be there; I didn't care about my good luck that I wasn't. I cried until I could cry no longer. Then I rose to my feet and started to walk back to the battalion area. It was getting dark, and I was totally drained. I can never go back out to the bush again, I thought. I was no good to them now.

RADIO LOG

TIME	FM	TO	
1740	60	0	We are going to put in another set of Spads and then we are going to SP our 96 element to link up with our 39 element.
1745	60	0	The total of people taken out was 6 KIA and 21 WIA.
1745	18	60	Night location for 80A 160774.
1800	60	bde	Requested permission to hang on to LOH to pick up some trip flares at our resupply pad and take them to our 39 element (granted).
1810	35	60	39 has a little shrapnel in the legs he says he is a little stiff other than that he is in good shape.
1811	gam	60	Gambler guns on station requested him to stick around a little while.
1828	60	bde	Requested a spooky NLT 1930 to come up on 96 internal.
1830	35	60	Have 2 or 3 MIA spotted about 75 meters outside of B co. perimeter

As we walked back, Mitch asked me if I was all right. I told him I wanted to be by myself, that I was tired. He told me to be ready at 0900 for R&R. I didn't answer; I couldn't. I went back to the transients' building, lay down, and tried to collect my thoughts. I couldn't.

RADIO LOG (cont.)

TIME	FM	TO	
1832	96	60	Getting sniper fire from the wood line. Have 1 WIA don't know how serious yet. There is only 1 gun firing at them.
1910	bde	60	Requested to know the strength of C co. (93–4–6 total 103)
1918	gam	60	Gambler 6 going off station at this time.
1920	bde	60	Spooky 23 coming up ETA 20 to 30 min haven't got final clearance for him to fire so don't use him until I give you clearance.
1920	bde	60	You have clearance for Spooky at 097781 a 3 K. radius.
1930	96	60	Have run into a machine gun nest about 150 meters between B co. and A co. Have 1 friendly KIA and 2 WIA.
1945	60	bde	Plans Summary: A co. will sweep south-southeast from night location OBJ 16 west of road vic ZAC88754, road running southeast will be boundary between A and B co. will make sweep with air cav. cover, will move slow.
			B co. will sweep south-southeast from night location on east side of road, will move slowly to obj 17.

C co. will continue to maintain defensive positions on LZ Nicole and will maintain present ambush.

D co. will remain at present night location and establish SRP Screen south of present location, linking up with 2/35 blocking position.

Recon will continue to maintain defensive positions on LZ Nicole and will maintain present ambush.

2000 20 60 The rap up on the contact his 70A had contact with 3 dinks they killed them, and the 80A had contact with 3 dinks and killed them also, the 70 went down to help them, they are still outside the perimeter they found 15 hand grenades, 1 AK-47, 1 B-40 rocket launcher, 3 B-40 rounds, 1 SKS, 3 B-40 Charges, 3 Rucks, 3 Ponchos, 3 Hammocks, 1 Firstaid kit 3 Magazines of AK-47, 1 Web belt with knife, and canteen they have 2 WIA they will send in tomorrow, 1 with a S/A in the arm the other with cuts in the hand from B-40.

Continued plans summary requested cav troop first light tomorrow also 1 LOH first light and 2 resupply slicks all day. Also will not have a company or plt size element on reactionary stand by due to the tactical situation as we are fully committed. (overlay will follow in LOH when we return it)

I lay on the bunk. My mind wrestled with my thoughts. What was I going to do? Everything was set up for me to leave in the morning. I had waited so long. My praying, was it my praying . . . I was so lucky not to have been with them. If I hadn't left on the twenty-ninth, I would have been there. Warner had my radio; he got wounded. I didn't know how bad.

I thought about Ginzo. He should have been leaving with me. Why didn't they let him come in? How many others were wounded or killed that I didn't know about.

Because I ran, I never found out the rest. I could take no more. I felt guilty and lucky at the same time.

After lying there for hours, I decided I needed the R & R to get away from this shit, even though it was only for five days. With luck I'd grab a couple of extra days in Cam Ranh Bay. I also decided that I wasn't going back out to the bush; I couldn't. No more insanity, no more pain; I only had about one hundred days left. I was almost at double digits. I would hit that in two days. Soon I would be a short-timer. That title came when you had less than ninety days. I had to get out of going back to the bush. I didn't care if I got a court-martial. I thought of my mother. If I was killed, it would destroy her will to live. I thought of Jim, and of Steve's mother, and all the others. Tears rolled down my face, I wept until I fell asleep.

RADIO LOG (cont.)

TIME FM   TO

2120   96   60   The MIA was recovered he is KIA.
                 They have 2 KIA and 1 WIA.

2145 comp 60   18,20,39,92,96 sitrep n/c

2400   —   —   LOG CLOSED

TOTALS	KIA	WIA
B Company	8	27
A Company	2	3
HQ	1	2
Engr		2
Arty		1

THE AMBUSH
(EYEWITNESS ACCOUNT)*

PFC Robert Noel (3d Platoon, machine-gun squad)
MAY 31, 1969

My recollection of the events of that day is only a partial account of the contact, which only goes to a certain point, and everything after that is a blank. I do not know why this is. I would like to know the whole story, but the idea of knowing all the facts scares the hell out of me. Maybe, during those last hours, I saw or did something so terrible that I shoved it deep into my subconscious, where I would never have to deal with it. I know it's all inside of me, ticking like a time bomb that could go off at any time. I just hope that when or if it does that I can deal with it.

Anyway, here is the way I remember that day. It has been almost twenty years, so you have to make allowances for the passage of time and the usual distortion of my imagination, but I believe it is accurate.

On that day, I had less than three months in country. I was in Bravo Company, 3d Platoon, with the gun squad. At that time, I should have been carrying the 60, having taken over the job from Mike Crawford on LZ Carmen. This is one of the puzzles about that day; I know I was the gunner then, but I cannot see me with the 60 when I think about that day. Why?

We started out that morning on a normal company sweep. I do not remember where we were, as far as a map is concerned, or how long we had been out when it all started. I believe it was late morning when word came down the line that the point had spotted about ten dinks up ahead. We should have been more suspicious, as this is something that just doesn't happen unless Charlie wants to be seen. The dinks began running, and LT made the decision to chase them. We chased them through the jungle for what seemed a short time when we came to an open area of shoulder-high grass surrounded by jungle. I do not remember how big it was, but it seemed pretty large. Charlie entered the grass and, I guess, went straight through. We entered and got about halfway through when all hell broke loose on us. I believe I was toward the front of the column

*Although taken twenty years later it is an accurate account because it is etched in the memories of those who experienced it and will never forget.

with the lead gun, but I couldn't swear to it. When the enemy opened up on us, it was total chaos. We all hit the ground where we were and started returning fire. I don't know what size enemy force we were up against, but they seemed to be all around us. We were receiving fire from every direction—small arms, automatic weapons, B-40s, and mortars. I believe the rear tried to go back the way we had come and found it sealed off. There was nowhere to go, and the only cover we had was the tall grass. It was a beautiful trap, and we stumbled right into it. I don't know how many people we lost in those first minutes. I could hear the screams of the wounded, over the shooting, all around me. I guess the medic was taking care of them, but I really didn't know. I don't remember anyone giving orders or in control at all. No one knew what to do, except to just keep shooting and pray for help of any kind. Although the grass wasn't much cover, it did conceal us pretty well. Charlie was walking his mortar fire around trying to locate our exact position. We were pretty strung out, everyone lying pretty much where they had been when this whole thing started. We crawled only a few feet on our bellies, for a little better cover. The way the rounds were whistling through the grass, you did not want to move very much. Mike Crawford was lying off to my left, and two others, whose names I can't remember, were to my rear. I remember them saying to me, "Noel, we're right behind you, don't forget about us," and I said, "Don't worry I won't." I did forget about them though, for a while, and they were killed. Although I cannot or will not remember their names, I have never forgotten about them since, and I never will. I carry a lot of guilt concerning those two nameless ghosts, as I believe they were killed as a direct result of my actions to save another. I don't know how long it had been since the first shots were fired, but it seemed like I had been lying there for days when I spotted some movement to my left front.

All I could see was his head above the grass; it was one of ours. He had blood on his face, no helmet, and he was crying for help. I don't know his name as I believe he was from a different squad and fairly new. I tried to get his attention, but he couldn't hear me over all the noise of gunfire and the confusion going on around us. He couldn't see me either, because as I found out later, he had been blinded by either a grenade or mortar round hitting close to him, filling his eyes with dirt from the explosion. By this time I gave up trying to get his attention and decided to go get him and bring him back to our position. I just couldn't lay there listening to him cry for help any longer. The enemy mortars still had not found our location and were working the area, searching for us. I knew Charlie had to have seen this guy wandering around out there, but I didn't consider why they didn't seem to be shooting at him. I didn't know or didn't think about the fact that Charlie was using this guy as bait, hoping that one of us would go after him and show them exactly where we were. And that's exactly what I did. I crawled out to him and wrestled him to the ground and tried to calm him down. I let him know who I was and began checking him for wounds. He was really terrified at first as he didn't know who had grabbed him. I could imagine how he felt. I mean, I was scared to death, and I could see what and who was where, but he had no idea if he was heading straight for the enemy or back to our location. It must have been hell for him. After doing a quick scan of his wounds, I could see his face was covered with blood, but he didn't seem to have any serious wounds anywhere else on his body. His main injury was to his eyes from the debris of the blast close to him.

Anyway, we must have made quite a commotion getting back to the platoon, which was exactly what Charlie wanted; they now had a pretty good idea of where we were. Shortly after I got him back into our perimeter—it seemed like just a few seconds, but I couldn't sever the fact that the first mortar rounds began falling inside our position. The first round landed right behind me, and I remember hearing a loud scream, only once, and then nothing. Then Crawford started yelling that he was hit. I forgot about that other scream, all hell was coming down on us then.

Crawford, who was to my left rear, was yelling that his ass was on fire. I went over to him. He was lying on his stomach and had taken a piece of shrapnel in the ass. He didn't have any other wounds that I could see; he just kept asking me to put that fire out.

Everything after that is a blank to me. I don't know how much longer it lasted or how we got out of it. At the time though, I knew I was going to die any second. My body went on automatic; my mind just couldn't take any more and just shut down.

The next thing I remember is when the shooting was all over. I remembered the two guys who'd been behind me, and that one loud scream. I went over to check on them, but all I found was a pile of green and red. The first mortar round must have hit right on top of them. It left something that didn't even look human. I'm not sure now if it was their scream that I heard. Looking at that bloody mess, I can't imagine them surviving long enough to scream.

I don't remember who came to our rescue or why the contact was broken. Charlie had us cold and could have wiped us out, so someone else must have come and chased them off. But I don't know who or when. I don't remember any details after the contact. The evacuation of the dead and wounded, the cleanup, and enemy body count are all blanks in my mind.

I do know that a lot of good men died that day; a lot more were fucked up physically, and who knows how many more are carrying mental scars, the kind that never heal and never go away. I know I carry a lot of guilt about that day, and I guess I will until the day I die. It's kind of funny—I thought for sure I was going to die, and when I didn't, I should have been happy, but I wasn't. I mean, sure, at first, I was relieved and happy to still be standing, without a scratch, but then the guilt started, and I began second guessing my actions and wondering, why?

Why, was I spared? Sometimes I think the lucky ones died that day; at least it's over for them, and they are at peace.

THE AMBUSH
An Eyewitness Account

Sp4. Ed Medors (1st Platoon, rifleman, 3d Squad)
May 31, 1969

I don't recall this one as well as the one in March. I do remember that our battalion was getting the shit kicked out of it. We knew that it was big because all the companies out in the field were getting hit on, all at the same time. C Company got hit the worst; they had walked into an ambush and knew it. I couldn't believe that our battalion commander sent them in there.

They sent us out to about the same area. Our platoon was in the rear when the company point spotted approximately ten NVA or more up ahead of us. Captain Patrick stopped the company and yelled for the 1st Platoon to move up front. I said to myself, I can't believe this shit. They're going to send us right into the same shit C Company just got out of?

Anyway, our platoon moved up front, and Captain Patrick told Lieutenant Scurr what he wanted, then Sergeant Cribb told us. We could not believe what they wanted—they put the first platoon on a straight line by a clearing. On command, we charged. We were in a straight line, charging the other side of the clearing that had bunkers all along it. About halfway across, Sergeant Cribb told us to drop our packs and to aim low at the bottom of the clearing's edge. We got about twenty-five yards from the edge of the clearing, and stopped. Then we stayed there for five to ten minutes. Sergeant Cribb called for my squad to come to his location, which was on our left. When we got there, they were shot up pretty bad. Lieutenant Scurr was dead, and so were quite a few others. I was wondering where the rest of the company was. I didn't know that they were getting the shit kicked out of them, too.

As you can see they had us pretty well trapped and the air force and the gun ships saved our asses.

THE AMBUSH
An Eyewitness Account

PFC Roger Ranker (Rifleman, 1st Platoon, 1st Squad)

We were in the grassy area where initial contact was made. Our squad entered the tree line, and we were engaged by enemy fire. The squad was proceeding up an incline when Sergeant Leonard walked by a bunker, he was shot, and went down. The gook grabbed his gun and shot Leonard several more times as he lay over the bunker where he died. We were pinned down and were told to pull back. Hoping to save Leonard, I crawled up to the bunker and unloaded my M-16 in the bunker but apparently missed the gook. He fired back, missing me, and I crawled back down the hill where the rest of the squad was. I asked who was going up to get Leonard. No one responded, so I said, "Cover me." Without a rifle and armed only with a frag, I crawled up to the bunker, popped the pin, counted to three, and threw it in. When it exploded, I grabbed Leonard. I knew he was dead. With the help of a squad member, we dragged Sergeant Leonard down the hill and put him on the pile of dead soldiers.

Eyewitness Account
May 31, 1969

Capt. Phil Patrick (B Company, Company Commander)

The fight on May 31, 1969, as I remember it, goes like this:

We started moving that morning to the west, I believe, and the word was that we were going to be picked up that evening or the next morning, and taken back for a stand-down. We had been out for quite a while by this time. I am sure you are aware of a lot of this, and I will try to make it as brief as possible.

As I remember, the order of march was 1st Platoon, CP, 2d Platoon, and 3d Platoon. The point called in that they had spotted ten dinks moving across a marshy area to our front. I called the company to a halt and moved forward to see if I could see the dinks. I started to have our forward observer call in artillery fire on the dinks when Major Owens came into the area in a LOH (light observation helicopter). The major started firing at the dinks and said he had some of them down in a meadow surrounded by a tree line to the front of us and to the right. Major Owens started taking heavy fire and was wounded. The pilot evacuated the major as he was seriously wounded, and I had the forward observer continue calling in artillery fire. Prior to being wounded, Major Owens reported bunkers and fortified positions in the tree line. The forward observer called in HE [high explosive] with time delays to get to the bunker before it exploded. Things were going pretty good, but the artillery had one gun shooting out of battery. The artillery was, I believe, B Battery of 1st or 2d of the 42d Artillery, a 105 howitzer battery. I told the forward observer that he needed to get the gun out of battery adjusted as it was coming closer to us than it was to the dinks. The artillery couldn't correct the problem, so I decided we would call it off and move in.

I instructed Lieutenant Scurr to take his platoon and go on line and attack the tree line to our front. As Lieutenant Scurr moved forward, so did I and my command group. I reached a position about the center of the clearing, near a large anthill, and stopped. The NVA, under heavy attack by Lieutenant Scurr's platoon, started leaving their positions and retreating to our left. At this time, I moved the 2d Platoon, under Lieutenant Murphy, on line and sent them on assault to the left. At almost the same time, Lieutenant Scurr informed me of movement to his right, so I decided to commit the 3d Platoon, under Lieutenant Nathan, to the right, on line. At this time, all hell broke loose.

The 1st and 3d platoons started taking heavy small-arms fire, and because of our position, the command post also started taking heavy fire. The 3d Platoon and CP also started taking mortar fire. Sergeant Sewell took a direct hit and was killed. The 3d Platoon was almost entirely killed or wounded in about five minutes. Lieutenant Scurr and Sergeant Leonard were killed in the 1st Platoon. I called for reinforcements so we could continue our assault, but with no results because the battalion did not keep any reaction force to back the companies up.

I then made the decision to move toward the 2d Platoon as they were the only platoon not under heavy fire. I called the 1st and 3d platoons and told them to pull back and move through the 2d Platoon and regroup. In the meantime, I took my command post and moved through the 2d Platoon to try to secure an area where the 1st and 3d could bring their dead and wounded. The CP had moved about twenty meters through the 2d Platoon when we ran into a group of NVA moving across our front. An NVA soldier took aim on me. Sp. 4. Stephen Turzilli jumped in front of me and started shooting. Steve and the NVA soldier both went down. I called for my head medic to help Steve. He checked him and told me there wasn't anything he could do for Steve. At about this time, another NVA soldier threw a hand grenade into the middle of the CP and wounded another of my RTOs. The whole CP was down on the ground by this time, setting up covering fire for the 1st Platoon and 3d Platoon. The first Sergeant (Top Page) was under a tree when an NVA fired a B-40 rocket into it. The entire CP was wounded by this time but continued to fight and put out covering fire. The 1st Platoon came in and took over a position on the west side of the perimeter we were setting up.

This action started about 11:00 in the morning, and we fought all day. We were under heavy fire most of that time. I had the antennas shot off of two radios and got hit in both legs by shrapnel. After we consolidated and secured the wounded, I called for an air strike on the enemy positions. The air force came in and dropped bombs, napalm, and strafed the enemy positions.

It was necessary to check casualties so I would know where we stood. Lieutenant Nathan, having had the most casualties and himself wounded three times, returned to the area of maximum concentration of NVA numerous times to retrieve his dead and wounded.

Even though I don't remember all their names, I know also that at least one sergeant went with Lieutenant Nathan during their numerous trips. I remember one medic of exceptional quality going up against the enemy to retrieve wounded, his name Lloyd Pelky (nicknamed Piggy Dumpy).

By the end of the day, we had accounted for and evacuated all but one man, who we couldn't find. His name was Patrick Haggerty. Haggerty was only an average soldier, but died in a way everyone could be proud of while facing enemy fire. As we could not find Haggerty, and I felt my wounds were not serious, I refused evacuation until he was found. At this time, we did not know he was dead. During the night, the NVA continued to move around our perimeter, but I gave orders not to engage them as by this time my company was only about one-half strength, and our position was only marginal at best.

The next morning at first light, I sent out patrols to inspect the battle area. The patrols found numerous dead NVA and recovered Haggerty's body. They also found an extensive bunker area which had been occupied by the NVA, which we had entered into through the marshy area.

This was the area of the main battle and the positions of the platoons when the heaviest casualties were taken.(Page 271)

THE AMBUSH
Eyewitness Account

E-5 Bill Butler (1st Platoon, 3d Squad Leader)
May 30, 1969

LOCATION:	Approximately five miles south of Highlander Heights, a fire base and landing zone. It is ten miles south of Kontum, on the west side of Highway 14, between Kontum and Pleiku. The Kontum River runs a few miles to the west, where it makes a ninety degree turn from south to west.
MISSION:	There is an NVA (North Vietnamese Army) regiment in the area, and our battalion is trying to push them west across the Kontum River. Major Owens, our battalion operations officer, is in charge of the sweep.

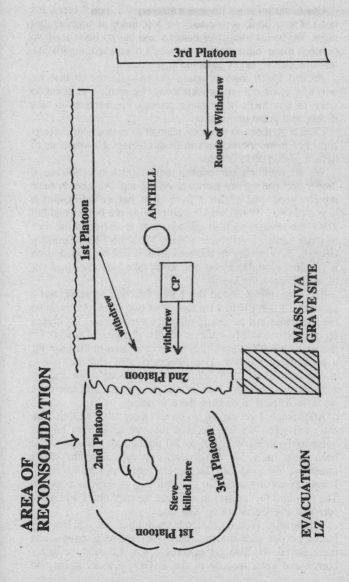

Our company is set up in a temporary PB (patrol base). It's not much to look at because we just threw it together last night. We built some small bunkers and put up hootches (two ponchos made into a tentlike covering.) If attacked in a PB like this one, we wouldn't have much protection.

Around 0800 hours, Captain Patrick informs us that we won't be going out on a sweep today. We aren't even going to send out any SRPs (short-range patrols). He wants us to take it easy and get rested up.

LT (Lt. Ken Scurr) tells our platoon to enlarge our bunkers and clear more of the brush in front of them. He wants us to have a greater field of fire.

We all work on our bunker until 1100 hours. We dig it deeper and place more sandbags on the top. We already have a pretty good field of fire in front of us, but we are making it larger, anyway. While working on clearing the bushes and tall grass, the new sergeant in my squad starts yelling at the men to work harder. I yell back at him, "This isn't Fort Benning, Georgia. Take it easy on the men. This is still my squad, even if you are my replacement! You won't take over my squad until after I leave the bush!"

The guys in my squad don't like this new sergeant, and I know that I don't either. He has about two weeks seniority on me and thinks that he should run the squad. He isn't my choice for a replacement. My squad is 1/3 (1st Platoon, 3d Squad). Of the six men in the squad, only three have been in the bush for a while: King Harrison, Don Elmore (Elmo), and me.

Approximately 1145 hours, we finish our work and sit around the hootch for lunch. It's amazing all the different ways we have learned to prepare these C rations.

After lunch, I get caught up on all of my letter writing. You can't tell when we will be able to write again with all this humping (walking with full packs) through the boonies we've been doing lately. We will probably go out on another sweep tomorrow. We were told that we are getting in supplies today. I want to get my letters in the mail bag as soon as possible. The first bird (helicopter) in will take the mail out. I will make sure that my letters are on that bird.

A little after 1300 hours, the birds bring in our supplies. My letters go out with the first bird. We receive C rations and more ammo. We also get in some FNGs. LT calls me to his hootch and gives me one of the FNGs. LT looks at me and says to be nice to the guy. I guess LT thinks I'm getting a little harsh with the FNGs.

I take the FNG back to the squad and introduce him to the gang. I tell him that it is good having another man for the squad and that he will learn quite a bit in the next few days. I tell him to feel free to ask questions.

By 1730 hours, the new sergeant starts giving the men hell again because he doesn't think the bunker is big enough. I tell him, "It looks fine to me. Stop giving the guys hell or one of them might shoot you in the next firefight. I am not going to put up with the way you are treating the men." He tells me again that he has seniority on me and he will do what he wants. I reply, "I don't give a shit how much seniority you have, my main concern is for the men in my squad!"

By now we are yelling at each other, and I am so mad that I can punch him. It's taking everything I have in me not to hit him. He finally tells me that he is going to get me when he has the chance. I respond with, "You'd better make the first one count because you won't get a second chance!" LT comes up to us and breaks up the fight before we start swinging.

LT tells the new sergeant that a few weeks seniority doesn't mean anything in Nam. He has had PFCs training sergeants on how to run SRPs the right way. You can't learn everything out of the books. You have to listen to the men with experience and ask them questions.

LT says that he wants to talk to me alone. We walk over to his hootch, and he tells me to calm down. I ask him to take the new sergeant out of my squad. I cannot stand him, and he is just too damn self-centered. LT replies that I should have patience with the new sergeant. The man is new and has a lot to learn. He goes on to say that he wants me to teach the new sergeant everything that I can. He says that he has watched me train other men and knows that I could do it if I wanted to.

I tell LT, "I only have thirty-eight more days before going home, and I don't think I can train any more men. I want to give my squad to one of the guys who has earned it, not a shake-and-bake sergeant. I just don't trust this man. He doesn't have what it takes to be a leader in combat."

LT tells me, "Not to worry, everything will turn out all right. The new sergeant will make it."

LT and I have a couple of beers. I received a package three days ago containing two six packs of Coors beer. LT likes Coors, so we drink the five remaining cans. I don't want to have them in my pack when we go out on another sweep anyway.

We talk about the things that we will do when we get home to the real world. We are both from the same hometown. We went to the same high school and knew each other before coming to Nam. We talk a long time about hunting, fishing, and sports we both enjoy. We plan on taking some trips together when we get home.

It starts to rain while we are talking. It is a light shower. It shouldn't rain very hard yet because the clouds are not dark.

LT says that if he doesn't make it back home that he wants Terry Mayfield (a friend of ours who is a cook for the officers open mess at Camp Enari) and me to have a party in memory of him. He goes on to say that he wrote a letter to his parents and told them to save some of his money for the party. If he gets killed, the money is to go to Terry.

I tell LT that I don't like him talking like this and that there isn't any reason for him not to make it back. We will both throw a big party when he gets home. Grass Valley won't be the same when we get back to the World.

I tell LT that I will see him in the morning and start back to my hootch.

As I'm walking back to my squad I see Steve Turzilli at the CP (command post) and stop to talk to him. Steve and I came to Nam around the same time. He is a RTO (radio telephone operator) and loves it. He doesn't have to go out on any platoon sweeps or SRPs.

We talk about how short we are getting and how great it will be to get homemade cooking and ice-cold beer again. Steve comments that New York doesn't have any jungles and he isn't going camping or hunting ever again. He's had enough of it and wants a roof over his head when he sleeps.

Steve and I should be going to Camp Enari next week or the week after to get ready to go home. The way we look and talk, it will take a lot to get us ready.

By now the sun is starting to go down, and the rain is getting harder. I tell Steve that I will see him later and walk back to my squad. Steve has a way about him that always calms me down. I sure enjoy talking to him. It is around 1945 hours.

The new sergeant is getting two of the FNGs prepared to go out on LP (listening post). I tell him I don't want the guy who came in to our squad today going out tonight. He asks King Harrison if he will go out, and King says that he doesn't mind.

King is getting short, but he will do anything if asked in the right way.

I walk the men out to the LP, and the new sergeant comes along. I want to see what the area looks like. The LP is only one hundred fifty meters from the PB perimeter.

When we get to the LP, we find two guys from the 2d squad who have been out here most of the day. They say that they haven't seen anything and everything is quiet.

The area that they are in is too open for my taste. I want my men set up in a more secure area. The place I find for them is very bushy, with a lot of cover. The dinks would have to walk on them before they would be seen.

I tell King to take care of the new guy. King asks to borrow my watch because he doesn't have one. I lend it to him and tell him not to lose it.

It is already dark when we get set up, so I use their Prick-25 (PRC-25 radio) to call Six (CP). I tell the new sergeant that it is better to be safe than sorry. With all of the FNGs at the PB, you can't tell when one may get nervous and shoot at us.

I tell Six that we are on our way in and to pass it along to the line. It is Steve on the radio, and he says that he will walk over to the line and tell them.

While walking in, I tell the new sergeant that I feel sorry for the new guy sitting out on the LP. I remember some of the LPs that I have been on and how scared I had been.

The new sergeant is lucky because he will never have to be with just one other guy to depend on out on a LP; sergeants don't pull LP duty.

We get back to our PB, and Elmo is standing guard at our bunker. I tell the men that I will stand the next guard because I'm not tired. Elmo says that he isn't tired either, so we stay up while the other three men go to sleep. Elmo wants to talk, so I tell him to talk softly. He is a great talker and says some pretty funny things. He calls everyone "Good Buddy."

Elmo goes to sleep around 2300 hours, but I'm still not tired. I've got another real bad headache. I reach into my shirt pocket and take out the pills the doctor in Camp Enari prescribed for me. I take a Valium and a codeine tablet. I am starting to run low on both of these drugs, so I take them only when I really need them.

I stay on guard duty until approximately 0030 hours, May 31, 1969. I wake up the new sergeant and tell him that it is his turn to stand guard. He gets right up and goes to the bunker. His gun and ammo are already lying on the bunker.

I hear Steve talking to the LPs on the Prick-25, and I want to know what's going on. I walk over to the CP and ask Steve. He remarks that one of the LPs from the 3d Platoon had heard noises, but they say it has stopped. Every time the wind blows and makes a noise, this LP calls in. At least they aren't sleeping.

I ask Steve how my LP is doing, and he replies that they haven't missed a call all night. This makes me feel better. King has a man out there that he can trust. I remember going on a lot of LPs with King before I made sergeant.

I tell Steve that I can't sleep again tonight. I am feeling somewhat nervous and have another damn headache. Steve says that everything will be okay because we have been through so much that nothing can happen to us now. The logo on our helmets reads INVINCIBLE, and we have come to believe it.

I light a cigarette, and the first sergeant yells at me, "Put the damn thing out. You can see the match flame for miles." He is right, and I put it out. I guess that I am getting a little careless.

I walk back to my hootch and fall over my pack. It is real dark tonight with this rain. I need to get some sleep. I tell the new sergeant to have the guard wake me up at 0600 hours. I take off my wet poncho, climb into my hootch, and lay down on my bed roll. Airborne (one of the FNGs) jumps up and asks, "What time is it?" He is the next one to watch guard. I tell him that it is almost 0200 hours and the new sergeant needs to be relieved. He gets up and leaves the bunker.

Not long after he leaves, the new sergeant comes in and lies down. He goes right to sleep. Boy, I wish I could drop off to sleep like he does.

I start to shake from the wet and cold. I reach into my pocket and take out a couple more pills. My headache is driving me crazy.

I think the reason I have been getting these headaches is the malaria I contracted last month while on R & R in Australia. When I came into Nam, I weighed 168 pounds; now I'm down to 127 pounds. My strength sure isn't as good as it was before I had malaria. This is the reason for getting rid of everything that I can out of my pack. I don't want to carry any extra weight.

Approximately 0500 hours, I decide to get up. There is no use trying to sleep this night. I go out to the bunker and relieve P.R. (He's from Puerto Rico.) I tell him to go get some more sleep. It might be another long day.

At 0600 hours, LT calls all the squad leaders to his hootch. He says that our company is going on a sweep today toward the Kontum River. Our platoon is going to walk rear guard this time. This makes me happy. We have been the point platoon so many times in the past few weeks, and I am getting tired of it.

LT says that we are leaving around 0700 hours. This doesn't give us much time to eat, pack up, and tear down our bunkers. I go back to the squad and tell them what is happening. P.R. and Airborne get their packs together very quickly. I have them go out and relieve the LP.

At 0700 hours, we call in the LPs and are ready to go out on the sweep. I am told that the other companies in our battalion will also be going out this morning on sweeps.

At 0725 hours, we leave the PB and start humping east toward the Kontum River. I think to myself that I hope this sweep doesn't take us all day. I guess I'm bitching about everything lately.

The humping isn't bad. We walk up a few small hills and cross some little valleys. Most of the terrain is pretty wooded, without too much underbrush. There are a few open fields of grass that we have to cross, and this makes for easy walking, but scary when we get into the wood lines. There aren't many places where the point element has to cut the trail. This keeps the noise level down.

As we cross a small blue line (creek), I observe some footprints. They look like treads from car tires. This is the type of print that the NVA sandals leave. The footprints don't look very old to me. At least they are heading north, and we are headed east.

We start up a small hill, and I see a low, long fence made out of bamboo. The fence is about two feet high and at least a hundred feet long. About every twenty feet, there is an opening. On top of the opening there are bamboo stakes with rocks tied to them. When rabbits go thru the openings, the stakes come down and impale them. This one is still in working order.

I have seen this type of rabbit trap around Montagnard villages. This is a strange place to have rabbit traps, with no villages close to us. Just after seeing this trap, the company halts. We are in a nice wooded area with lots of cover.

I hear on the radio that the point has seen some dinks (NVA) going across the hill in front of us. The dinks went through a grassy field and into a tree line. We take off our packs and wait to see what is going to happen.

Captain Patrick calls the three lieutenants to the CP and talks to them. They are deciding what we are going to do next.

While they are talking, a LOH comes into our area and starts shooting. They are shooting at the dinks that the point had seen. It seems strange to me that this LOH is in the area. I hear later that Major Owens, our battalion operations officer, is in the LOH.

We put our packs back on, and the 1st Platoon goes up to the rest of the company. Somehow we have become the center platoon. We have one platoon on our right and the other platoon on our left.

LT says that the LOH killed the dinks, and we are going up on the hill to see how many.

I place the new sergeant at the front of my squad, and I take a middle position. I want him to get the feel of leading his men. LT wants me to train him, and I think today is a good day to start.

We only walk a few meters when I hear small-weapons fire. I see movement in front and to the right. I fire a clip (eighteen M-16 rounds) into the area. Airborne also shoots a clip into the area. We shoot across a grassy field into some bamboo, which is on the edge of a wood line. After we shoot, we still hear other shooting around us.

Sergeant Cribb (our platoon sergeant) comes up to me and wants to know what I am shooting at. I tell him that I saw movement. He then asks me why I am not at the head of my squad. I tell him the reason, and he tells me to trade places with the new sergeant.

By now, the company was stopped again. We are told that there is a bunker complex on top of the hill. We take cover and wait to see what is going to happen.

I hope that we don't have to go up that damn hill. In front of my squad, it's all open ground until you crest the hill. There are a few bamboo thickets, but they are all small. The grass is about waist-high and doesn't offer much protection.

The artillery blasts the ridge around the hill. They pound the shit out of the hill. The artillery is coming in from different directions. We must be getting it from LZ Joyce, LZ Penny, and some other place. The whole hillside looks like it's getting destroyed.

The artillery stops, and it gets very quiet. To the north, I hear helicopters off in the distance. They are getting closer, and I can see that they are gunships. The gunships open up on the hill. They rake the whole area in front of us and put everything they have into the hill.

All of the time I have been in Vietnam, I haven't seen this amount of artillery or air strikes go into a small hill. I tell the new sergeant, "It must be a damn big bunker system to bring in all of this artillery and gunships."

I sure am praying that the NVA has left the bunker complex and that it has been completely destroyed. I knew better, but I can hope. I will never forget the smell of all this destruction. The heavy smell of sulfur is so strong that it makes your eyes water.

Everything gets real quiet again. The birds aren't singing, and the bugs aren't making any noise. You can hear a pin drop, it's that quiet. This isn't what I'm waiting for. I know now that we will be going up onto that small damn hill.

LT put us on line. He says that we are going to assault the bunker complex. We are going to have a platoon on either side of us as we push up the hill.

I put my squad on line, with myself in the middle. I can't see the 3d Platoon, which is on my right. I know that they are over there someplace, but they are out of my sight.

My squad is on the far right of the 1st Platoon. I can see the 2d Squad on my left. LT and Sergeant Cribb are with the 2d Squad.

LT gives the word, and we start pushing up the hill. This is the first time that I have seen a platoon assaulting a hill on line. It just doesn't seem right that we are doing this.

I tell my men to put their M-16s on semiautomatic and save their ammo until we get to the top of the hill. I tell them to shoot at places that look like possible dink hiding places.

My squad walks to the top of the hill, shooting at every place that looks like an area where the NVA could be concealed. We don't get any return fire until we crest the hill. About one hundred meters on the other side of the crest is a wood line. Around seventy-five meters to our right is another wood line. We are standing in the open grass, without any

cover. We hear the other platoons shooting and getting return
fire. My squad is the only one on top of the hill.

. All at once, the dinks in front of us open up with small-arms
fire. We drop to the ground and return fire. Small-arms fire
starts coming at us from the right. I yell at the men on my
right to shoot in that direction. We hear the rest of the platoon
in a firefight, just off of the hill to our left. Bullets are hitting
the grass and ground all around us. I yell at the men to keep
returning fire so the dinks can't come up on us. I hear the pop
of mortars—and, damn, if they aren't hitting near us. We don't
need these mortars coming in on us! Now, if this isn't enough,
we are getting shot at from our rear! I think one of our platoons is shooting at my squad. I yell into the Prick-25 at Six
to have the platoon quit shooting. I don't want us getting shot
by our own men. Six, Captain Patrick, comes on the radio and
says that it's not our men shooting at my squad. The dinks are
between us and the other platoon.

Now I'm really pissed off at the world, and to make matters
worse, the damn dinks are shooting B-40 rockets at us. One of
the rockets hits right behind P.R. and me, knocking us to the
ground. It knocks the wind out of us, but somehow, we don't
get a scratch.

I start to get up, and I hear a bullet whiz by my ear. I turn
around and see the new sergeant with his M-16 pointed at me.
My heart almost stops. He is on his knees, and his eyes have
a wild look in them. I yell at him to shoot in front of him;
that's where the dinks are. I just know that he is going to shoot
me, but he turns and starts shooting at the tree line.

Airborne and Elmo yell to me that they are out of ammo.
P.R. and King yell that they are getting low. I decide that we
are going to have to get off of this hill.

I tell the men to drop their packs and get all of the ammo
and hand grenades they have. We are getting back to the rest
of the platoon. We start crawling off the hill. The grass around
us is being cut down by the firepower of the dinks. They are
still hitting us with B-40 rockets, mortars, and now machine-
gun fire. There has to be a hell of a lot of dinks in this area!

The only way we can go is to our left. The dinks are on the
other three sides of us. I tell King Harrison to start toward the
rest of our platoon, and I will bring up the rear. I want to make
sure that all of my men get off the hill.

All of my men crawl by me except the new sergeant. I see
him lying down, covering his head. I tell him to start moving,

and he just stares at me with a blank look in his eyes. I finally get him moving after I take his gun away. It doesn't take us long to catch up with the rest of the squad. I give the gun to Airborne and tell him to watch the new sergeant because he's gone off the deep end. I take the sergeant's ammo because he won't be needing it again.

As we crawl toward the platoon, the dinks keep shooting at us. On the way I hear on the radio that LT has been shot and they need a medic. God, I hope he's not hurt bad! Next I hear that the medic has been hit, also, and can't help anyone. It seems like a lifetime until we find the rest of the platoon. We ran out of ammo ten minutes ago.

Sergeant Cribb yells at us to shoot at the tree line and the bunkers that are in front of him. I tell Sergeant Cribb that we are out of ammo and need more. He says, "Oh, shit!"

I go over to Sergeant Cribb, and he tells me that LT and Sergeant Leonard are both dead. I can't believe that both LT and Sergeant Leonard are dead. Sergeant Leonard and I go back to my first days in Nam. It's like a nightmare when I see the dead and wounded. The wounded need medical attention fast.

Sergeant Cribb says that we are pulling out. He tells me to find the rest of the company. I leave most of my squad to help carry the dead and wounded.

I take two of my men and start walking in the direction toward where we first started up the hill. After about one hundred yards, I hear voices up on a knoll. I stop the other guys and tell them that I will go up and find out if they are our men. I can't tell by the voices. I crawl up the knoll until I can hear the voices better. It is our men, and am I happy to hear them. I yell at them that we are coming in. They holler back that they are waiting for us.

I go back to the rest of the platoon and help carry LT.

Airborne tells me that he had to take a knife off of the new sergeant because he thought he was going to kill himself. The new sergeant is giving the men a hard time, and they have to tie him up. It is harder to bring him in than it is the dead or wounded.

When we get back to the rest of the company, we make a perimeter. We are all almost out of ammo now. I ask King to find us some. If anyone can find ammo, King can. We get a M-14 rifle and take some M-60 machine-gun belts apart for the clips. This will give us another weapon.

I look around at the wounded and wonder why the medic

isn't taking care of them. Then I remember that the medic has been shot. I go over to the wounded and start to give them first aid the best I can. I don't have any medical supplies, so I tear up some towels that we wear around our necks. I use them as bandages to stop the bleeding. I use insect repellent as a disinfectant.

One new guy from California has a bad head injury. He has a big open wound in the back of his head. He says that he is in a lot of pain, and he thinks that I am the medic. He wants something for the pain. I give him a couple of Valium pills and tell him they are morphine. In a little while, he says that he doesn't feel the pain as bad. By looking at him, I don't know if he will make it or not. Sergeant Cribb asks me about the guy, and I only shake my head.

I can still hear some small-arms fire going off around us, but I think the worst is over. Sergeant Cribb comes back over to me while I am still tending to some of the wounded.

Sergeant Cribb wants me to get a couple of other guys and cross the grassy field to our north and secure the area. I remind him that I am still working on the wounded. He tells me that we need to secure the area so that we can bring in the medevac helicopters and take out the wounded.

I grab the ammo that King Harrison has found and take a couple of guys across the field. I am scared crossing that field and looking at another tree line in front of me. We make it across the field and into the tree line. Just inside the tree line is a small gully with a lot of brush. On the other side of the gully, there is thick brush, a good place for the dinks to hide.

I use the Prick-25 to call Six and report that we have secured the area. Then I see a dink coming toward us. As I see him, he sees us. He is by an anthill. I shoot him. He grabs his stomach and falls behind the anthill. (The anthills in this area average about four feet high.) The anthill he fell behind turns out to be a bunker.

Now I am extremely nervous. I don't know how many more dinks will be coming up on us. As it turns out, this is the last shot that the company would fire today.

I wait for about an hour and watch the clouds get thicker. I hope that the medevacs will hurry and get here before it starts raining.

Sergeant Cribb sends out some replacements for us. We go back to the perimeter, and I start looking after the wounded again. The kid from California looks good, and he thanks me for taking care of him.

Sergeant Cribb comes up and asks me to talk to the new sergeant. "He needs someone to talk to." I tell Sergeant Cribb that I don't want to talk to the man because he tried to kill me up on the hill. I don't think Sergeant Cribb believes me. At least I know that because of his actions today, the new sergeant will not be taking over my squad when I leave.

Finally the medevacs come. I pick up the kid from California and carry him to the first bird that lands. As I get to the bird, a guy jumps out and tries to help me carry him. I tell him that I can do it myself. The guy says that the kid must be a close friend of mine. I look at the guy and say, "I don't even know the kid's name; but he has a lot of heart."

After we get all of the wounded on the medevacs, I go to talk to Captain Patrick. He has been wounded but wants to stay with his men. He tells me Steve Turzilli has been killed. When he says this, I feel like I am going to pass out. I go into a daze for a while. This is almost too much for me to take. Captain Patrick goes on with the list of the dead, but I don't hear him. I walk over and look at Steve because I just can't believe that it could happen to him. When I see him, I go numb. I don't care what is happening around me.

I walk back to my squad and lay down. When I wake up, I am wet and cold. It has started raining again. I look for my pack and bed roll and remember that they are still up on the hill.

I look around for something to put on to keep warm. I finally take a poncho from around one of the dead. I can smell the blood, but at least it will keep me warm and dry.

One of our sister companies is set up with us, and I am told that I don't have to stand guard tonight.

Our sister company lost a couple of their men trying to get to us. Their point element was shot up crossing a road not too far from us.

I take my last Valium pill and go right to sleep. I sleep all night and don't want to wake up when the sun shines into my eyes.

Today is June 1, 1969. I have thirty-six more days left before I go home. I block out everything that happened yesterday. I don't want to think about it.

The only thing I know is that my pack is up on the hill, and I need it. In my ammo can are all of the addresses of the guys who are already home. I want to look them up when I get home.

At 0730 hours, I am informed that we are going to make another sweep of the hill and see what type of injuries we inflicted on the NVA. This will be the only time I'll have to look for my pack.

We spend hours looking over the bunker complex. The bunkers are set up in a horseshoe shape around the hill. My squad had walked right into the center of the horseshoe. I don't know why we weren't all killed.

I look as long as I can for my pack but cannot find it. Airborne and King Harrison find their packs; but the rest of our packs are gone. I find an NVA helmet where my pack should have been.

In the bunker where LT was killed, I pick up an NVA knife. Elmo finds an old Chinese flare gun with flares.

Altogether, we count eighty-one dead NVA. We will never know how many were wounded.

Our company has eight KIAs and a hell of a lot of wounded. I wonder how many of the wounded will die before getting home. We never will hear if the wounded make it or not. I just hope the kid from California makes it.

When we left our last PB, we had over one hundred men. Now we are down to fifty-seven able-bodied men.

● ● ●

Morning came quickly. My head was heavy; my heart was heavier. I went over to HHQ to see Mitch for my last instructions for R & R. I told him that when I came back I wanted to see the guys who were wounded at the hospital, and asked where they were. He said that they were at the 71st Evac, on the other side of Pleiku by the airstrip, and that he would see what he could do while I am gone. I got on a deuce-and-a-half that took about eight of us to the airstrip, where we caught a plane to Can Ranh Bay.

RADIO LOG: 1 June S-3 1/12 Inf. Call Signs 13(A Co.) 39(B Co.) 67(C Co.) 43(D Co.) 90(E Co.) 0(Bde) 63(Batt.)

TIME	FM	TO	
0630	13, 39	63	13 and 39 have sp'd small elem to find their MIA's and KIA's.

| 0640 | 39 | 63 | Found 3 of his MIA they are KIA 099760. |

| 0645 | 0 | 63 | 1 Slick all day and 1 Slick 1200-1700 LOH All day. |

| 0705 | 13 | 63 | Have closed with KIA's at 097761 was the location they were found. |

| 0710 | 39 | 63 | Found estimated 30 bodies and 3 possible graves capable of holding 5 to 6 corpses (099760) 13 found 10 bunkers in a perimeter formation with 18 inches overhead and foxholes on (097761) each side. Main bunkers 3 ft. deep could hold 5 or 6 people. |

| 0730 | 39 | 63 | Just recovered all my MIA's there are 4 and they are all KIA. |

| 0735 | 63 | bde | Requested 2 slick sorties to move 3997A to 39C LZ on AL. |

| 0740 | 39 | 63 | Casualties 9 KIA 18 WIA 19 shock, 2 engineer WIA, 1 red leg wia. |

| 0744 | 39 | 63 | SOI went in with head RTO who was KIA, also lost X mode believe it is shot up and can recover it. |

After landing, we checked in and then went down to the beach. We would leave for Hong Kong in the AM. On the beach I met a guy named Mike Janeczko who was going on R & R to Hong Kong, too. He was from Chicago and was with the 1st of the 35th. That kind of broke me out of my thoughts; Chicago is close enough to Forest Park, my hometown. At the beach, there was a bar called Surfside 6. We sat down in the sand about ten meters away. All I wanted to do was get drunk, which didn't take me long in the heat and sun.

RADIO LOG: 1 June (cont.)

TIME	FM	TO	
1030	43	63	The only thing my 33 element found were 2 more KIA's found in bunkers there were found a little further down which weren't counted yesterday.
1203	13	63	Found a bunker complex found by Shamrock will take till 1500 not 1330 as planned. Will employ concrete piercing on complex.
1250	0	63	Reliable source says that at grid ZA-083714 there is a NVA Company and to the South of that there is a Village with 50 NVA's in it at this time cooking rice (Plei-Bok-Blei) they have 15 M-16's, and 2 M-60's and 15 captured packs, shift the Air Cav. over to 1/22 so they can check it out.
1255	63	13	Hold there until we get Air cover back.
1300	43	63	4357 closed and 4397 SP'd.
1310	43	63	4357 at grid 111751 found 3 B-40's a RPG 1 Chi Com grenade about 50 Bunkers 30 of them were dug into the side of a Ravine 3 ft. × 5 ft. × 3 ft. 2 Shiters, 1 Cooking bunker, some Commo wire, a large trail running South from the Bunker complex, the trail was heavily used by approx. 50 people within the last week.
1411	13	63	My element sweeping has found very large complex no count on bunkers yet. Also a lot of equipment both US and Dink. Also stumbled across 2 dead dink

bodies. Will get all the equipment together and go through it on the way back.

1500   13   63   Found at B Co. contact area some B-40's and some other equipment will send everything of intell. value back to FSB also found 3 dink KIA's with plain green fatigues, we will be moving out in 20 Minutes also found 1 M-16 and a flare gun, also the dinks were buried, the grid was 097760.

1544   39   63   Will SP in 15 Minutes and will be able to except resupply when they reach their objective.

1545   0   63   Release the LOH as soon as possible and send it to the 2/35.

1550   13   63   There was about 36 bunkers, 4 ft. × 5 ft. × 4 ft. 18″ of overhead, 1 kitchen 4–5 feet long the kitchen had 3 stoves, also the equipment that 13 found is 1 mosquito net, 100 pounds of rice, 1 gook watch, 1 flare gun and 13 flares for the gun, 1 diary, miscellaneous papers, 2 60mm fuses, 14 B-40 rockets, 2 GI ruck sacks, 1 GI grenade, 2 AK mag., 1 82mm motor round, 100 M-60 rounds, 16 M-16 Mag., 1 GI trip flare, 1 gook telephone, 2 large spools of commo wire, 7 60mm motor rounds, 1 GI protective, 1 GI towell, 5 Chi-com entrenching tools, 1 GI entrenching tools, assorted clothes, 1 2 quart canteen (US) 2 Chi-com grenades, 1 GI smoke grenade, 1 GI 1 quart canteen, 1 GI 1 quart canteen cover, 1 GI claymore, 2 gook picks, 5 1 quart gook canteens, 1 saw blade, medical supplies, (albumin bandages).

| 1646 | 39 | 63 | We have not got the x-mode [the radio for communicating between a battalion and its companies] with us, we could not find it on the sweep today but the last time we saw it, it was all shot up. |

| 1648 | 63 | bde | Plans summary: A co. will establish patrol base and sweep with patrols to the SE, SW and S. Will pull 1 patrol when Recon 2/35 starts his sweep. |

B co. will remain in patrol base and patrol to NE and E.

C co. will continue to maintain defensive positions on LZ Nicole also will maintain present ambush.

D co. will remain in present location and patrol to south SE and SW only 200 meters out.

Recon will sweep from LZ Nicole to LZ Carmen.

Request 1 LOH at 0730 for 2 hours to check in on our Cmd A push also 2 resupply slicks all day to check in on our AL push. Will not have a company or platoon element on stand by due to the tactical situation.

I don't remember how long we stayed at the beach. I do know I got so drunk that I did something I hadn't done in years—I passed out.

The following morning, June 2, we boarded a bus to the airstrip and left for Hong Kong. Away from the war, a war that I tried like hell to forget, at least for five days.

Hong Kong was a beautiful city. The harbor of Kowloon and Hong Kong was crowded with a mixture of boats, old and new, Chinese junks, ocean liners, cargo ships—all surrounded by skyscrapers and mountains. I saw all of this as the plane came in for a landing.

Once in Hong Kong, I caught a red cab, which drove on the wrong side of the street and looked like it had been imported from England. I had forgotten that Hong Kong was a British colony. The cab drove through immaculate streets. Shops crowded the sidewalk. There were signs, in English and Chinese, and bars and restaurants. People of all nationalities walked briskly along. The city was as intriguing as I pictured it. I couldn't wait to get into my civvies and become part of the flow. The cab took me to the Grand Hotel, where I was staying. It was a modern hotel, about thirty stories high. It was sure good to see civilization again.

After checking in, I hurried to my room, took a shower, put on a pair of pants and a short-sleeve shirt, and headed out on the town with about eight hundred dollars. I only got two buildings away before I saw a tailor shop, and headed in. I wanted a few suits made so I could be stylish. Three suits for 150 bucks was the price. I whipped out my wallet, still wrapped in plastic, and took out three pictures I had ripped out of someone's *Playboy* magazine and handed it to the tailor. "Can you make these?" I said.

"No problem," he answered. Then he said, "You pick material, I make real fine. One day."

I was amazed at the rolls of material that were on shelves from floor to ceiling around the shop. I picked out blue silk for a double-breasted suit, one gray wool, and a dark brown material for a short suit like James West wore in the program "Wild, Wild West." I was excited; I couldn't wait until tomorrow to get them. I also ordered three shirts for another thirty dollars. I had only been in Hong Kong about two hours, and already I'd spent $180.

I left the tailor and headed down the street. I made it about a half a block and saw a music store and headed in to buy Joe an AKAI 1800 SD. The store had so much music equipment, I almost fainted with shock. Fascinated, I looked around at all the makes and models. I found the reel-to-reel Joe wanted, and ordered it—three hundred dollars plus twenty dollars shipping. I wanted one myself, but I just didn't have the scratch to buy it.

Besides, I had my social life on my mind ... All I really wanted was to party, screw my brains out, and forget about Nam. At a club, I met a Chinese woman named Kim who spoke good English. She was a lot of fun, showed me the sites, and even took me home to meet the folks and have dinner.

After five days, I was headed back to Nam, hung over, my head in the ozone layer. I fell asleep on the plane and woke up when we landed at Cam Ranh Bay. A bus took us to the reception area and to a building where we were checked back in. After converting our greenbacks to MPC, we had to sign an affidavit stating that we had no more US currency in our possession. I signed it and turned it back in. My head was throbbing as I walked to a table. MPs were standing behind it and asked to see my wallet. He opened it. To my surprise, two twenty-dollar bills were stuck in front of my pictures behind the plastic. He looked at me and said, "What is this?"

"Looks like two twenty-dollar bills to me."

"You just signed an affidavit that said you didn't have any US currency. You know what that means?"

I was getting pissed off and said smartly, "Listen, man, I must have forgotten they were there. I wasn't trying to smuggle anything in. Besides it's only forty bucks. If I'd wanted to hide it, I would have hidden it where you couldn't find it, not in front of my pictures. Come on give me a break. I'm hung over, and I forgot, what's the big deal?"

He didn't like my tone of voice and said, "Follow me, wise guy. You're in some shit!"

By now I was getting scared. I followed him into an office. He handed my affidavit and my wallet to a captain sitting behind a desk, then told him the story, finishing up with his conclusion that I was a real smart ass. If I'd had a gun, I would have shot him in the leg.

The captain looked at me with hate in his eyes and said, "You are in very serious trouble, soldier, do you know that?"

I couldn't believe this was happening. I felt like puking on his desk. "Sir, believe me I wasn't trying to smuggle money in; I forgot I put it there; I got pretty drunk last night."

He was stern, a real lifer; he looked at my affidavit and looked at me. "That's no excuse, soldier, we are going to request that you be brought up for court-martial. What is your full name, rank, serial number, and unit?"

Him I wanted to kill with my bare hands. I gave him the information. He wrote it down and gave me back my wallet, then told me I could leave.

Outside, I threw up on the side of his building. Imagine, threatening me with LBJ for forty dollars! I was getting short—eighty-eight days—what was going to happen?

Chapter IX

SHORT TIMING

I was a nervous wreck by the time I got back to Camp Enari. The first thing I did was check back in, then I went to see our company clerk, Mitch. I told him what had happened in Cam Ranh; he told me he would rip the recommendation off for me when it came down, that it was "No big thing." That was a relief. Then I asked him if I could go to 71st Evac to see the guys.

"For sure," he said. "Why don't you go over to the mail room, pick up your mail, and take the stack of mail for the wounded at the 71st Evac. The mail truck will take you." I thanked him and started to the door, then he said, "Oh, when you come back, your CO, Captain Patrick, wants to see you."

"What about?"

"It's about what we discussed before you went on R & R."

I knew what it was about, going back out to the bush. A mail clerk named Arroyo was waiting in the mail room for me. I had three letters and read them as Arroyo and I drove toward Pleiku. Arroyo was from Puerto Rico. He drove the three-quarter-ton truck through the busy streets of Pleiku. As we talked, I kept my right hand on his M-16. He told me there was an opening for mail clerk for B Company because Jerry Sehman had gone home. "No shit," I said. "Jerry was in my squad for six months. He's my buddy. I *need* that mail clerk job; I can't go back out to the bush."

"I know. Mitch told me what happened; I hear where you're coming from."

At the hospital, I asked a nurse for the guys from B Company 1/12th. She gave me directions. As I walked through the wards, my eyes darted left and right, from bed to bed, searching for a familiar face; my heart was pounding. There were so many beds, and none were empty.

291

The first person I recognized was Bill Warner. He was talking to Top Page when I walked up to them. I suddenly realized I didn't know what to say. I didn't interrupt; I just stood there. Bill looked at me, looked right through me. I don't think he even saw me. He nodded and kept on talking to Top.

Top turned around. He had that look on his face, the one-thousand-meter stare, but he said, "Leninger, what are you doing here?"

"I . . . I brought your mail," I answered. I looked at the others huddled in groups down the aisle.

"Son, why don't you pass it out quietly. I thought you were on R & R?"

"I . . . I just got back. I don't know what to do, Top. I don't know what to say. I don't think I can do this."

"Be strong, son, be yourself, don't worry," he said to me. "They are glad to see you. They just can't relate to different things now; they'll snap out of it in a while."

As I passed out the mail, it was plain to see that most were still in shock. I tried not to look at their bloody bandages. A few managed to crack a smile. The more letters I passed out, the more guilty I felt. I had missed the biggest contact that my company was in since I arrived in country. I passed out the last letter, turned and walked away. Nobody noticed.

Arroyo talked all the way back to Camp Enari, but I didn't hear one word he said. I guess I had that one-thousand-meter stare. He dropped me off by the mail room. I walked down the wooden sidewalk toward headquarters, my eyes watching my boots. I have to get that mail clerk job, I thought.

My train of thought was broken when someone called, "Hey, Leninger!"

I looked up. It was Captain Patrick, my CO. He walked over. I was the first to talk, "Captain, I can't go back out to the bush, I just can't. I've had it. I can't take any more; I wouldn't be any good to anyone; I've seen too much."

"I know what you're saying; I understand. I have discussed this with a few others, and I have decided to keep you here in base camp as our mail clerk. The spot is open—Sehman went home, and you're already here."

I was overwhelmed. "Really, I'm mail clerk? Really, thanks, Captain, thanks. I'll be a good one. For sure, I won't fuck up." He smiled, I saluted, he walked away.

For the first time, I felt I'm going to get home! I'm a base-camp commando. Thanks to God, thanks to St. Jude. I was so overwhelmed, tears of joy rolled down my cheeks as I stood there, laughing. The captain wasn't so bad after all. He saved me. It took me ten minutes to control myself before I walked over to headquarters to tell Mitch, our clerk. I could tell by his facial expression that he knew before I told him. I believed he had something to do with it, but he denied it.

The following day, I met the other mail clerks, Lake from A Company, Holmes from C, Scoma from D, Pollar for HHQ and E. For the first week or so, I got into sorting mail and meeting guys who worked throughout our battalion area, especially LaDeaux, the guy who ran the beer hootch at the end of the street. LaDeaux had so much gray in his hair, I thought he was in his forties; he was twenty-two. We called him the Gray Fox or the old gray mare. And I got in with a group that smoked hootch, ree bar, rope, whatever you want to call it.

My third night as a mail clerk, I smoked a few bowls with five guys who were all former grunts and had been assigned around the battalion. I found out that grunts in the rear stuck together just the way we did in the bush—things didn't change much. I got so high that I went outside, lay down, and watched the clouds go by the moon. All the while Led Zeppelin danced through my head and blew me away. I spent three hours outside on the ground. Nobody noticed where I was; I didn't know either.

For the next few days, I sorted through the mail, finding mail for those who were killed, wounded, and those who survived. A blackboard next to the sorting table had a list for each company, listing KIAs, WIAs, those in hospitals, those at Trains.

I was put in 1st Reactionary, which meant in case of an attack, mortar or ground probe, we would be taken to the perimeter or wherever they wanted us. Most of those in 1st Reactionary were base-camp grunts, so I asked for the M-60 and got it. If I was going to sweep or whatever, I wanted some firepower. No way something was going to happen now. I had one foot on the stair of the freedom bird.

Base camp was a trip. There was so much going on and so many different types of people. Lifers, shammers, drunks, heads, black power, white power, whores, bores, wimps, pimps, fags, nags, fuck-ups, jack-offs, assholes, gooks, collies, cooks, clerks, grunts. At times it was enough to make a grunt want to be back to the bush to be with the "family." In a few weeks, I learned to cope; fuck, it don't mean nothin'.

One night, someone on the bunker line opened up. Then the

whole bunker line opened up; tracers filled the blackness with red streaks leaping toward a village about five hundred meters outside the wire. Who knows if any civilians were killed. We never heard.

Three times a week, we picked up mail at the Pleiku air force base, so we took turns jumping out in Pleiku to "socialize" while the others drove around the block. It never took very long. I was always done when they pulled up.

Before I knew it, it was the end of June. One day I was sorting mail when a letter crossed my hands addressed "To Whoever Knew Steven Turzilli." I opened it right away.

It was from a Jeanne Firriolo, one of Steve's cousins. Twelve years older than Steve, she had helped raise him when he was a child, and had loved him very much. In heartbreaking terms, she asked for details about his death—the why and the how—and about his life in the field.

After I read it, I placed it on the table, went in the other room, and sat. Tears rolled down my cheeks; the other guys saw me and came over. I told them to read the letter on the table top. They did. Nobody said a word.

Finally, I broke the silence and said, "I have to write her. Steve was my buddy."

Holmes gave me the letter and said, "You got to do what you got to do."

I stood up and walked out, thinking what to write. I went back to the barracks, sat down and started to write.

Dear Jeanne,

I was a close friend of Steve. We were in the same platoon, the 1st. When I arrived in B Company, he was in the machine-gun squad with Wayne Kahre, Pat Flynn, Larry Bond, Luke Whitaker and a guy named Roger. That was back in September. I was in the 1/3 Squad; my squad leader was Dean Johnson. All were there before me. Dean was very close to the machine-gun squad because most of them got there about the same time, around three months prior to my arrival. The machine-gun bunker was always next to ours, and when we moved, they were in back of us, so we all became very close. In fact our platoon was "family." Most were great guys. I was lucky to be in the best platoon. With each passing month, we grew very close. All we talked about was home, families, where we grew up, sports, girls, etc. For months, we lived together, battling the environment and the elements. We went from jungles to mountains. For four months, nothing happened except a small contact I was involved in a few weeks after I arrived. We were always scared something was going to happen, fear was a part of daily living. We were lucky until March. We were in the mountains somewhere northwest of Kontum. Our 3d Platoon was almost wiped out; Dean Johnson and Ray Bethea from our squad were killed along with about seven others. Of the rest of the 3d Platoon, most were wounded. We were devastated over our losses, mostly over Dean. He was a strong and respected leader and part of the "family." Our hearts were torn apart.

Steve was one of the "older guys," like Dean. He and a couple of others took over, to lead, to guide us other guys. Steve always would be himself. When he talked, we always listened. He had a way about him. He was one of the ones that held us together. He became head RTO (radio operator) about December. I became 1st Platoon RTO the end of January, so we always talked. He taught me the radio. He rubbed it in to everyone when the Jets won the Super Bowl. We were always joking around to keep our minds busy. In April, we had another contact, a few more were killed and wounded. We all were scared but tried not to show any sign of weakness. Steve was getting short when May rolled around, so were a lot of others from our platoon. You could sense the change in them. Steve was slated to go home in June. Everybody knew who was short; we all kept our own calendars on our helmet covers. The last week in May, we were humping through some medium jungle southwest of Kontum. We were out of the mountains. We were glad of that. On May 27, our battalion commander was killed, and our sister company, C, took a lot of casualties. From about a thousand meters away, we heard the battle. We had to walk at night through the jungle to set up a blocking position. To say the least, we were scared, everyone. Nothing happened; maybe it was luck, or prayers, I don't really know. The next day we pulled back, I was told by 1st Sergeant Page that I could go on R & R if we cut a good landing zone.

Steve and I organized the cut. We knew we could both get out together—him going home, me on my R & R. I waited the longest out of anybody for my R & R. Almost nine months. We cut like madmen—trees, jungle, etc. Steve would take time out and tried to get in contact with a helicopter; he wanted out as badly as I did. He thought for sure he would go in with me. He only had about three weeks left. At the end of the day, he finally got hold of a chopper. He yelled to me to get my gear ready. I ran to where my pack was; I could hear the chopper in the distance. I ran back up to the command post where Steve was still bringing the chopper in. He had tears in his eyes but kept on talking into the handset. I knew right away they weren't letting him go. The chopper was coming in; the noise was getting louder. He stood up and came over to me; we hugged each other. I yelled to him, "What is going on, aren't you coming?" He didn't say anything. By now the chopper had landed. Someone yelled for me to get going; I ran to the chopper. I felt so bad for him; it wasn't fair; why? I got on the chopper; it took off. I saw him standing below; we motioned thumbs-up to each other. I felt what he felt. On May 31, I was in base camp setting up my R & R when the news came down that B Company hit a battalion ambush. I ran to the radio hut and heard the casualties come over the radio. I wasn't there; I wanted to be, but I wasn't. I don't know what happened. I was broken. I wish I could tell you more, but I can't. I don't know what happened. All I can say is I loved him, too. He was a brother to me.

Sincerely,
J.G. Leninger

A few weeks went by. I continued to sort mail every day and got loaded a few times a week.

About the middle of July, I received a letter from Steve's cousin Jeanne. She wanted to know how it happened, why it happened. I couldn't answer her; I didn't know how. I never really found out the whole story, only bits and pieces from a few guys that were heading home.

Captain Patrick came into base camp for something, and when he came to pick up his mail, I gave him the letter to answer. I don't know if he ever did, but I knew it was his job to give her something I couldn't.

One day shortly thereafter, the battalion sergeant major started harassing me. He seemed to dislike grunts.

"What company are you with?" he asked.

"B Company!"

"What's your MOS?"

"Eleven Bravo Twenty ("11B20")" I answered, proudly but

nervously. I had heard this guy was a Dick with a capital *D*, a true lifer. He shipped a few guys back out to the bush who were in to go home and had three or four weeks left in country. Although they probably ended up back at Trains in Kontum, it was still a rip. I was also told that he had been fragged once or twice but somehow avoided getting killed. I could see why he was the most hated man in our battalion.

"Do you have a no-duty slip?" he asked.

"No!" Guys like this jerk were the reason companies held back on sending short-timers in at two or three weeks. I hated him and I didn't even know him.

The last thing he said to me was, "You're going back out to the bush, son!"

"Sergeant Major, I only have three weeks left!" I lied.

"You're not short enough; you will be brought in your last week."

I started to shake. I wanted to smash his head on the floor with my bare hands. He scared me into aggression. If I'd had an M-16 in my hands, I would have made him eat eighteen rounds. He looked at me with those lifer eyes, turned, and walked out.

I left the mail room, trying to think of a way out of my situation. On the way to the barracks, my back occurred to me. I had some kind of growth on it. I never complained about it, but since March, it had grown to the size of a large marble. I would go to the battalion surgeon to see what it could be. There was no way I was going back out. I had five weeks left.

The following day, I went to see Doc Goodin, I told him straight up about what happened. He told me that I had a sebaceous cyst and not to worry, the surgery was simple. He also told me not to worry about going back out to the bush, that I would be in the hospital about a week, and he would give me a no-duty slip for a few weeks that would take me till the end of August. He was a good guy no doubt about it. The surgery was set for July 31, two days away.

I returned to the mail room to tell the guys. When I got there, Pollar said, "I have some bad news for you. There was an accident in your company. One man was killed and six others were wounded."

"Who was killed?"

"A guy named Barbee!"

I knew him. He was in the 1st Platoon, a tall blond kid from

South Carolina who came to B Company after the contact we had in March. "What happened?"

"From what I heard, the platoon was on a sweep somewhere around a bridge in Kontum. A vine pulled a grenade off his pistol belt or something and blew up."

Another stroke of bad luck. Just like the tree back in April. The bush was a killer. I turned and walked out the door. I didn't tell them until the next day about my going into the hospital.

On July 31, I was in the hospital and had surgery. I was given a couple of shots to numb the area. I didn't feel anything; it was fairly simple. The doctor showed me a glop of fat that was taken out of my back; inside was a piece of metal the size of a pin-head. He asked me if I'd been in combat. I said I had been, back in March. "Then you must have been hit," he said.

"I didn't feel anything! You mean I should get a Purple Heart?" He laughed, and I said, "Forget it, they can keep the Purple Heart. I don't need it."

I was put in a ward with a lot of wounded, but I felt out of place. Some of the men were pretty messed up. I couldn't get up, so I just looked around at the beds close to me. On one side of me was a guy whose whole body was wrapped with bandages, except his face. He never said a word. On my other side was a guy who'd been shot through the shoulder. He talked, sometimes.

About the third day, I woke up at 2:00 AM. Some guy was walking from bed to bed with a flashlight. I didn't know what was going on until he reached me. It was an E-5 paymaster. He said, "Give me all of your MPC; I will give you a receipt."

"What for?" I asked.

"Come tomorrow, the MPC you have now won't be worth diddly squat. They're changing it tonight."

I gave him about eighty dollars, and he gave me a receipt. "I'll be back in the morning," he said.

I turned to the guy next to me and said, "Boy, this is going to piss off a lot of gooks with MPC, man."

He laughed, "Serves those motherfuckers right," he said.

The next day, before it got dark, nurses and interns were busy moving the seriously wounded to some other place. The rest of us were told to sleep under the beds. That night, rockets and explosions ripped through the air. Most were far away, but a few landed close. The gooks were pissed off big time. I didn't blame them; I'd be pissed off too.

On August 6, I was released from the hospital and given a

no-duty slip that read, "Retain in Camp Enari. No details involving stooping or carrying until 25 August." It was signed by a captain from 4th Med.

When I returned to the mail room, I found out more bad news had happened in B Company. A claymore had gone off in a trash barrel and wounded five guys. Then I was told somebody was cleaning his M-16, and it went off, killing a guy in the 3d Platoon. I couldn't believe it; who would throw a claymore in a trash barrel? The other must have been a terrible mistake for the guy cleaning his M-16. All I could figure out was that they must have been FNGs, it was shocking. After the May 31 contact, a lot of FNGs were assigned to my old company.

Sunday, August 10, 1969
Letter written to Bill Butler by Roger Ranker.

Hi Bill;

How in the hell are you getting along in the World? I sure wish I was there, too.

You left us in LZ Joyce, and several things have happened since then. We've been humping rice paddies and hills until a couple days ago.

We set up on the Kontum Bridge (Highway 14) for eleven days. What a sham. We went swimming, ate hot chow, drank cold beer, and saw a lot of Vietnamese women. It was really nice.

The twenty-fourth of last month, I went to NCO School. I came out fifth in our class of twenty-seven. It wasn't too bad, considering I screwed around a lot.

A lot happened the fifteen days I was gone. The day after I left, a claymore went off in a trash barrel and wounded five guys in the 2nd Platoon. That was on the Kontum Bridge, their last day.

Then the company started humping the hills behind LZ Joyce. Our 1-1 Squad was walking point, and a grenade came off of Barbee's belt and went off. It injured Tom LaRoe, Bo Williams, Ed Wiler, Airborne, Ron McKenney, and killed Barbee. I sure hated to hear it.

Last Friday night, another guy's gun went off and shot a guy in the 3d Platoon. He died later of a belly wound. We've had probably twelve casualties in about three weeks, and haven't had any contact since May 31.

Sergeant Burns went LRPs about a month ago, and that

left me team leader. Now Ed is in on R & R, and I've taken over the squad. In the squad there is Pecker, P.R., Williams, Kirt, Reed, and Bill.

The Bill you know went to the CP, and we got another Bill. As you can see, I've got a squad of FNGs.

The guy named Kirt is really a help. He went to jungle training in Panama for fourteen weeks. He's uptight as far as I can see.

Pecker told me to tell you hi. John went to the company's CP. It's been quite a change since you left.

Claiborne left today to see his brother in An Khe. I doubt if he'll be back since he is getting short. Luke leaves the twenty-eighth, and Ken Thomas and Reagan leave the twenty-ninth of this month. They got ten day drops. I'll be an old-timer when they leave.

I got your package in the mail the other day. That Coors beer was really good, along with the other goodies. The film you sent was all right. I'm taking pictures with it right now. I hope they turn out okay. Either make slides or have duplicates made. I'd like to have a copy of them. I'll repay you somehow.

Well, Bill, that's about all I have for now. I hope you are having fun back in the World.

Thanks for everything.

> *Good Buddy,*
> *Rog*

I came across five letters for the sergeant major, which I burned in the garbage can in the next room. He continued to harass me, even though I had a no-duty slip. I was safe until August 25. Every day, I scratched off another day on my short-timer's calendar.

About a week before the twenty-fifth, the sergeant major strolled into the mail room and said, "Leninger, the twenty-fifth is coming up, and I found out you're not going home until September 10; you're going back to the bush for a week at least!"

I hated him worse than the gooks, but he also had me worried. He asked if he had any mail. I told him no. When he left, I took out another one of his letters and burned it. He was fucking with the wrong person.

That night I went to Mitch and told him what had happened. He said there was a chance he could get me out of Nam before the twenty-fifth. Within two days he'd done it! My prayers were answered, and my orders were cut for August twenty-fourth. I couldn't believe that I'd be going home in five days!

For my last few days, every time the sergeant major came in to threaten me, I just stared at him and didn't say a word; I was over him and the army.

My last day in Camp Enari, I was totaled by noon. Before I knew it, the sun was going down. I got together with a bunch of guys, four from the mail room, and we continued to party. When we ran out of beer, I volunteered to go to the beer hootch to get some more, on me. As I stumbled to the street, I was looking directly at the bunker line in the distance because the street sloped to the west. I saw a flash in the distance, then a giant explosion. A fireball shot up a few hundred feet. It happened so quickly, I was stunned. Then the entire bunker line opened up, and tracers were flying, bouncing in semislow motion upwards from the horizon. The sirens went off, a single blast: we were being attacked and 1st Reactionary had to report! Guys were running in all directions to get to bunkers and to the weapons building. The situation was chaotic.

I headed to a nearby bunker, and others got there at the same time, so it was a mad shove to get in. I was trying to get my breath and my senses. Then, without warning, I started coughing and gagging, and my eyes burnt like hell. CS gas! I ran out of the bunker to get to the weapons hootch for a gas mask and a weapon. I couldn't help but think that on my last night in Vietnam we were going to be overrun. I *had* to get a weapon and a mask.

As I ran, everyone I passed was coughing and hacking. By the time I reached the weapons building, my eyes and nose were running like a faucet. Smitty quickly gave me a mask, and I gasped for air as I put it on. Then the all-clear siren sounded, and everyone calmed down. Guys started laughing while I was still coughing. About five minutes later, someone came in and said, "A bolt of lightning hit the fougasse and CS on the bunker line."

I broke out laughing myself. I saw the flash myself, but I was too drunk and high to realize what it was. By the time I got back to the party, the guys had all disappeared, so I headed back to my bunk and had a few beers with Arroyo until midnight. Then I hit the hay.

Chapter X

FREEDOM BIRD

In the morning, I pulled out a freshly pressed, starched pair of tapered jungle fatigues. The shirt had all the patches on it, Spec Four, 4th Division, Combat Infantry Badge, my last name. I said my good-byes, picked up my orders, and got on the truck that took me and ten others to the airstrip on the other side of Pleiku. All I had was my duffel bag with a few war souvenirs and my clothes. The plane took us to Cam Ranh Bay. I couldn't believe how many guys were waiting to go home when we got there. There must have been a few thousand guys waiting for that Freedom Bird to home.

We were told it would be two or three days before it would be our turn. What a bummer. What to do for two or three more days? No way I was going to do details; they weren't going to catch me.

The heat and humidity were unbearable, so almost everyone stayed in the barracks, out of the sun. There was no wind. That night, it was so hot inside that some guys stayed outside; it was too hot to sleep. I was too nervous and excited. A thought did cross my mind—what if there was an attack? What would we all do? Nobody had any weapons. We had turned in everything in base camp.

Word spread that our hair would be checked at the plane, and that if anyone needed a haircut, he would be bounced off his flight. Word also was spread that everyone's duffel bag would be checked for war souvenirs or anything made in north Vietnam. If "they" found any, they would hold you also. Worst of all, if "they" caught you with any dope, you would go straight to LBJ (Long Binh Jail) without passing go.

About twenty of us were outside the barracks talking about

all of the rumors we heard. I certainly didn't know what to believe.

I got the bag of weed I had hidden in my duffel bag, brought it outside and asked, "Who wants to smoke some boo!" About half said yeah, so we went to a nearby bunker and smoked some bowls. I gave the rest away. The souvenirs I would hide. As to my hair . . . my hair was long, especially the sides. Over the ear, and you needed one. When I combed mine down, it covered the ear. I had some thinking to do.

Those of us who got high, stayed awake until dawn. Then most hit the showers before the others were up. When I returned to the barracks, my duffel bag was open. I yelled out, "Who the fuck was in my bag?" Everyone was up, walking around; nobody said a word. The lock on the ring was open, but I thought I'd locked it. I hadn't. I laid everything out on the bunk, and my heart sank. My war souvenirs were gone.

I was heartbroken; those things meant a lot to me. The two knives and the NVA belt meant the most; the AK-47 mags and the gook letters didn't mean that much.

At 9:00 AM and 1:00 PM, a captain would get up on the podium and call off names alphabetically for the two flights that day. About 250 names each time. Everyone was so anxious that when you didn't hear your name, it was a giant letdown.

That night we were sitting around outside again. All of a sudden, six rockets exploded about a mile away. The sirens went off, everyone ran around like chickens with their heads cut off. I ran to a shelter that was just a hole big enough for about fifty guys, open on all sides, with sandbags about five deep on top. I dove in, and it filled in a few seconds. Guys were screaming, "What do we do?" If sappers got in, we were in deep trouble. Cam Ranh was huge. A sapper attack was possible—two weeks earlier the 91st Evac hospital was blown up, and a lot of guys were killed. The hospital was down close to the beach, about a mile away. I had heard the news back at Enari.

Flares lit the sky. It was scary. I picked up a rock. I thought that if I saw a gook, I'd hit him in the head with it, then run over and take his AK-47! Not the brightest idea, but I was desperate.

After an hour of wondering, the all clear sounded. Everyone crawled out, joking around, laughing, trying not to show how scared they'd been. I returned to the barracks and went to sleep, convinced I'd be leaving the next day. I had to. Enough was enough.

The next morning, August 26, after the roll call for the first flight, I broke down and got a haircut. I told the guy to just give me a trim; he gave me the usual "white-wall," so I looked like a real asshole.

At the 1:00 PM roll call, my name came up. I had an hour to report back. I reported back in ten minutes, and a bus took thirty of us to the airstrip. When we got off the bus, we had to wait in a roped-off area. I was so excited. The Flying Tigers Freedom Bird was just pulling up, the sun reflecting from its wings. My Freedom Bird, the plane I thought I would never see. It was beautiful. I tingled.

We were put in single file. The doors opened; guys, decked out in new fatigues, filed down the stairs. They walked past us, and I wanted to say something, but I couldn't talk; I was speechless. Their eyes, their faces showed how green they were. I immediately thought, They don't know what they are coming into. How many of these kids aren't going home? Which ones would lose limbs? I felt like shit as they passed.

Some looked at us, waiting to get on, and said, "Hey, man, what's it like?" Nobody answered. They would find out like we did.

After the plane had refueled, we headed to the stairs and up, some guys yelled, "Fuck you, Nam," but a lot were silent, buried in their own thoughts, like me. I took a window seat and just looked out. The Freedom Bird took off and rose quickly. I looked down at the coastline as it vanished from view. All I could think about was those friends of mine who I left behind, both living and dead.

As the plane ascended, I thought that although I was never really wounded, a wound had been cut deep inside of me. I should have been happy that I was out of the godforsaken place; I wasn't. Maybe if I'd been going home with somebody I'd served in the bush with; but I wasn't. I went over alone, I was going home alone. Vietnam I would never forget.

AFTERTHOUGHTS

It has been twenty-four years since I served in Vietnam. And after researching my year in depth, I have more burning questions than I had before. Why? How?

A lot of my questions deal with strategy, and I know that strategy comes from higher up than company commander or battalion. When President Johnson stopped bombing the north on November 1, 1968, the enemy came down by regiments and divisions. A massive build-up of enemy troops took place in the south. As many as three divisions were staged throughout the Plei Trap Valley, in some of the most rugged terrain in the world. This was known by OPLAN 24–68 (DEAD END–TOLL ROAD–U CAN DUONG), dated November 1968, (INTELLIGENCE). On November 6, 1968, a recon plane spotted twenty-one trucks and four tanks using the Plei Trap Road in one day. The Plei Trap Road was a main cutoff from the Ho Chi Minh trail. The division's 8th PSYOP Battalion made up leaflets telling the enemy to get off the road, that we were going to bomb it! We gave them early warning, and the division didn't commit most of the infantry battalions until late February and early March, 1969. Why? And when our battalion was deployed, *Why* were we so spread out? In March of 1969, D Company was put on Hill 1483, two klicks away from where we were on Hill 1018. Between us was a Hill 994 that an NVA regiment had somehow occupied. *How?* And it just so happens that seven klicks to our south, where the rest of our battalion was (around Fire Base Mile High), was another NVA regiment. *How?* And in every radio log, battalion tells brigade "Will not have a company- or platoon-size element on reactionary standby due to the tactical situation as we are fully committed." *Why?* Somebody had to know what was going on. We didn't in my platoon, and I'm sure my company commander didn't know either. He just followed orders. Every battalion made contact in the Plei Trap and got hit hard in March of 1969. For every battalion we had in the Plei Trap, the enemy had two or three *regiments*; we were outnumbered six or eight to one. Then in May we're pulled back towards Kontum. Our sister company hit a regiment on May 27, 1969. Our battalion pursued, only to get stopped in place three days later for a one-day "cessation of offensive operations." *Why?* And the following day my company walked into a battalion ambush. *Why?* If I'd been a company commander, commanding one hundred men, I'm really not sure what I would have done when faced with such difficult decisions and mismanaged situations. I am sure that the years have taken their toll on the omniscient of some commanders and that they now ask the same questions I do.

Why and how? These questions may never be completely answered, but a better understanding of the whole picture may heal some of the wounds that just never go away.

I hope this book encourages others to write their stories. The only way that people will learn the truth is from those that experienced it. Like so many who served in Vietnam, I have never claimed to be a hero, but I was fortunate enough to have known a few whom I will never forget.

EPILOGUE

Many books have been written on the Vietnam War, and I am sure many more will be. The emotional scars of that war will never go away for the hundreds of thousands of us who served in various line units or in LRRPs, Recon, and hunter-killer teams. Those who fought the war in the bush, no matter the unit or the service, know the true meaning of war.

War is a true hell, and it does not single out individuals by race, color, creed, or religious preference; bullets, rockets, mortars, and booby traps do not have names written on them. Life in Vietnam, no matter how long you lived there and fought there, cannot be compared to anything known in our society. Yet, for many of us, the society that we fought for—or thought we fought for—has become a society that doesn't care about the past. This society has become something like Vietnam, a living hell for those of us who survived.

People who care are far outnumbered by those who don't. With what we know now, would most of us who served go if we were called on today? Was it worth the carnage that it caused for over a decade? For me the answer is simple— *No!*—but, paradoxically, I would not trade the experience for anything.

Few historians would argue the fact that the key to victory for the North Vietnamese in Vietnam was in II Corps, the Central Highlands.

The II Corps area, the largest geographically, included almost half the total land area of South Vietnam, although it was sparsely populated. The major cities or provincial capitals of Dak To and Kontum Pleiku and Plei Me, Ban Me Thuot, dotted the landscape north to south, and in the east lay An Khe and Qui Nhon.

There were only three strategic highways. Highway 14 connected Kontum, Pleiku, and Ban Me Thuot in the center of II Corps. Highway 19 connected Pleiku with An Khe and Highway 1 along the coast. Highway 21 connected Ban Me Thuot to Highway 1 in the southern region of II Corps.

In the spring of 1975, the NVA launched regimental attacks, cutting the highways in many places, thus isolating Pleiku from Kontum and Ban Me Thuot, and the Central Highlands from the east coast. The NVA, who vastly outnumbered the ARVN, quickly annihilated the two divisions in the area and moved on to Qui Nhon, thus cutting the country in two. The debacle followed. The war might have ended earlier, during the Easter offensive of 1972, if Kontum and Pleiku had fallen, but massive B-52 strikes ended that threat at Kontum.

From September 1966 to December 1970, the 4th Infantry Division and supporting units thwarted many enemy attacks that tried to accomplish the main objective of the entire war, the capture of the Central Highlands. For those who fought and died in the Central Highlands, this says something of the esprit de corps of a unit that is truly a forgotten division in the history of the Vietnam War.

GLOSSARY

AGENT ORANGE:	Very toxic chemical used to defoliate vegetation.
AIR BURST:	Time fuse.
AID:	(United States) Agency for International Development. An agency which helped provide humanitarian aid.
AIT:	Advanced Individual Training; specialized instruction in a soldier's field of specialty. Sometimes incorrectly referred to as Advanced Infantry Training.
AK-47:	Communist manufactured automatic assault rifle.
ALPHA:	Phonetic word for letter *A*.
AO:	Area of operation.
APC:	Armored personnel carrier; a tracked vehicle used to transport troops or supplies, armed usually with a .50-caliber machine gun, at least.
ARC LIGHT:	Bomb strike from a B-52.
ARVN:	Army of the Republic of Vietnam. A member of the army.
AWOL:	Absent without leave.
BANJO:	Company strength.
BASE CAMP:	A fortified, generally rear area containing a brigade or division headquarters, main logistic center for division. For supplies, paperwork, done by clerks, etc., people who worked in base camp known as base-camp commandos.

BASIC:	Basic training.
BANGALORE TORPEDO:	Two-inch-diameter tube, approximately eight feet long, explosive used in clearing areas.
BANJO:	Company Strength.
BATTALION:	A military unit with two or more companies, batteries, or similar units, usually four companies A,B,C,D, and E, a reinforced platoon, known better as recon.
BATTERY:	An artillery unit equivalent to a company. (Six gun emplacements with crews.)
BDA:	Bomb damage assessment.
BIRD:	Slang for any aircraft, most often a helicopter.
BLUE LINE:	River or stream.
BODY BAG:	A zippered plastic bag used to hold and transport dead bodies.
BOO KOO:	Bastardized French for beaucoup, meaning much or many.
BOO KOO DINKY DAU:	Much crazy (Vietnamese/GI slang).
BOONIES:	Slang term for unsecured areas—jungle, mountains, etc.
BOOM-BOOM GIRL:	Slang for prostitute.
BOOM-BOOM:	Intercourse, belly slapping.
BOUNCING BETTY:	A mine, when tripped, that springs up in the air about waist-high, then explodes.
BRAVO:	Phonetic word for letter *B*.
BRIGADE:	A military unit composed of two or more battalions or equivalent units.
BUSH:	Same as boonies.
B-40:	A communist shoulder-fired rocket, used against bunkers, tanks, etc.
CA:	Combat assault by helicopter.
CARE PACKAGE:	Goodies from home.
CIDER:	Call sign of forward observer (Battalion LOH [Loach].)
CHARLIE:	Phonetic word for the letter *C*. Also slang term for communist soldiers, sometimes used as Charles or Mr. Charles.
CHICOM:	Chinese Communist.

CHIEU HOI:	The Open Arms program to entice members of the Viet Cong and NVA to defect to the South Vietnamese side.
CHINOOK:	A CH-47, twin-rotor helicopter used to transport supplies or personnel. Nicknamed Shithook.
CIB:	Combat Infantryman's Badge, an army award given to infantrymen who have been under enemy fire in a combat zone.
CLAYMORE:	A curved antipersonnel mine, which when detonated, propels 200 small steel balls in a sixty degree arc to its front.
C-4:	Plastic explosive one-pound bricks.
CO:	Commanding officer.
COBRA:	An AH-1G gunship helicopter armed with rockets and machine guns.
COMMO:	Slang for communications.
COMPANY:	Military unit consisting of two or more platoons, whose strength can vary between 100 or so (in combat) to 200 (authorized).
CONCERTINA WIRE:	Coiled barbed wire, stretched out along the ground to provide protection from infiltrating enemy troops.
COSVN:	"Central Office for South Vietnam"— Communist headquarters for military and political operations in South Vietnam.
CP:	Command post.
C RATIONS:	Combat rations; canned meals used by the military in the field.
CSS:	Combat sky spot; an observation helicopter sent to a location where a unit is engaged with the enemy, used to plot air strike.
DAILY JOURNALS:	Battalion account of company strength.
DELTA:	Phonetic word for the letter *D*.
DEROS:	Date eligible to return from overseas.
DI DI:	Vietnamese for get moving.
DI DI BOP or DIDLY BOP:	Walk slack, not caring.
DI DI MAU:	Slang Vietnamese for "go quickly."
DIEN KY DAU:	Crazy (Vietnamese).

DINK: Derogatory term for a Vietnamese; also
                         Gook, Slope, Slant Eye.

DUSTOFF: Medical evacuation helicopter, also
                         medevac or evac.

DUD: Unexploded bomb or artillery shell.

ECHO: Phonetic word for the letter *E*.

ELEPHANT GRASS: Tall, wide-bladed grass with razor-sharp
                         edges.

ETA: Estimated time arrival.

FAC: Forward air controller, used to coordinate
                         air strikes.

FIRE BASE: A temporary base set up in hostile
                         territory from which patrols are sent out to
                         search for the enemy. If artillery is
                         present, fire support base.

FIREFIGHT: Contact with enemy. Battle using small
                         arms, rifles, machine guns, etc.

FLAK JACKET: Heavy, vestlike protective armor for
                         protection against shrapnel.

FLANK: Two or more soldiers put on both sides of
                         column when marching in single file.

FO: Forward observer; an attached person to
                         an infantry company to coordinate
                         artillery fire support, lieutenant or
                         sergeant.

FNG: Fucking new guy.

FOXTROT: Phonetic word for the letter *F*.

FREEDOM BIRD: Airplane to take you back to the World
                         (home).

FREE-FIRE ZONE: An area where a soldier was free to fire at
                         anything.

FTA: Fuck the army.

GOOK: Slang for Vietnamese.

GOLF: Phonetic word for the letter *G*.

GOOFY GRAPE: Purple smoke grenade.

GUNSHIP: Armed helicopter used to support the
                         infantry.

GRUNT: Name given to infantry soldier 11B MOS.
                         Also nicknamed ground pounder.

H AND I FIRE:	Harassment and interdiction artillery fire fired at random into areas suspected to contain enemy troops.
HE:	High explosive.
HHQ:	Headquarters.
HOOTCH:	A shelter or dwelling, no matter how primitive.
HOT LZ:	A landing zone under enemy fire.
HOTEL:	Phonetic word for the letter *H*.
HUMPING:	Marching through the boonies with a heavy loaded backpack.
HUEY:	Slang for the UH-1 series helicopter.
I CORPS:	I (eye) Corps, the northernmost military region in South Vietnam.
II CORPS:	Two Corps, the Central Highlands military region.
III CORPS:	Three Corps, the highly populated military region between Saigon and the Central Highlands.
IV CORPS:	Four Corps, the southernmost military region covering the Mekong River Delta.
IN COUNTRY:	Vietnam.
INDIA:	The phonetic word for the letter *I*.
INCOMING:	Enemy mortar rounds, artillery, rockets, etc.
JUNGLE ROT:	Infection, festering white pus.
JANUARY:	The phonetic word for the letter *J*.
JODY:	The guy who was supposed to run off with your girl while you were in the army.
KIA:	Killed in action.
KILLING ZONE:	The area within an ambush where all enemy are expected to be killed or at least wounded.
KILO:	The phonetic word for the letter *K*.
KLICK:	Kilometer. One thousand meters.
LAW:	Light antitank weapon, shoulder-fired rocket for use against tanks or bunkers, with a disposable launcher.
LARGE ORGANIC:	105mm or 155mm artillery.

LBJ:	Long Binh Jail, military stockade.
LIMA:	Phonetic word for the letter *L*.
LT:	Lieutenant.
LP:	Listening post, a forward position of two men set up about fifty meters from perimeter at night to help guard a perimeter by listening for enemy movement toward perimeter. Usually located in thick foliage, with radio for communication.
LRRP:	Long-range reconnaissance patrol, a specially trained four- to seven-man team sent into enemy territory to observe enemy activity and harass.
LOH:	Light observation helicopter.
LZ:	Landing zone. Area where helicopters discharge troops or supplies.
MACV:	Military Assistance Command Vietnam, the main American military command with authority over all U.S. troops.
MEDEVAC:	Same as dustoff.
MIA:	Missing in action.
METER:	3.2 feet.
MIKE:	Phonetic word for the letter *M*.
MILLION-DOLLAR WOUND:	A wound serious enough to cause return to the United States but not serious enough to cause permanent disability.
MONTAGNARD:	Mountain people; numerous tribes of primitive people living in the Central Highlands.
MPC:	Military Payment Certificate, script used to pay U.S. personnel in lieu of American money. Also called play money or monopoly money, funny money.
M-16:	Standard U.S. rifle used in Vietnam.
M-60:	Standard U.S. light machine gun used in Vietnam.
M-79:	Single-barreled shotgunlike weapon used to launch grenades and shotgun rounds.
NOVEMBER:	Phonetic word for the letter *N*.
NUMBER 1:	The best.

NUMBER 10:	The worst. Screwed up to the max.
NL:	Night location.
NVA:	North Vietnamese Army.
OP:	Observation post. Two- or three-man group sent out from a perimeter during the day to watch for enemy infiltrators.
ORLL:	Operational Report Lessons Learned.
OSCAR:	Phonetic word for letter *O*.
PAPA:	Phonetic word for letter *P*.
PATROL BASE:	Company perimeter (PB).
PERIMETER:	Outer ring of defenses of a military position.
PIASTER:	Vietnam money.
PLATOON:	A military unit with two or more squads. Usually three squads approximately thirty men.
POINT OR POINT MAN:	The first man or element of a military unit on a combat patrol.
PONCHO:	Hooded plastic rain wear.
PONCHO LINER:	Lightweight liner for poncho used as a blanket by the infantry.
POP SMOKE:	To ignite a smoke grenade to mark a unit's position or signal an aircraft.
PRC-25:	Radio carried by the infantry.
PUNGI:	A sharpened bamboo stick, stuck in the ground at an angle in order to stab a GI in the leg.
PUNGI PIT:	A foot trap lined with pungi stakes.
QUEBEC:	Phonetic word for letter *Q*.
RADIO LOG:	Official radio transmissions
RECON:	Sweep-area patrol (also recon platoon, approximately forty men).
RIDGELINE:	The sloping finger of a mountain or hilltop.
ROMEO:	Phonetic word for letter *R*.
RPG:	Communist rocket-propelled grenade.
R & R:	Rest and recuperation (five-day vacation), one per year. (In-country R & R—three days.)

RTO:	Radiotelephone operator, the man who carried the radio for a unit, usually a PRC-25, or PRC-70.
R/L:	Red Leg—artillery (105s or 155s, 175s).
SADDLE:	A low area connecting two hills.
SADDLE UP:	A call to the infantry to put on their packs and get ready to move out.
SHORT ROUND:	Artillery round short of target.
SHORT-TIMER:	A soldier nearing the end of his tour, ninety days or less.
SHAM:	To waste time, also called shamming.
SIERRA:	Phonetic word for letter *S*.
SP4. OR SPEC FOUR:	Rank—Specialist Fourth Class.
SITREP:	Situation report.
SLICK:	Slang term for an unarmed UH-1 series helicopter or one from which the doors had been removed.
SMALL ORGANIC:	Usually mortars, 81mm or 4.2-inch.
SPOOKY:	(Also known as Puff The Magic Dragon.) AC-47, AC-119, or AC-130 aircraft armed with miniguns.
SOP:	Standard operating procedure.
SRRP:	Short-range recon patrol, a four-man patrol sent out about three thousand meters to observe enemy activity for three nights and four days, without special training and only used by the 4th Infantry Division.
SPs:	Special privileges, cigarettes, candy, etc.
STAND-DOWN:	A rest period for infantry units when they are brought in from the field to a base camp.
SP'D:	Leaving position.
STARLIGHT SCOPE:	A special scope which intensified very minute amounts of light from stars, etc. to enable the user to see at night.
STEP-AND-A-HALF:	Slang for bamboo viper—highly poisonous snake, florescent green in color.
TANGO:	Phonetic word for letter *T*.

TET:	Lunar New Year, Vietnam's biggest holiday.
TI TI:	A little bit (Vietnamese).
TRACER:	A round of ammunition treated to glow when fired so you can see its flight. Used mostly in machine guns, generally every fifth round.
TOP:	First sergeant of company, E-8.
TRACKS:	Slang term for any vehicle which moved by tracks rather than wheels.
TRIP FLARE:	A ground flare triggered by a trip wire, used to illuminate infiltrating enemy troops.
UNIFORM:	Phonetic word for letter *U*.
UNK.:	Unknown (U/K).
VC:	Viet Cong.
VICTOR:	Phonetic word for letter *V*.
VIET MINH:	Experienced fighters that fought and defeated French.
VILLE:	A Vietnamese village or hamlet.
WASTED:	Killed.
"WAIT-A-MINUTE VINES":	Vines with small three-prong claws that rip at your skin and you say, "Wait a minute."
WHISKEY:	Phonetic word for the letter *W*.
WIA:	Wounded in action.
WILLY PETER:	White phosphorous, used in grenades or shells for incendiary purposes. Also Willy Pete or WP.
WORLD:	The United States.
XIN LOI:	Vietnamese for too bad, also used as sorry about that.
XRAY:	Phonetic word for letter *X*.
YANKEE:	Phonetic word for letter *Y*.
ZAPPED:	Killed. Bought the farm.
ZEBRA:	Phonetic word for letter *Z*.